# FOR EVERY SEASON,

## VOL. 2

# FOR EVERY SEASON, VOL. 2

*by Greg Laurie*

ALLEN DAVID™
PUBLISHERS  Dana Point, California

# For Every Season

Unless otherwise indicated, all Scripture quotations are taken from the New King James Version. Copyright © 1982 by Thomas Nelson, Inc. Used by permission. All rights reserved.

Scripture quotations marked (NLT) are taken from the Holy Bible, New Living Translation, copyright © 1986. Used by permission of Tyndale House Publishers, Inc., Wheaton, Illinois 60189. All rights reserved.

Scripture quotations marked (AMP) are taken from the Amplified® Bible, copyright © 1954, 1958, 1962, 1964, 1965, 1987 by The Lockman Foundation. Used by permission. (www.Lockman.org)

ISBN 0-9777103-4-3

Printed in the United States of America.

| | |
|---|---|
| *Published by:* | Allen David Publishers—Dana Point, California |
| *Coordination:* | FM Management, Ltd. |
| *Cover photo:* | Peter Barrett for Masterfile ©2004 |
| *Editor:* | Karla Pedrow |
| *Design:* | Highgate Cross+Cathey, Ltd. |

*But they delight in doing everything the Lord wants;*

*day and night they think about his law.*

*They are like trees planted along the riverbank,*

*bearing fruit each season without fail.*

*Their leaves never wither,*

*and in all they do, they prosper.*

*Psalm 1:2—3* NLT

# INTRODUCTION

Since the publication of *For Every Season*, I have heard from a number of people who have told me how God has used those daily devotions to encourage and strengthen them in their daily walk with Christ. The experiences they have described, from a variety of seasons and stages of their lives, serve to confirm the words of Isaiah 55:11, in which God says, "So shall My word be that goes forth from My mouth; it shall not return to Me void, but it shall accomplish what I please, and it shall prosper in the thing for which I sent it."

When we spend time in God's Word, it is always a good investment—one that is sure to bring a profitable return. In fact, Psalm 1 tells us,

> Blessed is the man who walks not in the counsel of the ungodly, nor stands in the path of sinners, nor sits in the seat of the scornful; but his delight is in the law of the Lord, and in His law he meditates day and night. He shall be like a tree planted by the rivers of water, that brings forth its fruit in its season, whose leaf also shall not wither; and whatever he does shall prosper. (vv. 1–3)

The word "blessed" used here could be translated "happy." Your life is going to go well as you meditate in God's Word day and night. Notice this passage doesn't say, "His drudgery is in the law of the Lord," or even "His duty is in the law of the Lord," though a good case could be made for dutiful Bible study. Rather, it says, "His delight is in the law of the Lord." It something the blessed man (or woman) looks forward to—opening up God's Word.

If you want to be a happy person, then it is found in doing the right things. You can take God at His Word and learn the easy way. Or you can learn the hard way. It is your choice. God tells us how to be happy. He tells us how to be fulfilled. It is in keeping His commandments. So stay away from sinful influences and embrace those things that will build you up spiritually—things such as prayer, sharing your faith, fellowshipping with other Christians, and reading God's Word.

If you want to be a happy person, then you need to live according to God's ways. It is my prayer that *For Every Season*, vol. 2 will encourage and challenge you to walk in more of His ways as you explore more of His Word.

Greg Laurie
August 2006

## *Monday*

# POUR IT ON!

> *"But none of these things move me; nor do I count my life dear to myself,*
> *so that I may finish my race with joy, and the ministry which I received*
> *from the Lord Jesus, to testify to the gospel of the grace of God."*
> *(Acts 20:24)*

I magine for a moment that you are running a race that is ten laps long. And let's just say that you are in first place for nine of those ten laps. Not only are you in first, but you are creaming the competition. So when you come to the tenth lap, you think, "What's the point? I'm obviously the winner here. I'm going home." Guess what? You don't get first place, second place, or even an honorable mention. You don't get a gold medal, silver medal, or bronze medal. You are disqualified, because you didn't finish the race.

In the same way, it isn't enough for you to do well in the first five years or the next twenty years of your Christian life. You have to cross the finish line. That is why the apostle Paul, when he was leaving the elders of Ephesus, said in his departure speech, "But none of these things move me; nor do I count my life dear to myself, so that I may finish my race with joy, and the ministry which I received from the Lord Jesus, to testify to the gospel of the grace of God" (Acts 20:24).

That is what we should all be aiming for. The apostle Paul wanted to win the spiritual race. We should want to win it as well. And that is why this is not the time to be easing up. This is the time to pick up the pace. This is the time to pour it on.

# Tuesday

## FULL SPEED AHEAD

*Beware, brethren, lest there be in any of you an evil heart*
*of unbelief in departing from the living God.*
*(Hebrews 3:12)*

We all know of situations, activities, and places we can go that make it easier for the devil to tempt us. But now that we have been delivered from his power, we don't want to put ourselves in a position of vulnerability again.

Why do I bring this up? Because I believe that we are living in the last days. And one of the prophetic signs we sometimes forget about is that in the last days, there will be a great apostasy, meaning that people will fall away from the Lord. According to 1 Timothy 4:1, "Now the Spirit expressly says that in latter times some will depart from the faith, giving heed to deceiving spirits and doctrines of demons." This means that in these critical days in which we are living, the devil is walking around like a roaring lion and is looking for people that he can pull down (see 1 Peter 5:8).

The Book of Hebrews warns about the perils of spiritually turning away. Hebrews 3:12 tells us, "Beware, brethren, lest there be in any of you an evil heart of unbelief in departing from the living God." Notice this verse doesn't address unbelievers. Rather, it is a warning to Christians. The passage continues, "But exhort one another daily, while it is called 'Today,' lest any of you be hardened through the deceitfulness of sin. For we have become partakers of Christ if we hold the beginning of our confidence steadfast to the end" (vv. 13–14). Did you catch that? You will "become partakers of Christ"—if you are faithful to the end. In other words, you need to cross the finish line.

# Protecting His Investment

*Therefore He is also able to save to the uttermost those who come to
God through Him, since He always lives to make intercession for them.*
*(Hebrews 7:25)*

The Bible tells us to keep ourselves in the love of God
(see Jude 21). But we are also told in the same passage
that God will keep us (see v. 1). Is this a contradiction? Not at all. These verses complement one another. They
show us God's part and our part. We don't keep ourselves
saved, but we can keep ourselves safe.

God's love is unconditional. And fortunately for us, Jesus
Christ loves, preserves, and intercedes for us before the Father.
But we can do things that will get us out of harmony with His
love. That's why we are reminded to keep ourselves in the love
of God, which means that we are to keep away from all that
is unlike Him. We are to keep away from any influence that
would violate God's love and bring sorrow to His heart.

We are loved by God, and He will protect His investment.
For example, if you own an inexpensive pair of sunglasses,
you may not be all that concerned about where they are. But
if you have a more expensive pair, then you will tend to know
their whereabouts. Or, if you went to Disneyland with your
children, you wouldn't just forget about them. Instead, you
would keep your eye on them, because you want to protect
what is dear to you.

In the same way, we are preserved, we are protected, and
we are being kept by the power of God. But we need to keep
ourselves in a place where He can actively show His love to us.
We need to keep ourselves in the love of God.

# *Thursday*

# OUR REASON FOR RUNNING

*And let us run with endurance the race that God has set before us.*
*(Hebrews 12:1 NLT)*

When I was in high school, I was in track and field. I always noticed that I ran faster when a pretty girl was watching me, because I wanted to impress the pretty girl.

But there is a better motivation than that for running this race of life: the Lord Jesus is watching us. Hebrews 12:1–2 says, "Let us run with endurance the race that God has set before us. We do this by keeping our eyes on Jesus, on whom our faith depends from start to finish" (NLT).

That is what will keep you going. You have to keep following the Lord, even if your friends aren't there with you. As the song, *I Have Decided to Follow Jesus,* says, "Though none go with me, still I will follow." We all know that people do turn away from the Lord. But if you are living this Christian life because of what people have to say about it, then you are not going to make it. People will let you down. People will disappoint you. Circumstances are going to be hard. You should do this because you love Jesus.

When you face all of the garbage out there, remember that it is the Lord Jesus Christ you are running for. That is the reason you should be running this race.

Is this why you are running it right now? When you are maintaining a love relationship with Jesus Christ, you will see this world for what it really is—empty, futile, and meaningless. On the other hand, if you are just giving it your bare minimum, then you are not going to make it. So let's make every day of this spiritual race count.

# THE IMPORTANCE OF PACING

*Enoch walked with God three hundred years, and had sons and daughters.*
*(Genesis 5:22)*

I'm glad the Bible compares the Christian life not to only running a race, but also to walking a walk. Isaiah 40:31 says, "But those who wait on the Lord shall renew their strength; they shall mount up with wings like eagles, they shall run and not be weary, they shall walk and not faint."

The Book of Genesis tells us about a man named Enoch who walked with God for three hundred years. Enoch teaches us the importance of pacing ourselves in the spiritual race. I bring this up because there are people who have a yo-yo relationship with God. Either they are fully backslidden, or they are passionate to the point of being obnoxious. They haven't learned to pace themselves.

I learned the importance of this one day on a twenty-five-mile bike ride with some friends. I had a lot of energy, so I would pedal ahead of the pack. But then I would run out of steam and have to pull back. I would get another burst of energy and pedal ahead of everyone else. Then they would catch up and pass me. Once we reached our destination and were on our way back, one of the guys I had been cycling with had to actually push me, because I had no strength left. That is not the way to do it. The objective is to get there and back.

The same is true in the spiritual race. The objective is not to just run fast. It is to run long. Finish. That is the objective. If you want to grow up spiritually, then you need to pace yourself in this race of life—because you are in it for the long haul.

# *Weekend*

# FOR THE LONG-TERM

*Create in me a clean heart, O God, and renew a steadfast spirit within me.*
*(Psalm 51:10)*

If you're married, then you remember when you first met your wife or husband-to-be, and how you probably had the feeling of butterflies in your stomach and even a loss of appetite. You felt nervous when he or she was around. You wanted to make the best impression. But I hope you understand that those emotions aren't going to last throughout your entire marriage. I'm not saying that you won't have a deep, passionate love that will grow. But I am saying that I hope you're not expecting to always have the butterflies you once did.

It is kind of like driving a car. There is the love that brings you together, like an explosion that starts the engine. Next comes the actual driving of the car, which means that now you need to understand what real love is. The problem is that some people don't understand that. They think that when the emotional excitement is not there on a daily basis, they have fallen out of love and it is not working out. "I suppose we have irreconcilable differences," they say, "so let's just dissolve it." Then they move on to another relationship because they don't have a clue as to what real love is.

The idea is that first there is an excitement and passion that brings you together. Then you deepen and grow in what real love is.

In the same way, we need to mature in our relationship with God. It is more than a journey of feeling. It is also a journey of faith. So we must deepen in our love for God, because we are in it for the long-term. And we want to finish this race well.

*Monday*

# STAYING IN STEP

*"Can two walk together, unless they are agreed?"*
*(Amos 3:3)*

A while ago, I was having problems with my German shepherd whenever we went for a walk. If another dog came anywhere near him, he would go crazy and lunge out at the dog, even if it wasn't bothering him. When I shared this with the people who gave him to us, they asked me how I was walking him. I told them how, a lot of times, I would take him out, turn him loose, and let him go wherever he wanted to. Sometimes he would chase rabbits. When he was done, I would take him home.

They told me I couldn't do that anymore, because I was letting him run wild. They said, "The problem is that he is too 'doggy.' " They went on to explain how he needed to be reminded of who his master was. They said I needed to get him on his leash and use a muzzle device. I started using it, and I found that it did work. I would just pull on his muzzle a little bit and he couldn't go after that rabbit. He had to go where I wanted him to go. After awhile, I took the muzzle off. Now he no longer needs that device. I am the master, and he is the dog. He just goes where I go.

We can be like that with God. We say, "Here is what I want to do, Lord. You come with me."

But God says, "That is not the way it works. I want you to be more like Me. I want you to get in step with Me. I want you to go where I am going." When we do, we are living the Christian life to its fullest.

# *Tuesday*

# THE KEY TO ANSWERED PRAYER

*"If you abide in Me, and My words abide in you,*
*you will ask what you desire, and it shall be done for you."*
*(John 15:7)*

How often have you felt that your prayers were hitting a glass ceiling—as though the Lord were saying no? Maybe it is because you were praying outside of His will. Maybe it is because you were praying for something that God didn't want you to have.

We need to remember the promise Jesus spoke of in John 15, which says, "If you abide in Me, and My words abide in you, you will ask what you desire, and it shall be done for you." Another translation puts it this way: "If you maintain a living communion with Me and My words are at home with you, you can ask at once for yourself whatever your heart desires, and it is yours." I really like that translation—especially the part that tells us to ask at once whatever our hearts desire. But let's remember the condition: "If you maintain a living communion with Me and My words are at home with you. . . . " If you are maintaining a living communion with God, and His words are at home with you, then your desires are going to change. Your prayers will not necessarily be the same as they were before. As you get in sync with the will of God, you'll see that prayer is not getting God to do what you want Him to do, but that prayer is getting you to do what God wants you to do.

You will discover the important truth that prayer is not bending God our way—it is bending us His way. And then, you just may see your prayers being answered in the affirmative.

# THE URGENCY OF THE HOUR

*Then He said to His disciples,*
*"The harvest truly is plentiful, but the laborers are few."*
*(Matthew 9:37)*

I n his poem entitled, "The Second Coming," William Butler Yeats wrote, "The best lack all conviction, while the worst are full of passionate intensity." What a summary of the times in which we are living today: the worst have their passionate intensity, while the best lack all conviction.

While the church today dabbles with liberal concepts and even questions the authority of the Word of God in some aspects, the world outside our doors is running headlong into sin. When will we wake up? When are we going to get out there and get the gospel to the world? The world is pursuing its wickedness like never before. It is amazing how some people who believe in wicked, vile things will dedicate their entire lives to the promotion of those concepts. Meanwhile, there are so many Christians who know the Bible more than adequately, but who won't even lift a finger to get the gospel out to someone who lives right next to them. What is it going to take? We need to wake up to the urgency of the hour.

A survey among evangelical Christians revealed that 95 percent of those polled had never led another person to Christ. Yet Jesus gave us His marching orders. He said, "Go therefore and make disciples of all the nations, baptizing them in the name of the Father and of the Son and of the Holy Spirit, teaching them to observe all things that I have commanded you . . . " (Matt. 28:19–20). This is an order from our Commander in Chief, and it isn't merely addressed to pastors or missionaries. It's addressed to every man or woman who names the name of Christ.

## *Thursday*

# THROUGH HIS EYES

*But when He saw the multitudes, He was moved with compassion for them, because they were weary and scattered, like sheep having no shepherd. (Matthew 9:36)*

Everywhere Jesus went, He was very much in demand. There was always a crowd around Him, and understandably so. He was God in human form, walking through their streets. Everyone wanted something. There would be those who always wanted a touch, like the woman who had spent all of her money on doctors, trying to be cured, but to no avail. When she touched the hem of His garment, she was restored and healed. There is the story of the Syro-Phoenician woman who brought her demon-possessed child to Jesus, and the story of Jairus, who came and asked Jesus to touch his sick daughter.

Everyone needed something, but Jesus knew they needed more than just a healing, more than just a touch, and more than just a word. He knew the deepest need was in their soul. We see this demonstrated time and again. Despite His incredibly busy schedule, He went out of His way to meet someone in a little town where Jacob's well was located, even though she had no idea she had an appointment with God. She went to that well at that time of day, because she was a social outcast.

Sometimes when people do things that are wrong, we get angry with them. Not only do we hate the sin, but we end up hating the sinner also. Yet God wants us to see that while we can hate the sin, there is still a sinner who is loved by God. Maybe no one has ever told him or her there is another way to live. May God give us eyes to see this world as He sees it.

# JUST SHARE IT

*How then shall they call on Him in whom they have not believed?*
*And how shall they believe in Him of whom they have not heard?*
*And how shall they hear without a preacher?*
*(Romans 10:14)*

C ritics of mass evangelism, or crusade evangelism, say it is not effective. They say it is much better to share the gospel one-on-one, because trying to gather them in large stadiums is really not an effective way to reach people.

I would have to disagree. First of all, we find two forms of evangelism in the Book of Acts. We see what we might term as mass evangelism at work, and we also see examples of personal evangelism. Second, we have found that 85 percent of the people who come forward at a Harvest Crusade were brought by a friend. So essentially, one-on-one evangelism—personal evangelism, that is—was coupled with large-scale evangelism.

Therefore, a Harvest Crusade can be a catalyst for a believer to utilize in his or her evangelistic efforts. After all, there are a lot of unbelievers who won't go to church when Christians invite them. The reason is that something about the idea of going to church intimidates them. But when you invite them to a stadium, however, they are more likely to go with you. Of course, a Harvest Crusade is church too. In fact, it's a larger church than they would go to with their Christian friends. But whatever the motive an unbeliever may have for coming to a Harvest Crusade, they will hear the gospel.

God can use both large-scale evangelism and personal evangelism to get the gospel out. Both are important. It's vital that we share our faith one-on-one with people. But it's also important that we throw out the seeds of the gospel to as many people as we can.

# FOUR THINGS
# WE SHOULD KNOW

*He has planted eternity in the human heart.*
*(Ecclesiastes 3:11 NLT)*

There are four things we should know about every person on Earth. No matter how successful or unsuccessful they are, how famous or obscure they are, or how attractive or unattractive they may be, everyone shares these four traits.

One, there is an essential emptiness in every person who hasn't yet come to Christ. Everyone is essentially empty. No matter how much money or prestige someone has, everyone has to deal with that emptiness. Scripture says that God made His creation subject to vanity or emptiness, meaning there is a void, a hole if you will, inside every man, woman, and child.

Two, people are lonely. We can assume there is a sense of loneliness in every individual. Albert Einstein once wrote, "It is strange to be known so universally and yet be so lonely." People are lonely. We need to know that.

Three, people have a sense of guilt. They may try to mask it with alcohol or have a psychologist or psychiatrist tell them it is not there. But they have to deal with their guilt over the things they have done wrong. The head of a mental institution in London said, "I could release half of my patients if I could find a way to relieve them of their sense of guilt."

Four, people are afraid to die. Some may strut around and say, "Not me. I'm not afraid to die." But they are.

So don't be so intimidated by the facades that people hide behind and assume they don't want to hear what you have to say about your faith in Christ. Remember, you used to be one of those people. I used to be one of those people. We responded to the gospel. And so will they.

*Monday*

# FOLLOWING PHILIP'S EXAMPLE

*Then Philip went down to the city of Samaria and preached Christ to them.*
*(Acts 8:5)*

Acts 8 tells us that Philip went to Samaria. We may read that in passing and not think much of it. But it actually brings out an important point. Philip went to where people were. Here was a man overcoming his natural prejudice to bring the gospel to a group of people with whom he would not even have communicated under normal circumstances.

The Samaritans and the Jews hated each other. That is why, when Jesus asked the woman at the well for a drink, she said to Him, "How is it that You, being a Jew, ask a drink from me, a Samaritan woman?" (John 4:9).

Yet Philip went down to Samaria. He was not going to let prejudice keep him from bringing the message to someone who needed to hear it. He put those things aside. It is a reminder that there is no room for bigotry, no room for prejudice, and no room for bias in the life of the child of God. It also reminds us that we should not try to communicate only with people who look just like us. We may be more comfortable talking to someone who is basically our equal in age, gender, economic background, race, or whatever. But God wants us to take the gospel to all people. They may be younger. They may be older. They may be of a different race or background. It doesn't matter. Everyone needs Jesus.

There is another thing: Philip was essentially watering seeds that Jesus had sown a few years earlier. When Jesus spoke with the Samaritan woman, she came to faith and went out and told others. Now Philip was laboring in the same area. It reminds us that the process of conversion happens through reaping and sowing, often over a period of years.

# Tuesday

## SEIZE THE MOMENT

*Now an angel of the Lord spoke to Philip, saying, "Arise and go toward the south along the road which goes down from Jerusalem to Gaza." This is desert. So he arose and went.*
*(Acts 8:26–27)*

Have you ever been someplace where a baby is screaming so loudly that people are practically running away with their hands over their ears? Meanwhile, the baby's mother is sitting there as though nothing is happening. She has managed to tune this out, which is an uncanny ability that mothers possess.

We can do the same thing with God. He may be speaking to us, but we have essentially tuned Him out. Like Samuel, we might say, "Speak, Lord, your servant is listening," but we are not listening. And when He does speak, we aren't responding.

Philip was not this way, however. When we read in Acts 8 that an angel of the Lord told him to go to the desert, he went. How easily Philip could have argued. How easily he could have said, "What do you mean, 'Go to the desert'? For what? To do what? I am having a fruitful ministry here in Samaria. Get somebody else to go to the desert. I have work to do."

But the Spirit led Philip, and he responded to what God wanted him to do. That is very important. Philip responded, and he seized the moment. Why? Because he was the right person for the right job. God had uniquely equipped him to minister to the man from Ethiopia that he would meet there in the desert. And God has uniquely equipped you. Will you be available? Will you be open? If you will, then I believe God will call on you and give you the privilege of reaching others with the gospel.

# Going Fishing?

*Then He said to them, "Follow Me, and I will make you fishers of men."*
*(Matthew 4:19)*

While I am not in the ranks of great anglers and seasoned fishermen, I have fished a few times. I know that I need to use different kinds of bait for different kinds of situations, because different types of bait are required to catch different types of fish.

In the same way, as we share the gospel, we might bring up different aspects of it to speak to a person's situation. To someone who is filled with anguish, we might speak to them of the peace that God can bring. If we are talking with someone on his or her deathbed, we would address the subject of death and the certainty of heaven for those who put their faith in Christ. Another person might be plagued with personal guilt, so we might speak to him or her about God's offer of complete forgiveness.

These are various types of bait, so to speak, to bring us to a decision for Christ. And for our example, we can look to Jesus, the Master Communicator, who never dealt with any two people in exactly the same way. There was the woman at the well who had spent a lifetime trying to fill a void in her life with relationships with men. To her, Jesus spoke to her of her deep spiritual thirst. Then there was a man who was an expert in theology and a great intellectual. With him, Jesus spoke in almost childlike terms as He told him, "You must be born again." Jesus adapted to their situation and appropriately applied the truth of God's Word.

Jesus had time for the multitudes, but He also took time for the individual. And we should take time as well.

# *Thursday*

# AN EVANGELISM ESSENTIAL

*"Is not My word like a fire?" says the Lord,*
*"And like a hammer that breaks the rock in pieces?"*
*(Jeremiah 23:29)*

B illy Graham once said, "Time and time again in my ministry, I have quoted a Bible verse in a sermon, sometimes without planning to do so in advance, only to have someone tell me afterward it was that verse which the Holy Spirit used to bring conviction of faith to him."

Knowing God's Word is essential for any person who wants to lead others to Jesus Christ. Anyone who shares the gospel needs to use the Word of God.

When Philip met the Ethiopian in the desert, the Bible tells us, "Then Philip opened his mouth, and beginning at this Scripture, preached Jesus to him" (Acts 8:35). What if Philip had not been a student of Scripture when the Ethiopian was looking for answers? He would have had to say, "I don't know. ... that's a good question. Uh, can I get back to you?" Fortunately, Philip was well-versed in what the Scripture taught.

That is why we are told in 2 Timothy 2:15, "Be diligent to present yourself approved to God, a worker who does not need to be ashamed, rightly dividing the word of truth." I am not saying we need to have the answer to every question. But I am saying that we need to study and prepare ourselves as effectively as possible. And if we don't have the answer, let that propel us back into the pages of Scripture to find it for the next time that question arises.

# THE WHOLE TRUTH

*For if the word spoken through angels proved steadfast,*
*and every transgression and disobedience received a just reward,*
*how shall we escape if we neglect so great a salvation? (Hebrews 2:2–3)*

A doctor called one of his patients into his office and said, "I have some good news and some bad news." The patient said, "What's the good news?"
The doctor said, "You have only three weeks to live."
"That's the good news? Then what's the bad news?" asked the patient.

"I should have told you two weeks ago. I forgot. I'm so sorry."

How can people appreciate the good news about God's love and forgiveness in Jesus Christ if they don't understand the bad news about sin and judgment? Some people present the gospel as though Jesus were some kind of additive in life: "Accept Jesus and your teeth will be whiter and your clothes will be cleaner and your life will be better. And everything will be great." But here is the problem. What about the person who says, "You know what? I can see that you were once a miserable person. I can see that this has made you a happier person, and I am glad you have found religion. I am glad you have found God. But I'm not miserable like you were. I'm pretty happy with the things are going."

You see, it's not just about being happier. It's not about being a little bit more fulfilled. It's about facing a certain judgment if you reject God's offer of forgiveness through Jesus Christ. It's about not going to hell. We don't want to say these things, because it might be offensive. Yes, it might. But it just might be offensive enough for someone to start thinking about his or her life.

If we don't deliver the whole truth of the gospel, then we are not proclaiming the gospel. It's good news and it's bad news. Before we can appreciate the good news of forgiveness, we need to know the bad news about judgment.

# *Weekend*

# THE SIMPLE TRUTH

*I passed on to you what was most important and what had also been passed on to me—that Christ died for our sins, just as the Scriptures said. He was buried, and he was raised from the dead on the third day, as the Scriptures said.*
*(1 Corinthians 15:3–4 NLT)*

Someone once asked the great British preacher C. H. Spurgeon if he could put into a few words his Christian faith. He said, "Yes. I can give it to you in four words: Jesus died for me." That is what it comes down to.

The gospel in a nutshell is that Jesus Christ died for our sins and was buried and raised on the third day. That is the cornerstone. So when you are sharing the gospel, remind those you are speaking to that Jesus died for them. He shed His blood for them.

Paul the apostle was a brilliant person, known for his great skills of oratory. He was known for his grasp of culture and languages. And if anyone could have intellectually convinced a person of the validity of something, it was Paul. Yet here is what he said when it came to preaching the gospel: "Dear brothers and sisters, when I first came to you I didn't use lofty words and brilliant ideas to tell you God's message. For I decided to concentrate only on Jesus Christ and his death on the cross" (1 Cor. 2:1 NLT).

He also said, "For Christ didn't send me to baptize, but to preach the Good News—and not with clever speeches and high-sounding ideas, for fear that the cross of Christ would lose its power" (1 Cor. 1:17 NLT).

We can actually hinder the message of the gospel by complicating it. It's that simple, powerful, yet profound message that can change lives—that changed your life and mine.

*Monday*

# TELL YOUR STORY

*And this is the testimony:*
*that God has given us eternal life, and this life is in His Son.*
*(1 John 5:11)*

I have heard people talk about their life and all the horrible things they used to do before they became Christians. And as they are describing this, it almost seems as though they had more fun before they were Christians than they are having now. While they are talking, I'm thinking, *Something isn't right here.*

When you share your testimony, never glorify or exaggerate the past. You can essentially let people know that you weren't always the way you are. You can say, "I wasn't always this way. There was a moment when Christ came into my life. Here is what Jesus did for me." You can show people what has taken place in your life. It becomes a great bridge as you are sharing the gospel.

Often when I share my testimony, I will say things like, "This is the way I used to view Christians," and then I will describe how I viewed them, which was not in a very favorable light. The person I'm speaking with is usually nodding, probably because that is how they are viewing me at the moment. I will say, "And this is the way that I used to think. ... But here is what happened to me. Here is what Christ has done for me."

You see, for the person who was among the lowest of the low or the person who has been living a relatively moral life, the effect is still the same. We were all sinners separated from God and going to hell. But Christ died for us. We put our faith in Him. And we were forgiven.

People need to hear your testimony. Because everyone has a story to tell.

# *Tuesday*

# READY WITH THE REASON

*But sanctify the Lord God in your hearts,*
*and always be ready to give a defense to everyone who asks you*
*a reason for the hope that is in you, with meekness and fear.*
*(1 Peter 3:15)*

The Bible is a spiritual book, but it is also a logical book, and the Christian faith is a logical faith. Clearly there has to come a moment in every person's life in which he or she takes a step of faith, but there is a logical progression to the truths that are found in the Bible. They fit together. They make sense. And the more you understand them, the more you see that the other philosophies of the world do not really make sense.

We need to recognize that when we are seeking to share the gospel with people, they will often try to get us off track with their so-called reasons for why they do not come to Christ or with a great question that has really been troubling them.

We need to know what the Scripture teaches. The Bible tells us that, as believers, we should always be ready to give a defense to everyone who asks the reason for the hope that we have (see 1 Pet. 3:15). The phrase used for "answer" in this verse is a fascinating one, because it comes from the Greek word, *apologia*, from which we get our English word, apologetic. This word means to give a verbal defense to anyone who would ask us for a logical explanation.

However, we should do this with gentleness and respect, keeping a clear conscience, so those who speak maliciously against our good behavior in Christ will be ashamed of their slander. We should have answers. But we are to give those answers with gentleness and respect, not with arrogance, not with a know-it-all attitude, but with humility.

# OUR DUTY TO DISCIPLE

*And Jesus came and spoke to them, saying,*
*"All authority has been given to Me in heaven and on earth.*
*Go therefore and make disciples of all the nations."*
*(Matthew 28:18–19)*

After I became a Christian, I wasn't really sure of what to do next. I was seventeen years old and in high school. No one told me that I needed to read the Bible. No one told me that I should pray. No one told me that I should go to church. No one gave me any materials to read, much less a Bible.

So for a few days, I was in sort of a spiritual no-man's-land. I didn't really feel comfortable with my old friends that I had been hanging around with, but I didn't feel comfortable with the Christians either. One reason was that I could hardly understand what they were talking about as they spoke to each other in their cryptic, Christianese type of language.

Thankfully, a young man named Mark took me under his wing. He invited me to come to church with him and began to help me grow spiritually. He taught me how to read the Bible, and he prayed with me. He was the first actual Christian I knew who modeled for me what it meant to be a follower of Jesus. He wasn't a Bible scholar, but he was a real believer. He made an impact on my life and put me on the path of spiritual growth. In short, what Mark did was disciple me.

What he did for me is what we need to do for others—to not only seek to win men and women to Jesus Christ, but also disciple them. Anything less than this is falling short of the Great Commission.

# *Thursday*

# Marching Orders

*"Therefore go and make disciples of all nations, baptizing them
in the name of the Father and of the Son and of the Holy Spirit,
teaching them to observe all things that I have commanded you;
and lo, I am with you always, even to the end of the age."*
*(Matthew 28:19–20)*

Before we can effectively obey this command of Jesus to "make disciples of all nations," we must first be disciples ourselves. Having understood the prerequisite of this command, we are then to go and make disciples of others.

However, there are two important things to note. First, in the original language, this passage in Matthew 28 is not a suggestion; it is a command given to every Christian. That is why we call it the Great Commission and not the Great Suggestion. It is something our Commander in Chief has ordered us to do.

Second, these words were not merely directed to the original Twelve, nor are they meant today only for those we would classify as professionals, such as members of the clergy. These words are given to every follower of Jesus. We all are to obey them.

If I am a disciple, then I am to go and make disciples of others. And if I am not making disciples of others, then I am not being the disciple He wants me to be. Let me emphasize, however, that God never asks us to do something that He will not give us the power to do. The calling of God is the enabling of God. So if Jesus has commanded us to go and make disciples, then we must be confident that He will give us the ability to see it through.

# MAKING DISCIPLES

*So everywhere we go, we tell everyone about Christ.*
*We warn them and teach them with all the wisdom God has given us,*
*for we want to present them to God, perfect in their relationship to Christ.*
*(Colossians 1:28 NLT)*

What does it mean to make disciples? Matthew 28:20 defines it for us. Simply put, it means to teach others to observe what Jesus has said. To disciple people is to live out our faith in this world, to share it with others, to teach it by word, and to model it by example. The concept of going into all the world and making disciples is to share our faith, to seek to lead people to Christ, and then to the best of our ability, help them become spiritually mature.

Somewhere along the way, we have separated evange-lism from discipleship, but no such distinction is given in Scripture. They are part of each other. The idea is not just to share the gospel, lead someone to a decision for Christ, and then say, "God bless you. See you later." We wouldn't do that any more than a doctor delivering a baby would give the newborn a package of diapers, set him out on the sidewalk, and then say, "OK, son. It has been good to be with you for this brief time. All the best to you." A baby needs to be nur-tured, loved, and cared for. And so does a new believer.

To make disciples is to help new believers grow spiritually and become dedicated, committed, faithful, mature disciples of Jesus, and in turn, repeat the process with someone else. To make disciples is to reproduce yourself. It is to bring others to Christ, help them get on their feet spiritually, and then do that again and again.

# *Weekend*

# TRUE DISCIPLESHIP

*And when Saul had come to Jerusalem, he tried to join the disciples;*
*but they were all afraid of him, and did not believe that he was a disciple.*
*But Barnabas took him and brought him to the apostles.*
*(Acts 9:26–27)*

After Saul's conversion, there was great doubt among the believers as to whether he had really put his faith in Jesus Christ. After all, he had been a relentless persecutor of the early church. Some even thought his alleged conversion might have been a scheme to infiltrate their ranks.

So God spoke to a man named Ananias and instructed him to go and visit Saul. Ananias probably couldn't believe his ears: *Are we talking about the same Saul here? Are you talking about Saul of Tarsus?* But God told Ananias, "Go, for he is a chosen vessel of Mine to bear My name before Gentiles, kings, and the children of Israel. For I will show him how many things he must suffer for My name's sake" (Acts 9:15–16).

Then God brought another man into Saul's (or Paul's) life. His name was Barnabas, and he personally introduced Paul to all the other disciples and reassured them that his conversion was sincere.

Many of us would like to be a Paul. We would love to turn our world upside-down. But the question is, how many of us are willing to be an Ananias or a Barnabas? You may not be the next Paul. You may not be the next Billy Graham. But you might have an impact on the one who will be. That person you take under your wing could shake his or her world.

What Barnabas did is a good illustration of true discipleship, because discipling is not just teaching; it is also being a friend.

*Monday*

# EVANGELIZE OR FOSSILIZE

*The generous soul will be made rich,*
*and he who waters will also be watered himself.*
*(Proverbs 11:25)*

I f we were to be brutally honest, maybe the real reason we do not want to take a new believer under our wings is because we know we are not living the Christian life as it ought to be lived. We don't want that new believer to see our inconsistencies or our hypocrisies. Therefore we say, "I don't want to take on that responsibility."

But there is another way to look at it. Maybe we need to make some changes in our lives so we can be good examples to new believers. That doesn't mean we have to be perfect. Christians make mistakes too, and a mature believer can be a model for applying the truths of God. This is all part of the discipleship process.

There can come a point in your Christian life in which you face spiritual dryness. Has that ever happened to you? It may be that you don't necessarily need to attend more Bible studies, read more Christian books, go to more church services, or even pray more. The real problem may be that you don't have an outlet for what you are taking in. You need an outlet for your intake, or else you will stagnate. You have a choice: either evangelize or fossilize. When you take a new believer under your wing, you are not only helping him or her, but you are saving yourself from spiritual stagnation. New believers need our wisdom, knowledge, and experience. And we need their zeal, spark, and childlike faith.

Show me a church that does not have a constant flow of new believers, and I will show a church that is stagnating.

# Tuesday

# THE PEOPLE GOD CHOOSES

*"For the Lord does not see as man sees; for man looks at the outward appearance, but the Lord looks at the heart." (1 Samuel 16:7)*

Today we have those who consider themselves experts in the field of church growth. But quite honestly, I believe that a number of these "experts" have deviated from the principles for churches as given in Scripture. They will use modern techniques and supposedly proven methods that should result in a large church.

I wonder how the disciples would have fared if they had been subjected to the scrutiny of many of our church-growth experts today? I wonder how many of them would have approved of the people whom Jesus selected to change their world. What if Jesus had submitted the résumés of this ragtag bunch to a modern management group? The response may have been something like this:

> Dear Jesus, Thank you for submitting the résumés of the twelve candidates for management positions in your new organization. It is a staff opinion that most of your nominees are lacking in background, education, and vocational aptitude for the type of enterprise you are undertaking. They do not have the team concept. We would recommend that you continue your search for persons of experience, managerial ability, and proven capability.

Look at the people God chose, yet look at the results. God did extraordinary things through normal, average people—people like you and me. These were not people who were supernatural in their own abilities; rather, God supernaturally touched them. It was the work of the Holy Spirit through them that enabled them to change their world. We can all be encouraged and realize that God can use each of us to impact our culture and our world.

# It Takes One to Make One

*So the disciples did as Jesus had directed them.*
*(Matthew 26:19)*

I t is my belief that every disciple is a Christian, but not every Christian is necessarily a disciple. The very word "disciple" means "a learner." A disciple is a pupil, one who comes to be taught. But a disciple is not just a passively interested listener. The idea of a disciple is that of someone who listens to someone else who possesses full knowledge, and they drink in every word and mark every inflection of the voice with an intense desire to apply what has been taught. A disciple really wants to learn.

I daydreamed my way through a good portion of my early education. But I have found that I will listen when something is important to me. I have also found that I will listen if I think my life might depend on it. I must admit that when I fly, I don't listen all that closely to the flight attendants' safety procedures at the beginning of the flight. I will note where the emergency exits are and then go on with whatever I am doing. However, if the plane were going down and I knew that I had twenty minutes before impact, you can be sure I would listen carefully if that announcement were given one more time. Why? Because my life would depend upon it.

A disciple is one who listens carefully and pays attention, because the most important thing is to know what God requires, what God desires, and what God wills. Does that describe you? Are you His disciple? To obey His marching orders to go into all the world and make disciples, we need to know what a disciple really is. After all, it takes one to make one.

# *Thursday*

# GOD'S POP QUIZZES

*"And whoever does not bear his cross and come after Me cannot be My disciple. For which of you, intending to build a tower, does not sit down first and count the cost, whether he has enough to finish it?"*
*(Luke 14:27–28)*

Evangelist John Wesley said, "Give me a hundred men who love God with all of their hearts and fear nothing but sin, and I will move the world." I think that is still true today. God is looking for men and women who will love Him more than anyone or anything else.

God will bring tests into our lives to find out if we are really His disciples, if we are really going to stand tough. It's easy to mouth the concepts we find in Scripture. It's easy to say we believe those things. But what about when we really need to walk by faith and not by sight or by feeling? What about when we need to really trust the Lord? God will bring pop quizzes into our lives.

I remember when I was in school, my heart would always sink when the teacher stood up and said, "We are going to have a pop quiz today. I didn't tell you it was coming, but get out a piece of paper, because I am going to test you."

God tests us too. So if you are looking for a life of ease with no conflict or sacrifice, then the life of a disciple is not for you. But let me also add that if you don't want to be a disciple, then you don't want to be a true follower of Jesus Christ, because this is normal Christian living. And anything short of this is abnormal.

# CAN'T WE ALL JUST GET ALONG?

*Then He said to another, "Follow Me."*
*(Luke 9:59)*

In Luke 9 we read that when Jesus called a certain man to follow Him, He received an interesting response. "Lord, let me first go and bury my father," the man said (v. 59).

Jesus responded, "Let the dead bury their own dead, but you go and preach the kingdom of God" (v. 60). Our first reaction might be, "What a heartless statement that was! This guy's father is lying dead out in the street somewhere." Of course, that wasn't the case at all. The phrase, "Let me bury my father," was often used in that culture to speak of waiting until your parents eventually died. This man was saying, in other words, "Let me wait until my parents are gone. I can't do this right now."

Jesus was saying, "Follow Me," but this man was saying, "I don't want to right now." Why? Maybe he thought if he told his parents he was going to follow Jesus as his Messiah, they wouldn't like it. There might be conflict. There might be friction. So he may have been saying, in reality, "Lord, I don't want conflict. I don't want hardship. I don't want friction. I will follow You at another time, when it's more convenient."

If we decide to be true disciples of Jesus, it will cause conflict in some of our relationships. If you say to your parents, husband or wife, or some of your friends, "I am going to follow Christ," they won't always applaud your decision. They may disagree with you.

Here is what it comes down to: Either you will have harmony with God and friction with people, or you will have harmony with people and friction with God. But you can't have it both ways.

# *Weekend*

# A LOVE THAT PREVAILS

*"If anyone comes to Me and does not hate his father and mother,
wife and children, brothers and sisters, yes, and his own life also,
he cannot be My disciple."*
*(Luke 14:26)*

I f ever there comes a time when the call of the highest
earthly love and the cross of Christ conflict, then the
call of Christ must prevail.

A good illustration of one's love for God being stronger
than his love for others can be found in the life of Abraham.
God told Abraham that he would have a son. But eventually Abraham took things into his own hands and had a son
named Ishmael with Sarah's handmaid. However, this was not
the fulfillment of God's plan. Then in Abraham and Sarah's
later years, they finally had a son, Isaac, whose name meant
"laughter." God had told Abraham that his seed would be as
the sand of the sea and the stars of the sky. Abraham knew it was
through this child Isaac that all this would happen. But one day
God told Abraham to take Isaac to the land of Moriah and sacrifice him there (see Gen. 22). Of course, God spared Isaac.
He never intended to take his life. Instead, God was testing
Abraham's commitment.

First and foremost, God tells us, "Love Me above everyone
else. And if you are going to be My disciple, then your love for
others must seem like hatred in comparison to your love for
Me." Is that true of you today?

Maybe some of us need to bring our Isaacs, so to speak, to
the Lord. Do you know what God will do then? He will say,
"Just testing you. Now I am going to bless you." He may even
do above and beyond what you had ever planned for yourself.

*Monday*

# WHAT JESUS ASKS

*But know this, that in the last days perilous times will come:*
*For men will be lovers of themselves.*
*(2 Timothy 3:1–2)*

When Jesus told His disciples, "If anyone desires to come after Me, let him deny himself, and take up his cross daily, and follow Me" (Luke 9:23), He was telling them (and us) that if we try to save our lives, we will lose them. But if we lose our lives for His sake, we will find them. It means that we must deny ourselves.

Of course, this goes against the pervading philosophy of today. After all, we need self-love, we are told. We need to realize our self-worth. We need a better self-image and more self-esteem.

In short, we are a self-obsessed culture. Yet according to the Bible, our problem is not low self-esteem or a poor self-image. The problem is that we are too preoccupied with ourselves. The Bible does not teach that we should love ourselves. Rather, the Bible teaches that we *do* love ourselves.

In fact, the Bible says this will be one of the characteristics of the last days: "For men will be lovers of themselves, lovers of money, boasters, proud, blasphemers, disobedient to parents, unthankful, unholy, unloving, unforgiving, slanderers, without self-control, brutal, despisers of good, traitors, headstrong, haughty, lovers of pleasure rather than lovers of God ..." (2 Tim. 3:2–4). These things are the outgrowth of loving ourselves rather than loving God.

Jesus did not say that we need to love ourselves. We already do that well. He was saying, "I want you to love Me more than yourself. I want you to love Me more than anyone and anything else." This is what Jesus asked of His disciples. And this is what He asks of us.

# Tuesday

# WHAT SELF-DENIAL MEANS

*Then He said to them all,*
*"If anyone desires to come after Me, let him deny himself."*
*(Luke 9:23)*

What did Jesus mean when He said, "If anyone desires to come after Me, let him deny himself ... "? The phrase "deny" used in Luke 9:23 could be translated, "repudiate," "disown," "forfeit," or "totally disregard."

As C. S. Lewis wrote in *Mere Christianity*, "The real test of being in the presence of God is, that you either forget about yourself altogether or see yourself as a small, dirty object. It is better to forget about yourself altogether."[1] Understand, the Bible is not teaching self-hate. It is not teaching that we should be miserable, self-loathing people. Rather, it is saying that we are to see ourselves as we are. You already love yourself. So instead of loving yourself, deny yourself, and love God more than you love your own life. If you will take your life and give it to Him, then He will give you His life in its place. If you lose your life, then you will find it.

So when we hear people say they are trying to find themselves, what they really need to do is lose themselves. We need to say, "Lord, here is my life." That may sound like the more miserable thing to do, yet it is the greatest thing you could possibly do. What God will give you in the place of what you give Him is infinitely better. If I have learned nothing else about God in my years as a Christian, I have learned that God's plans are better than my plans. So we should not be afraid to commit an unknown future to a known God.

# BEARING THE CROSS

*Then He said to them all, "If anyone desires to come after Me,*
*let him deny himself, and take up his cross daily, and follow Me."*
*(Luke 9:23)*

I f you were visiting first-century Jerusalem and happened to see a contingent of Roman soldiers come down the street with a man bearing his cross, you would think, *That poor guy is going to die today.* It was a shameful thing to be crucified. It was a long, tortuous, and painful death reserved for the most hardened criminals. The Romans would utilize this horrible form of torture to make an example of people. It was common knowledge that any man bearing his cross was going to die.

So when Jesus said, "If anyone desires to come after Me, let him deny himself, and take up his cross daily," it meant dying to yourself. Some people will misunderstand this. They say, "We all have a cross to bear. My cross to bear is my career," or "My cross to bear is this physical impairment," or "My cross to bear is this difficult circumstance." But that is not really using the phrase properly. The cross is the same for every man and woman; it doesn't vary from person to person. Bearing the cross simply means dying to self.

This means exchanging your life for the life of God, your plans for His plans, and your goals for His goals. Samuel Rutherford said, "His cross is the sweetest burden that I ever bare. It is such a burden as wings are to a bird, or sails are to a ship, to carry me forward to my harbor."[2] Rutherford discovered what we can know as well: When you really die to yourself, you will find yourself.

# Thursday

# TRUE DISCIPLES

*Do not love the world or the things in the world.*
*If anyone loves the world, the love of the Father is not in him.*
*(1 John 5:15)*

I've never been one for long, drawn-out emotional appeals for people to do certain things, especially when it's making a decision to follow Christ. I want a person to come forward during an evangelistic invitation because they have chosen to. And I would rather have fewer come forward who mean it than more come forward who don't mean it. Jesus wants people who have counted the cost and are His true followers. And what is the cost of discipleship?

First, we must pay the price of the sins that we now cherish. We must give them up—every single one. As disciples of Jesus, we cannot cling to a single sin and pretend that we are still following Him. Instead, we must walk in friendship and fellowship with God. There is no room for a double life here.

Second, we must pay the price of this world's friendship. James 4:4 says, "Whoever therefore wants to be a friend of the world makes himself an enemy of God." We must not allow worldly and secular philosophy to color our thinking and living. We may be laughed at for our convictions, mocked for our beliefs, and scorned for trying to live by what the Bible teaches. But in place of the world's friendship, we will have God's.

Third, we must pay the price of the plans for our own lives. We may have ideas of what we want to do or don't want to do. But we must be willing to give them up if God asks us to.

If we will live as true disciples, then we will impact our world.

# IN HIS STRENGTH

*"For the battle is the Lord's, and He will give you into our hands."*
*(1 Samuel 17:47)*

The Greek historian Herodotus told the story of three hundred men from Sparta who bravely defended their country against the invasion of the Persian army. When the Persians launched an attack against Greece with a force of more than two million fighting men led by Xerxes, they had to pass through a little area known as the pass of Thermopylae, which was a small opening through some jagged cliffs.

The armies of Greece, obviously wanting to turn back their attackers, called for troops, but all they were able to rally were three hundred soldiers from Sparta, led by their king, Leonidas. He thought that if he could just hold the area for awhile, reinforcements would come. So he led his three hundred men against the two million Persians at Thermopylae. Much to the surprise of everyone, the Spartans fought bravely and valiantly, and they were winning. Persian soldiers dropped one after the other. So Xerxes sent in his elite troops called the Immortals. These were the best men in his army, but the Spartans slaughtered the Immortals like everyone else. Eventually the Persians prevailed when a Greek traitor showed them the way to attack the Spartans from behind. All three hundred men were killed. And though they lost the battle, they did not lose the war, because the reinforcements finally came. The Spartans had bought much-needed time, and the armies of Greece ultimately prevailed against the Persians.

The same is true in the spiritual world as we fight a spiritual war. God can do a lot with a little. Our numbers may not be large. But our God is all-powerful. And as we go forward in His strength, we can make a difference.

# *Weekend*

# LIFE TO THE FULLEST

*"I have come that they may have life, and that they may have it more abundantly."*
*(John 10:10)*

A missionary went to Africa to bring the gospel to a tribe of cannibals. The men in this tribe were so vicious, they would carve their teeth into points in preparation for their attacks. The missionary thought, *If I could reach the chief of this tribe, if he would put his faith in Christ, then the others would soon follow.*

The problem was this missionary tended to emphasize the negatives of Scripture. So instead of telling the chief about the wonderful liberty and freedom that can be found in Christ, this missionary kept hammering on the importance of keeping certain rules.

After listening to the missionary for awhile, the chief said, "So you are telling me that I can't take my neighbor's wife."

"That's right," the missionary said.

"Or his oxen or his ivory."

"Right again" the missionary said.

"And I must not dance the war dance and then go out and ambush my enemies on the trail and kill them."

"Right again" the missionary said.

"But I cannot do any of these things," the chief said. "I am too old. It seems to me that being old and being a Christian are being the same thing."

That is how a lot of people view the Christian life. They see Christians living by certain standards, and it bothers them that we have the audacity, in their minds, to try to push our supposedly outmoded views on them.

If only they could see that God's commandments were given not to make our lives miserable, but to make our lives full. His commandments are barriers He has erected around our lives to protect us so that we might live our lives to the fullest.

*Monday*

# HOLDING TO THE TRUTH

*Instead, we will hold to the truth in love, becoming more and more in every way like Christ, who is the head of his body, the church.*
*(Ephesians 4:15 NLT)*

In 1991, an interesting little book was published called *The Day America Told the Truth*. The authors polled Americans with the assurance they would remain anonymous. They asked only that their questions be answered truthfully, and they received some very amazing answers. It was shocking to find how many Americans lie and steal and are immoral on a regular basis. The authors concluded that when it comes to right and wrong, Americans were a law unto themselves. Of those surveyed for the book, 93 percent declared that they, and no one else, determine what is and isn't moral in their lives.

It seems we have developed a have-it-our-way approach to faith in God. We want God to conform to our wishes. It is religion à la carte, where we choose only what appeals to us. In some churches today, pastors are giving shorter and shorter sermons. They say their congregations don't have the attention spans to listen any longer. The problem is that these sermonettes are producing Christianettes. I would venture to say that more people in the church today know more about self-esteem than they know about self-denial. They know more about inner healing than they do about outward obedience. We are living in a day in which many Christians place psychology on the same level as the Bible—or above it.

This is a dangerous time. We should heed the warning of C. S. Lewis, who, many years ago, said, "If you do not listen to theology, that will not mean that you have no ideas about God. It will mean that you have a lot of wrong ones."

# Tuesday

# THE MIRROR OF GOD'S LAW

*The law was our guardian and teacher to lead us until Christ came.*
*So now, through faith in Christ, we are made right with God.*
*(Galatians 3:24 NLT)*

Some people really like mirrors. They are always looking in them. When they are driving along, they have their rearview mirror pointed at themselves instead of the road behind them. If they are in a restaurant that has a mirror on the wall, they want to be seated across from it so they can look at themselves. They never miss an opportunity to catch a quick glance at themselves if a mirror is nearby. On the other hand, some of us don't like mirrors that much. In fact, we have come to dislike mirrors, especially first thing in the morning.

A mirror reflects your image, and that isn't necessarily a bad thing. For example, imagine that you're leaving a restaurant on your way back to work, and you notice everyone is smiling at you. You think, "I'm feeling good. Everyone loves me." Then you catch a glimpse of yourself in a mirror, and you find out why they are smiling. You didn't just eat your lunch—you're wearing it. A piece of pasta is affixed to your chin, marinara sauce and all. It's embarrassing. But better that you saw it in the mirror and dealt with the problem than spend the rest of the day with that noodle on your chin. The mirror showed you something about yourself that needed to be fixed.

In the same way, the law of God is like a moral mirror. When we look in the mirror of God's law, we see that major changes need to take place. We also realize that we can't keep things as they were. So that mirror drives us to Jesus.

# THE GREATEST COMMANDMENT

*"I will put My law in their minds, and write it on their hearts;*
*and I will be their God, and they shall be My people."*
*(Jeremiah 31:33)*

O n one occasion a scribe came to Jesus and asked, "Which is the first commandment of all?"

Jesus said, " 'And you shall love the Lord your God with all your heart, with all your soul, with all your mind, and with all your strength.' This is the first commandment. And the second, like it, is this: 'You shall love your neighbor as yourself.' There is no other commandment greater than these" (Mark 12:30–31).

That must have been somewhat troubling to this scribe: *Of all the commandments, there is none greater than these?* But when you get down to it, those two commandments summarize them all. If you really love God with all your heart, with all your soul, with all your strength, and with all your mind, then you will not want to break the other commandments. If you really love God as you ought to, then you will not take His name in vain, have other gods before Him, or make images that you bow down before. And if you really love your neighbor as yourself, you will not steal from him. You will not covet what belongs to him. And certainly you will not kill him. So if we get these basics down of loving God and loving others as we ought to, then obeying the Ten Commandments will come naturally.

Augustine said, "Love God and do as you please." It is a provocative statement, but it makes sense. If you really love God as you ought to—with all of your heart, soul, mind and strength—then you will naturally do the things the commandments teach.

# *Thursday*

# UNCONDITIONAL LOVE

*For there is one God and one Mediator between God and men,*
*the Man Christ Jesus. (1 Timothy 2:5)*

Many people have gone to church their entire lives and may think of themselves as Christians, but their concept of God is that of One who needs to be appeased. They believe the more good works they do, the more they will appease God. They are not able to say with complete confidence, "I know that if I were to die today, I would go to heaven." They want to go there. They think there is a very good chance they will go there. But they are not certain.

God wants us to have assurance of our salvation. But here is what it comes down to: No matter how good of a life we live, no matter how many laws we keep and rituals we observe, we are never going to satisfy the requirements of God on our own.

But if we realize that Jesus Christ died on that cross in our place, that He and He alone satisfied the righteous demands of God, and if we put our faith in Him, then we will be just fine. The way I am going to get into heaven on that final day is not because I am a pastor. I am going to get into heaven because of the shed blood of Christ, because I admitted I was a sinner, and because I repented of my sin and put my faith in Him.

That's the same way we all get in. Everyone comes in through the shed blood of Christ. Maybe you have been trying to please God all these years and have never known that He loves you. You don't have to earn His love. You have it. It's there. Unconditionally.

# *Friday*

# Our Privilege

*And God spoke all these words, saying:*
*"I am the Lord your God, who brought you out of the land of Egypt,*
*out of the house of bondage."*
*(Exodus 20:1–2)*

Before the Lord gave the first of the Ten Commandments to Moses, He offered a reminder of what He has done for His people, the Israelites. He was saying, "Remember, I brought you out of Egypt. You were slaves. You were in bitter bondage. You were in misery. You called out, and I sent a deliverer, Moses. He brought you out of that land of oppression and slavery. Remember that I did this for you."

In the same way, we were once living under the power of sin. We were facing a Christless eternity and a certain judgment. But God, in His great mercy, loved us and reached out to us. And when we put our faith in Him through His Son, Jesus Christ, He pardoned us and forgave us of every sin that we had ever committed.

God was saying to the Israelites, "Before I tell you what I want you to do for Me, I want to remind you of what I have done for you." The same principle is true for us. God is saying to us, "Before I give you My laws and standards, I want to remind you of what I have done for each of you."

Now if I really appreciate what God has done for me, it should be my privilege and pleasure to seek to live a life that is pleasing to Him. It is not because I have to, but because I want to. As 1 John 4:19 reminds us, "We love Him because He first loved us." Our obedience to God's commandments should spring from our love for Him.

# *Weekend*

# A HIGHER MOTIVE

*You know how we exhorted, and comforted, and charged every one of you ... that you would walk worthy of God who calls you into His own kingdom and glory. (1 Thessalonians 2:11–12)*

The great British preacher, C. H. Spurgeon, said, "What is the value of the grace we profess to receive which leaves us exactly the same kind of people as we were before we received it? An unholy life is an evidence of an unchanged heart and an unchanged heart is an evidence of an unsaved soul."

Some people have an image of God and His laws in which they believe that if they fall short, God is going to punish them. And while it is true there are repercussions for disobedience to God, we should not merely obey God because we are afraid of what will happen to us if we don't. The higher motive, the better motive, and the purer motive is to obey God out of love for Him. In recognition of all that God has done for us, we should now want to reciprocate and show Him our gratitude by obeying Him.

Jesus said, "If you love Me, keep My commandments" (John 14:15). Why? Because as James tells us, faith without works is dead (see James 2:17). If someone says they have truly committed their life to Christ, if someone says they really love God and yet live in open sin, then their love for Him seems highly unlikely.

I am not suggesting that a Christian will not violate God's commands. I am not even suggesting that we will never fall short of them. But what I am saying is that if we really are children of God, we should be seeking to lead lives that are pleasing to Him.

*Monday*

# THE FIRST COMMANDMENT

> *"You shall have no other gods before Me."*
> *(Exodus 20:3)*

A lan Redpath said, "Our god is the person we think the most precious, for whom we would make the greatest sacrifice, and moves our hearts with the warmest love. He or it is the person who, if we lost him, would leave us desolate."

That really opens up the possibilities. There are many things that can be gods in our lives. It is basically what we live for, what we think about, and what we get up for in the morning. For many, their god is themselves. They worship themselves. Romans 1:25 describes those "who exchanged the truth of God for the lie, and worshiped and served the creature rather than the Creator, who is blessed forever." Some people worship their bodies. And though I am not against keeping yourself in shape, the pendulum can swing too far that way. There are people who are absolutely absorbed with their appearance. They invest hours and hours into trying to look a certain way. Others worship the god of success or the god of pleasure. Philippians 3:19 refers to people "whose god is their belly, and whose glory is in their shame—who set their mind on earthly things." Then there is the god of possessions. Jesus said, "No one can serve two masters; for either he will hate the one and love the other, or else he will be loyal to the one and despise the other. You cannot serve God and mammon" (Matt. 6:24).

Every man, every woman, has a god—someone or something they live for, some pursuit in life they get passionate about. And the true but terrifying thought is that a person can worship in church every Sunday, but in fact be a full-tilt idolater.

# Tuesday

## UNEXPECTED IDOLS

*He said to him, "Follow Me." (John 21:19)*

There might be a man or a woman that God has used in your life, perhaps a pastor, a teacher, a parent, or a friend who has had a dramatic influence on you. Then one day, you discovered they were human, and yes, that they even make mistakes. You were devastated. Maybe you thought, "If a person like that would make a mistake, then I'm not going to be a Christian."

But let me ask this: whom you are following? If you are ready to abandon your faith because someone you respected slipped up, that would suggest to me that you are not worshiping the Lord, but instead have made a god out of a person. Other people can be a good influence on us, but they will fail now and then. All of us will fail at one time or another.

We can also make a god out of tradition. When the Israelites were rebelling against God, He judged them by sending venomous serpents into their midst. Then He instructed Moses to make a serpent out of bronze and put it up on a pole. Those who had been bitten by the serpents saw it and were healed. But years later, they ended up worshiping that image of the snake wrapped around the pole, and King Hezekiah had to destroy it (see 2 Kings 18:4). Something that had been legitimately used of God became an idol.

Sometimes we think only bad things can become idols. But idols can be things that are good, but that we put in an improper place in our lives. You can make a good thing into an idol that can eventually get in the way of the Lord. That is why we need to be careful.

# IN SPIRIT AND TRUTH

*Their idols are silver and gold, the work of men's hands. …*
*Those who make them are like them; so is everyone who trusts in them.*
*(Psalm 115:4, 8)*

Some people say they need a picture or an image to help them visualize God. But Jesus said, "God is Spirit, and those who worship Him must worship in spirit and truth" (John 4:24). God doesn't want us to have any image to help us in our worship. After all, who can paint God? Who can give us an accurate representation of who God is? I'm not saying that every painting of Jesus is bad. But I will say this: it probably isn't very accurate. None of us know what Jesus looked like.

I find it interesting that of all the details we find about Jesus in the Bible, not one person took the time to give us a physical description of Him. Couldn't one writer have said, "Oh, by the way, Jesus was about 5" 11", and the color of His hair was. … "? But we don't have anything. God did not give us a picture, and I think I know why. With our penchant for idolatry, no doubt we would have made an image out of Him.

"God is Spirit, and those who worship Him must worship in spirit and truth." If I need some holy object to help me worship God, then something is wrong. Whatever that image, no matter how beautifully it is done, it will not be accurate. It will give me a false concept of what God is really like. And if the image is false, then the thought of God is false. And that will produce a character that is false, because we become like the god we worship.

# Thursday

## THE UNBREAKABLE LAWS OF GOD

*Let us hear the conclusion of the whole matter: Fear God and keep His commandments, for this is man's all.*
*(Ecclesiastes 12:13)*

I t is my belief that one of the reasons for the great success of the United States of America over our two hundred-plus years can be found in our origins, the fact that our founding fathers built this country on a belief in Scripture and in the Ten Commandments. To quote James Madison, our fourth president, "We stake the future of this country on our ability to govern ourselves under the principles of the Ten Commandments."

Now that certainly is a far cry from where we are now. But we desperately need the Ten Commandments today, and we desperately need to follow them. We can either accept the truths of these commandments or fight against them as a nation and as individuals. And, I might add, we will reap the inevitable results.

As Vance Havner once said, "You cannot break the laws of God. You break yourself against them. You might as well try to attack Gibraltar with a pop gun as to go up against the laws of God. You can jump off a skyscraper, but you do not break the law of gravitation. You break your neck, but not the law of gravitation." He is right. You cannot break the laws of God, but you will break yourself against them. You can buck against these truths and say, "These don't apply to me, and I will live the way that I want to live." Or, you can see the wisdom God has in giving these commandments to us. It's your choice. You can do it the easy way. Or you can do it the hard way.

*Friday*

# MAKE THE RIGHT CHOICE

*The laws of the Lord are true. . . . They are a warning to those who hear them; there is great reward for those who obey them. (Psalm 19:9–11 NLT)*

Solomon was a man who rebelled against the truth he had learned from God and decided to sample just about everything the world had to offer. And basically having unlimited resources, he went on a sinful binge. Afterward he said that it was all vanity, like chasing after the wind. The Book of Ecclesiastes records his conclusion for us: "Here is my final conclusion: Fear God and obey his commands, for this is the duty of every person" (Eccl. 12:13 NLT). In other words, "Don't fight against the laws of God. They were given to us for a reason."

God in His commandments, has given us the blueprint for a fulfilled life, a blueprint for happiness, if you will. Psalm 1 says,

> Oh, the joys of those who do not follow the advice of the wicked, or stand around with sinners, or join in with scoffers. But they delight in doing everything the Lord wants; day and night they think about his law. They are like trees planted along the riverbank, bearing fruit each season without fail. Their leaves never wither, and in all they do, they prosper.
> (vv. 1–3 NLT)

In contrast, the psalm continues, "But this is not true of the wicked. They are like worthless chaff, scattered by the wind" (v. 4 NLT). You can either be like the happy person who avoids the things that will drag him or her down and embraces the truth and the commandments of God. Or, you can be like the ungodly person who chases after the wind, as Solomon once tried to do. There is your choice.

# Weekend

# WILLING TO FORGIVE

*Let all bitterness, wrath, anger, clamor, and evil speaking be put away from you, with all malice. And be kind to one another, tenderhearted, forgiving one another, even as God in Christ forgave you. (Ephesians 4:31–32)*

Have you ever been angry with someone without cause? Or to rephrase that, have you ever driven on a freeway?

Many people, in the depths of their heart, have anger and hatred to such a degree that their true desire would be for the one they hate to be dead. But that is clearly forbidden in Scripture. We read in I John 3:15, "Whoever hates his brother is a murderer, and you know that no murderer has eternal life abiding in him." The word used here for "hates" means "to habitually despise." It implies not just a transient emotion of the affections, but a deep-rooted loathing. The Bible is not saying that it is always a sin to be angry. But the idea in I John 3:15 is that of deep-seated anger and continuing resentment. It is to habitually despise.

Some people hold grudges. They operate by the phrase, "Don't get mad. Get even." Maybe someone has wronged you. Maybe they have taken advantage of you or slandered you, and you've thought, "I hate them. I wish they would just drop dead." But there is no place for thinking like this on the part of the believer. God says, "Vengeance is mine" (Heb. 10:30). You have to let it go and forgive that person, whether or not he or she deserves it.

You have been forgiven a great debt, and as a child of God, you must forgive others. If we know anything of what God has done for us, then we must extend the forgiveness we have received to others as well.

*Monday*

# THE ENEMY ON THE INSIDE

*"Look, this was the iniquity of your sister Sodom:*
*She and her daughter had pride, fullness of food, and abundance of idleness;*
*neither did she strengthen the hand of the poor and needy."*
*(Ezekiel 16:49)*

Jesus described His time as a wicked and an adulterous generation. And if it was true of the generation that He spoke to, how much more true is it today? There was a time when America was that "city on a hill," setting the example for the rest of the world of faith, freedom, and family. In ideology, we were without peer. The Protestant work ethic brought by the Pilgrims, which some make fun of now, produced a robust, productive, and powerful force for good—not only in our nation but also around the world. But it seems America has begun to rot from within. We have effectively resisted enemies on the outside, yet we have forgotten about the enemy on the inside. We have gone in the ways of Sodom.

When we think of Sodom and Gomorrah, we immediately remember the gross immorality. But consider the sins that led up to it. In speaking to Sodom, God said, "Look, this was the iniquity of your sister Sodom: She and her daughter had pride, fullness of food, and abundance of idleness; neither did she strengthen the hand of the poor and needy" (Ezekiel 16:49). That describes our country today: We are proud. We have fullness of food. We have abundance of idleness.

Today we celebrate the very things that the Bible says we should have no part of. And while some people see God's commands as restrictive, even oppressive, in reality they are God's grid for right living, the set of absolutes we have been searching for in an ever-changing time of moral relativism.

# Tuesday

# THINK BEFORE YOU SPEAK

*The lips of the righteous know what is acceptable,*
*but the mouth of the wicked what is perverse.*
*(Proverbs 10:32)*

J Vernon McGee used to say, "The only exercise some Christians get is running down others and jumping to conclusions."

Slander and gossip are sins that, unfortunately, are far too common in the church today. How many times have rumors been spread that are based on information that simply is not factual, because a person did not take the time to look into it? The Bible says, "He who answers a matter before he hears it, it is folly and shame to him" (Proverbs 18:13).

Gossip and slander are far easier to dish out than they are to take, aren't they? Has someone ever gossiped about you? Has something ever been said about you that simply was not true? Proverbs 18:8 says, "The words of a talebearer are like tasty trifles, and they go down into the inmost body." Gossip is like that. "Did you hear about this?" someone might say. So we take that tasty little trifle of information. We may swallow it easily, but in the end, it is like a wound. It hurts other people, and it can hurt us.

So when we hear gossip or slander, what should we do? Here is a little acronym that we need to remember: THINK. Is it *true*? If it is not true, then don't repeat it. Will it *help*? Is it *inspiring*? Is it *necessary*? Is it *kind*?

*Well, Greg,* you might be thinking, *If I applied that principle all the time, there would be a lot of things I wouldn't say.* Good. Then don't say them. You will be better for it. And so will many other people.

# The Many Faces of Deceit

*These six things the Lord hates, Yes, seven are an abomination to Him:*
*A proud look, a lying tongue, hands that shed innocent blood,*
*a heart that devises wicked plans, feet that are swift in running to evil,*
*a false witness who speaks lies, and one who sows discord among*
*brethren. (Proverbs 6:16–19)*

F lattery has been defined as saying things to someone's face that you would never say behind his or her back. It is one of the most subtle forms of deceit. We often flatter people when we want something from them. And it can be a form of lying.

There are many other ways in which we can lie. Exaggeration is a form of lying, and it is very easy to do. We tell our tales about the one that got away, and the fish gets bigger with each telling. I must say, in all honesty, that preachers have a real problem with this one—stretching the truth or exaggerating things so they will look good for us. We call it "evangelistically speaking," and I have seen it happen far too often.

Another way we can lie is through silence. How can we lie by being quiet? It is when we hear something being said about someone that we know is not true. We have the opportunity to refute it and say, "I know this person. I know the facts, and that is wrong." But we stay silent, because we don't want to get involved. But that can be lying too.

Three of the seven things that God specifically says He hates have to do with lying: A lying tongue, a false witness who pours out lies, and a person who sows discord among the brothers. From this we can safely conclude that God truly hates lying.

# *Thursday*

# THE UNDERESTIMATED SIN

*Therefore put to death your members which are on the earth: fornication,
uncleanness, passion, evil desire, and covetousness, which is idolatry.
(Colossians 3:5)*

A Roman Catholic priest who had heard the confessions of two thousand people said he had heard people confess iniquity of every kind, including adultery and even murder. But he had never heard anyone confessing to the sin of covetousness.

Coveting is a very subtle sin that can lead to things that are far worse. To covet is to eagerly desire that which belongs to another, to set the heart on something. A literal translation of the word means "to pant after something," almost suggesting the idea of an animal. Coveting is not just admiring your neighbor's car. It is wanting your neighbor's car—not one like it, but *his* car. And coveting usually leads to action. Coveting is a powerful and underestimated sin that can cripple us spiritually and ultimately destroy us. It should not be underestimated or left unchecked.

Think of the people in the Bible who tragically gave in to the sin of coveting. Consider Eve and how sin came into the human race. Genesis tells us, "So when the woman saw that the tree was good for food, that it was pleasant to the eyes, and a tree desirable to make one wise, she took of its fruit and ate … " (Gen. 3:6). She saw. She delighted. She desired. She took. She gave.

So coveting works like this. The eyes admire an object. The mind considers it. The will goes over it. The body moves into possession. That is coveting. And it is a sin that we can so easily commit.

# FINDING THE GOOD
# IN BAD TIMES

*Now no chastening seems to be joyful for the present, but painful;*
*nevertheless, afterward it yields the peaceable fruit of*
*righteousness to those who have been trained by it.*
*(Hebrews 12:11)*

Have you ever had the bottom drop out of life? Suddenly and without warning, one problem after another comes tumbling into your life. And then when it seems completely hopeless, like there is no way out, everything improves.

Why does God allow calamities into our lives as Christians? Why does God allow tragedy into the life of the believer? Why do we experience trials? James addresses these questions in the first chapter of his epistle. But the first thing he tells us is, "My brethren, count it all joy when you fall into various trials" (v. 2). What kind of thing is that to say to someone who is suffering? And what does it mean? Is it like saying to someone who is going through really hard times, "Don't worry. Be happy!"? Is that what James is saying? Yes and no. He encourages us to rejoice. But there is a reason for what he is saying.

James is not suggesting that we should necessarily be experiencing some all-encompassing emotion of joy or happiness in our times of hardship. Nor is he demanding that we must necessarily enjoy our trials in life. James is not saying that trials themselves are a joy, because usually they are not. But yet James says, "Count it all joy." He is saying, "Make a deliberate and careful decision to experience joy in your troubles and trials." It is not easy, but it is possible.

You see, there are lessons to be learned during times of trial. And there are lessons that can only be learned through times of trial. Just remember, they won't last forever.

# *Weekend*

# THE HARDEST
# PEOPLE TO REACH

*For even His brothers did not believe in Him. (John 7:5)*

It is interesting to note that neither James nor any of Jesus' brothers or sisters believed in Him prior to His resurrection. At one point, the Bible tells us, they came to take Him home, thinking He had taken leave of His senses. So His own family had not really accepted the fact that Jesus was the Messiah.

If you were Mary and Joseph, imagine how tempting it would be to say to the kids, "Why can't you be more like your brother Jesus? He never does anything wrong."

"But Mom, he's like, perfect. I don't know what the problem is with him."

In James' defense, however, one can see how hard it would be for him to accept that his own flesh and blood was the very Messiah of Israel. It was not until his eyes were spiritually opened that he saw that this was indeed the real Lord. It was the Resurrection that turned James around, because 1 Corinthians 15 says, "He rose again the third day according to the Scriptures, and that He was seen by Cephas, then by the twelve. ... After that He was seen by James, then by all the apostles" (vv. 4–7).

This just goes to show that even living a perfect and flawless life is not necessarily enough to convince someone of the truth of the gospel. After all, who lived a more perfect life than Jesus? He never once sinned in any capacity. But as Jesus himself said, "A prophet is not without honor except in his own country and in his own house" (Matt. 13:57). It just reminds us that the hardest people to reach are those who are the closest to us, especially our families.

*Monday*

# TRIALS OF OUR OWN MAKING

*Let no one say when he is tempted, "I am tempted by God";*
*for God cannot be tempted by evil, nor does He Himself tempt anyone.*
*(James 1:13)*

Sometimes we walk into trials of our own making, because they are a direct result of our own selfishness or pride or greed or lust. Then when this happens and we reap the results of our sin, we get angry at God.

But James says, "Let no one say when he is tempted, 'I am tempted by God'; for God cannot be tempted by evil, nor does He Himself tempt anyone. But each one is tempted when he is drawn away by his own desires and enticed. Then, when desire has conceived, it gives birth to sin; and sin, when it is full-grown, brings forth death" (James 1:13–15). We forge the links of small, compromising actions, and before we know it, a mighty chain is wound around us, and we are helpless.

I used to be able to outrun my oldest son Christopher, who is now an adult. But a few years ago, we were at the beach, and I picked a spot and said, "OK, Christopher, I will race you to that spot." We took off, and much to my surprise, he outran me. I thought, "How is that possible? I held this child in my hands when he was born. I watched him grow." Well, he grew up. That's what happened.

That is the way it can be with sin. We think we can handle it. We think it's so small. But James says that when sin is full-grown, it brings forth death. One of these days that sin will grow up, and it will outrun you. It will overpower you. That's what happens.

# Tuesday

# THE LASTING EFFECTS OF SIN

*Beloved, I beg you as sojourners and pilgrims,*
*abstain from fleshly lusts which war against the soul.*
*(1 Peter 2:11)*

I once read a strange story in the news about a plumber who was called in to unclog a drain. He had one of those snake-like devices that runs down into a drain and keeps running until the drain is cleaned out. But this time, the "snake" did a strange thing. It went outside of the house through an open vent and into the house next door. Then it went down through a vent, came out, and grabbed a ten-year-old girl who was playing in her backyard. Fortunately her little brother started crying, and they stopped. The fire department had to use cable cutters to set the girl free.

After reading that story, I thought about how sin can be that way. You never know where it's going to go. When we commit a sinful act, we don't realize the repercussions that can take place and the other lives that can be impacted by it. Billy Graham once said, "Immorality is an epidemic in our churches just as it is in the secular world at large. ... No wonder the world is in crisis."

God has a lot to say about immorality, and specifically adultery, in Scripture. It made His Top Ten list, the Ten Commandments. It was, in some cases, punishable by death. And we see it addressed in the New Testament as well.

God has told us not to commit adultery for good reason. When you cross that line of protection that God has placed around your and your spouse's life, you do so at your own peril. And the repercussions of that sin can last for months, years, and yes, even a lifetime.

# SIMPLY RUN

*Flee also youthful lusts; but pursue righteousness, faith, love,*
*peace with those who call on the Lord out of a pure heart.*
*(2 Timothy 2:22)*

J ust as surely as we count the cost to follow Christ, we ought to count the cost of what it is to sin. The warnings we find in Scripture, along with an intense love for God, will see you through the rough waters of temptation. No, you will never be temptation-proof. You never will outgrow temptation.

But we must always remember the wonderful promise of 1 Corinthians 10:13, a verse every believer ought to commit to memory: "No temptation has overtaken you except such as is common to man; but God is faithful, who will not allow you to be tempted beyond what you are able, but with the temptation will also make the way of escape, that you may be able to bear it." Allow me to loosely paraphrase: God won't give you more than you can handle. There is always a way out. So take it. Don't be foolish.

If you are in the way of temptation right now, stop. Repent. Hang a U-turn. And if you have already given in to temptation and are wondering whether there is any hope for you, whether God ever will forgive you, and whether He would give you a second chance, the answer is a resounding yes. The Bible says, "If we confess our sins, He is faithful and just to forgive us our sins and to cleanse us from all unrighteousness" (1 John 1:9). So there is forgiveness.

When we are tempted, the best thing we can do is to simply run, to literally get out of the situation that perhaps we have put ourselves in. We should flee temptation and never leave a forwarding address.

# *Thursday*

# HOW'S YOUR APPETITE?

*And they continued steadfastly in the apostles' doctrine and fellowship,*
*in the breaking of bread, and in prayers.*
*(Acts 2:42)*

I was once talking to a friend who was just starting out in the pastorate and told him that people will develop an appetite for what you feed them. If you build a church on programs, then that is what is what people will have an appetite for. If you build it on entertainment, then that is what people will have an appetite for. If you build it on other things, the same will be true. But if you build it on the teaching of the Word of God, then people will have an appetite for that. When I am giving a message at Harvest Christian Fellowship, one of the sweetest sounds to my ears is the rustling of Bible pages filling the sanctuary.

In Acts 2:42–47 we read, "And they continued steadfastly in the apostles' doctrine and fellowship, in the breaking of bread, and in prayers. … And the Lord added to the church daily those who were being saved." Here in this passage, we can find four important principles of the early church:

1. They were a learning church.
2. They were a loving church.
3. They were a worshiping church.
4. They were an evangelistic church.

I was told some time ago that Harvest Christian Fellowship is among the largest churches in the U. S. That was amazing to me, because we never tried to be a large church—we just wanted to be a strong one. We felt that if we took care of the quality, then God would take care of the quantity. And that is exactly what has happened.

# It Doesn't Hurt to Ask

*If any of you lacks wisdom, let him ask of God, who gives to all liberally
and without reproach, and it will be given to him.*
*(James 1:5)*

One of the first things that we ask when the bottom drops out, when trials come our way (and there can be so many ways they manifest themselves), is "Why Lord? Why are You allowing this to happen? What have I done to deserve such a fate?"

Maybe you've lost your job. Maybe you've suddenly become ill. Maybe you've lost a loved one. It has brought great anguish to you. It just goes on and on, and you wonder why. James 1:5 says, "If any of you lacks wisdom, let him ask of God, who gives to all liberally and without reproach, and it will be given to him." Or, as another translation puts it, "If you need wisdom—if you want to know what God wants you to do—ask him, and he will gladly tell you. He will not resent your asking" (NLT).

When you are going through these times of hardship, there is nothing wrong with saying, "Lord, what are You trying to teach me? Lord, is there a lesson to be learned here? Because if there is, then I want to learn it. I want to get through this as quickly as possible. If this is going to go on for awhile and there is nothing I can do to change that, fine. But if there is something I need to learn that will cause this to come to an end, then tell me now, Lord."

It's important for us to know that God does have lessons He wants us to learn in times of trial. And many times, it is simply to see if we have learned the material.

# Weekend

# NOT IF, BUT WHEN

*My brethren, count it all joy when you fall into various trials, knowing that the testing of your faith produces patience. But let patience have its perfect work, that you may be perfect and complete, lacking nothing. (James 1:2–4)*

It would be nice if we could see the trials in our lives as options, as electives. It would be nice if we could say, "I'm going to skip the trials course." But trials are going to happen in the life of every believer. Notice that James says, "Count it all joy when you fall into various trials ..." (James 1:2, emphasis mine). The phrase "various trials" could also be translated, "many-colored trials." So no two trials or experiences are necessarily alike. You will be tested. The question is will you pass or fail? We must remember that God never tests us without a reason.

God's ultimate purpose is to conform us into the image of Jesus Christ. God wants to produce a family likeness in us. This means that some trials and testings will show us immediate results, while others will produce long term ones. In other words, there are times when I can come through a trial, look back, and say, "I learned this when I went through that experience." But then there are times when I come through a difficulty, and I can't tell you what I have learned.

But what has happened, maybe unnoticed by me, is that I have become a little bit more like Jesus. He has worked in my life to mold me and shape me into His own image. It's hard to say what has resulted sometimes. But we can know that God is in control. And His ultimate purpose is to conform us into the image of His own dear Son.

*Monday*

# INTENDED FOR CHOICE WORK

*For whom He foreknew, He also predestined to be conformed to the image*
*of His Son, that He might be the firstborn among many brethren.*
*(Romans 8:29)*

I read about a traveler who was visiting a logging area in the Pacific Northwest. He watched with great curiosity as a logger, working alongside a mountain stream, would periodically jab his sharp hook into a log as it went past and separate it from the others. This visitor could not see any reason as to why the logger would grab certain logs and let others go by.

When the visitor asked the logger about it, he replied, "These logs may all look alike to you, but I can recognize that a few of them are quite different. The ones that I let pass by grew in a valley where they were always protected from the storms. Their grain is rather course. But the logs that I have pulled aside come from high up on the mountains. They were beaten by strong winds from the time they were quite small. This toughens the trees and gives them a fine grain. We save these logs for choice work. They are too good to be used for ordinary lumber."

Maybe God is saving you for a choice work. Maybe you have been going through hardships and have asked, "Why, Lord? What is the purpose?" Maybe He has made it known to you. Or maybe He has not. Know this: He is seeking to make you more like Jesus and create in you a family likeness. It's part of the Christian life. It is also part of every life. Everyone goes through hardship. But for the child of God, whatever comes into our lives comes first through the grid of God's plan and purpose for us.

# Tuesday

# THERE'S NO ESCAPING IT

*Blessed is the man who endures temptation; for when he has been approved, he will receive the crown of life which the Lord has promised to those who love Him. (James 1:12)*

It was Martin Luther who said, "One Christian who has been tempted is worth a thousand who haven't been." Temptation is a subject we are all familiar with. None of us enjoy it, but it is a reality of the Christian life. No doubt we would rather there were no such thing as temptation. But it may surprise you to know that testing—even temptation—can have a positive effect in the life of a Christian.

It has been said, "Christians are a lot like tea bags. You don't know what they are made of until you put them into hot water." It is in the hot water of testing and temptation that we see what we are really made of. Everyone faces temptation in their lives. As James 1:13 says, "Let no one say when he is tempted. … " This verse does not say *if* one is tempted, but *when*. Temptation is inevitable. There is no escaping it.

The word "tempt" means "to entice to do wrong by a promise of pleasure or gain." We must realize that it is not a sin to be tempted. Jesus himself was tempted, after all. Paul certainly grappled with it as well. But it is a sin when we give in to the temptation.

We don't want to underestimate the seductive power and pull of temptation. We make a big mistake when we say, "I can handle this." Famous last words. Even the strongest Christians are vulnerable to the enticements of the devil. Even those who have known the Lord for years are still susceptible to enemy's attacks.

# CAUGHT IN ITS CURRENT

*But each one is tempted when he is drawn away*
*by his own desires and enticed.*
*(James 1:14)*

Y ears ago, I was at the beach with my young son Jonathan, and we decided to go swimming. We weren't very far from the shore. Suddenly there was one of those drops in the sand, and for a few moments, my feet did not really touch the ground. As I was holding on to Jonathan, a little riptide began to pull us over to the right, just enough to move us along. We were originally lined up with a lifeguard stand, but I noticed that it had moved quite a distance. Obviously it had not moved; we had moved. We were being pulled along. I could not stop myself. I kept reaching for the ground with my feet, but I could not get my footing.

Suddenly the lifeguard came down from his stand and began running toward us with his flotation device. I didn't mind being saved, but I was only a few feet from the shore.

"I'm all right," I said, trying to wave him off.

But you know what? I wasn't all right. I couldn't stop myself. As he began swimming out, I thought, "I have got to get my feet on the ground." Finally, I planted myself.

"I'm OK," I shouted to him, and he waved and swam back in.

That is what temptation is like. You think you can handle it, but suddenly you are caught in its current.

To pray we won't be tempted and then place ourselves in a vulnerable situation is like thrusting our fingers into a fire and praying they won't be burned. We need a healthy respect of the enemy we face and of the temptation that he will utilize in our lives.

# *Thursday*

## ACQUAINTED WITH HIS STRATEGIES

*For we are very familiar with his evil schemes.*
*(2 Corinthians 2:11 NLT)*

Billy Sunday said, "One reason that sin flourishes is that we treat it like a cream puff instead of a rattlesnake."

Not only do we need to recognize the power of temptation, but we also need to realize that our adversary, the devil, is powerful. We do not want to underestimate him. He is a powerful spirit being with a well-organized network of demon powers ready to do his bidding. The apostle Paul said he was not "ignorant of his devices," or literally, his strategies and his deceits (see 2 Cor. 2:11).

Jesus told us what the ultimate agenda of the devil is: "The thief does not come except to steal, and to kill, and to destroy" (John 10:10). But then in contrast, He added, "I have come that they may have life, and that they may have it more abundantly."

Christ wants us to have life and that more abundantly, not to mention life in heaven, beyond the grave. The devil wants to steal us from God's protection. He wants to destroy us. He wants to kill us.

And while we don't want to underestimate the devil's power, neither do we want to overestimate what he can do or have an overblown concept of who he is. As 1 John 4:4 says, "He who is in you is greater than he who is in the world."

God has put a hedge of protection around every one of His children. That is not to say He will not allow hardship. Nor is it to say that He will keep us free from all temptation. But it is to say that God will never let us be tempted beyond what we are able to withstand.

# TEMPTATION'S TIMING

*Therefore let him who thinks he stands take heed lest he fall.*
*(1 Corinthians 10:12)*

History tells us that during World War II, Hitler had an interesting strategy for attacking the various European nations: he always did it on a weekend. Hitler knew the various parliaments would not be in session, making it more difficult to react swiftly to an invasion.

In the same way, the devil will wait for an opportune moment, that decisive time to attack. It may be when our guard is down, when we are not expecting it. It may even come when we think we are the strongest, when we think, "I am doing pretty well spiritually. I think I am really growing. Everything is going great." Often weaker believers are less vulnerable than stronger ones, because weaker believers recognize their frailty and vulnerability. The Bible says, "Let him who thinks he stands take heed lest he fall."

Perhaps recently you have experienced a great blessing in your life. That blessing may involve your family, your career, your ministry, or your personal walk with God. But the enemy wants to rob you of it. Remember, when Jesus was baptized in the Jordan River, the Holy Spirit came upon Him in the form of a dove, and a voice was heard from heaven from the Father saying, "You are My beloved Son; in You I am well pleased" (Luke 3:22). The Bible says that after this, Jesus was tempted by the devil in the wilderness (see Luke 4:1–14).

Remember, it's not a sin to be tempted. Even Jesus was tempted. The sin takes place only when we give in to that temptation, when we open the door to it and entertain it. That is why we should flee temptation and never leave a forwarding address.

# Weekend

## ENEMY TARGETS

*"Behold, a sower went out to sow. And it happened, as he sowed, that some seed fell by the wayside; and the birds of the air came and devoured it."*
*(Mark 4:3–4)*

Without question, the devil focuses his attacks on those who are often young in the faith and those who are making a difference in the kingdom of God.

You probably remember that when you first put your faith in Christ, the enemy was there to attack you. Maybe the day after you had made that commitment to Christ, you started thinking, "Am I really forgiven by God? Has something really happened to me? Maybe I just psyched myself into this." Or maybe you remember some very strong temptations that came your way right after you became a Christian. Obviously, temptation has to be tempting, so the devil will offer you things that are attractive.

Jesus told the story of a sower who sowed his seed, and it fell by the roadside, where the birds came and ate it. He said, "These are the ones by the wayside where the word is sown. When they hear, Satan comes immediately and takes away the word that was sown in their hearts" (Mark 4:15). This is why we should pray for new believers. The enemy will be there, trying to rob them of what God has done.

Then of course, the devil will attack those who are making a difference in the kingdom, those who are seeking to walk with God and reach others with the gospel. When believers step up and say, "Use me, Lord. I want my life to make a difference," they should brace themselves. The enemy will not take that sitting down. Expect opposition. It comes to those who are making a difference in the kingdom.

*Monday*

# It Starts with the Mind

*But I fear, lest somehow, as the serpent deceived Eve by his craftiness,*
*so your minds may be corrupted from the simplicity that is in Christ.*
*(2 Corinthians 11:3)*

In not all cases, but in most, temptation comes through the doorway of the mind. When Satan wanted to lead the first man and woman into sin, he began by attacking Eve's mind. Why? Because it is there that we think. It is there that we reason. We contemplate. We fantasize. We imagine.

That is why the Bible says, "For the weapons of our warfare are not carnal but mighty in God for pulling down strongholds, casting down arguments and every high thing that exalts itself against the knowledge of God, bringing every thought into captivity to the obedience of Christ" (2 Cor. 10:4–5).

When someone falls into sin, whatever kind it is, I can tell you that it first began in the realm of the mind. You may think that someone in an adulterous relationship suddenly fell into it. But it probably started weeks or months earlier with something small, but significant. Maybe it was something they watched on television. Maybe it was a little flirting with a coworker. Then the next thing they knew, they had committed adultery.

But how did they get there? It started in their mind. They played with an idea, and then the idea rooted itself. That is why we want to draw the line with sin and not even entertain it. Think about what happened to Eve. She started conversing with the serpent. That is why the Bible says not to give place to the devil (see Eph. 4:27). Anyone who has fallen away from the Lord began by thinking about it first. Because the first step toward going back is looking back.

# Tuesday

# Don't Look Back

*But Jesus told him, "Anyone who puts a hand to the plow*
*and then looks back is not fit for the Kingdom of God."*
*(Luke 9:62 NLT)*

I find it interesting how we can look at the past through
rose-colored glasses. Remember the children of Israel?
They had been delivered from the tyranny and bondage
of Egypt, where they had been slaves for years. They cried out
to God for deliverance, and the Lord answered their prayers
through a man named Moses.

As they were making their way through the wilderness, God
supernaturally fed them with an incredible substance called
manna. It was like bread from heaven. They had it daily for
breakfast, lunch, and dinner. But after awhile, they got a little
tired of it. They said, "We are sick of manna. We remember the
good old days back in Egypt, where we used to eat garlic, leeks
and onions. [Their breath must have really stunk, by the way.]
Those were the good old days. ... If we could only go back."

They spoke of the good old days, but they basically ate table
scraps in Egypt, because they were slaves. Their lives were
miserable. Yet in their imaginations, they had magnified these
scraps to some sumptuous feast they had each and every day.
They were not looking at the past accurately. In the same way,
the devil may remind you of the old days: "Remember the good
old days? Remember the fun you used to have? Remember that
old flame? If only you could reignite that." And suddenly you
begin to think about it.

Don't build up the past in your mind. Remember it for what
it was. Don't allow the enemy to pull you down by fantasizing
about it. Protect your mind, and don't look back.

# THE BEST PLACE TO BE

*Then Jesus, being filled with the Holy Spirit, returned from the Jordan and was
led by the Spirit into the wilderness, being tempted for forty days by the devil.
(Luke 4:1–2)*

Far too often, we unnecessarily put ourselves in the way
of temptation. We put ourselves in the wrong place
with the wrong people, leading to our doing the wrong
things. Look at Peter, for example. Where was he when he
denied the Lord? He was warming himself by the enemy's fire.
He was at the wrong place, listening to the wrong voice, which
led him to do the wrong thing. And where was Eve when she
fell into sin? She was at the tree that God had told her not to
eat from. She was listening to the wrong voice, leading her
to do the wrong thing.

Do you find it surprising when you are tempted over and
over again? Maybe it is because you are out of the will of
God. So where is the best place to be when temptation
comes? Answer: in the will of God. Even then, temptation
can still come.

The Bible tells us that Jesus was led by the Holy Spirit into
the wilderness when He was tempted by the devil (see Luke
4:1–2). Does that mean God led Him into temptation? No.
Because Jesus taught us to pray, "Do not lead us into temptation … " (Matt. 6:13). Even in the will of God, even when we
are doing what God wants us to do, we will still face temptation.

Maybe you have faced opposition lately and you are wondering if you are in the will of God. Maybe it is confirma-
tion that you really are in the will of God, that you really are
making a difference.

# Thursday

## THE BEST WEAPON

*For we do not have a High Priest who cannot sympathize with our weaknesses, but was in all points tempted as we are, yet without sin.*
*(Hebrews 4:15)*

When Jesus was tempted in the wilderness, He responded to every enticement of the enemy by beginning with the words, "It is written. . . ." When the devil suggested that Jesus turn a stone into bread, He replied, "It is written, 'Man shall not live by bread alone, but by every word of God' " (Luke 4:4).

When the devil promised to give Him all the world's kingdoms if Jesus worshipped him, Jesus responded, "Get behind Me, Satan! For it is written, 'You shall worship the Lord your God, and Him only you shall serve' " (Luke 4:8).

Then the devil pulled a fast one. He quoted Scripture too. The devil knows Scripture and knows it pretty well. Of course, he pulls it out of context and twists it, but he can quote it. So he said, "If You are the Son of God, throw Yourself down from here. For it is written: 'He shall give His angels charge over you, to keep you,' and, 'In their hands they shall bear you up, lest you dash your foot against a stone' " (Luke 4:10–11).

Jesus brought it back into context and responded, "It has been said, 'You shall not tempt the Lord your God' " (Luke 4:12). Christ faced temptation as a human being. He didn't use His executive privilege as God to get out of the situation. When the devil attacked, He quoted Scripture. And He occupied ground that we, too, can occupy.

So when temptation comes our way, it's important that we know the Word of God. God has given us the weapons for winning the spiritual battle.

# FIRST THINGS FIRST

*"Therefore you shall lay up these words of mine in your heart and in your soul, and bind them as a sign on your hand, and they shall be as frontlets between your eyes. You shall teach them to your children, speaking of them when you sit in your house, when you walk by the way, when you lie down, and when you rise up."*
*(Deuteronomy 11:18–19)*

I have often said of the Bible, "Sin will keep you from this book, and this book will keep you from sin." If you obey God's Word, it will keep you from sin. But sin will keep you from God's Word.

The devil will do everything in his power to keep you from reading and memorizing Scripture. As he did with Eve by first questioning God's Word, then distorting it, and finally adding to it, he will keep you from it as well. In Ephesians 6, we are told as believers to take up the whole armor of God. But have you ever noticed there is only one weapon listed that is both defensive and offensive? God has given us the Sword of the Spirit, which is the Word of God. That is what Jesus used. And that is what we need to use. As the psalmist said, "Your word I have hidden in my heart, that I might not sin against You" (Ps. 119:11).

What shape is your sword in today? Is it polished from daily use and sharpened on the anvil of experience? Or is it rusty from lack of preparation or dulled by disobedience?

Take time for the Word of God. Make it a top priority to not only read the Bible, but to memorize it. It will prepare your heart for what you will face throughout the day.

*Weekend*

# At an Advantage

*He canceled the record that contained the charges against us.*
*He took it and destroyed it by nailing it to Christ's cross.*
*In this way, God disarmed the evil rulers and authorities.*
*He shamed them publicly by his victory over them on the cross of Christ.*
*(Colossians 2:14–15 NLT)*

When I was a kid, I was walking down the street one day with some little cap guns that looked like six shooters, complete with holsters. I was feeling pretty good as I made my way down the street, firing these things off. But then I encountered some kids on the corner who grabbed my guns, pushed me, and told me to go away. I went home crying. Then I found my brother, who was five years older than me, and said, "Let's go back there. I want to get those guns." We went back to the same street, where I found the kids with my cap guns. Suddenly I had courage like never before. With my brother behind me, I successfully retrieved my cap guns.

Instead of facing the enemy in our own strength, instead of going out and trying to do this or that for God, we need to stay as close to Christ as possible. We can stand in Christ, and in His protection, because He dealt a decisive blow against Satan and his minions at the cross of Calvary.

So in spiritual battles, when temptation comes, we as Christians are not fighting *for* victory. We are fighting *from* it. In other words, we are resting in the work that Christ has done for us. Therefore, we should never want to stray from Him, because if we are caught alone, we would be weak and vulnerable. But thankfully, He is with us. The question is, are we with Him?

*Monday*

# THE BENEFITS OF TEMPTATION

*But each one is tempted when he is drawn away by his own desires and enticed.*
*Then, when desire has conceived, it gives birth to sin; and sin,*
*when it is full-grown, brings forth death.*
*(James 1:14–15)*

Did you know that temptation can have a positive effect in your life as a Christian? If you really want to follow God, you will cling to Him all the tighter during temptation. As A. B. Simpson said, "Temptation exercises our faith and teaches us to pray. ... Every victory gives us new confidence in our victorious leader and new courage for the next onslaught of the foe."

Some people are under the impression their sin won't catch up with them. But the Bible says that not only will it catch up with them, but it will ultimately bring forth death. Sooner or later, it is going to happen. They are not the sole exceptions to the verse that says, "Take note, you have sinned against the Lord; and be sure your sin will find you out" (Num. 32:23). Trust me. The Bible warns us about this. We have seen the ruin that sin has brought in the lives of those who have given in to it.

But let's look at the other side of the coin. James 1:12 tells us, "Blessed is the man who endures temptation; for when he has been approved, he will receive the crown of life which the Lord has promised to those who love Him." Another way to translate the word "blessed" is "happy."

So we see that temptation toughens us up. It makes us stronger. It teaches us to depend totally on Him. It's not easy at the time. But what a blessing it is to know that you have passed the test.

# Tuesday
# A Mark of True Spirituality

*For if you just listen and don't obey, it is like looking at your face*
*in a mirror but doing nothing to improve your appearance.*
*You see yourself, walk away, and forget what you look like.*
*(James 1:23–24 NLT)*

I have had the opportunity to meet many Christian people over the years. I have had the opportunity to sit down with many Christian leaders, household names, if you will, in the evangelical world. And I can say that, without reservation, the most spiritual people I have met have always been the most humble. They were not proud, not arrogant, but humble men and women of God.

It was after years of walking with the Lord that the apostle Paul referred not to himself as the chief of all saints, but rather the chief of all sinners (see 1 Tim. 1:15). This was not a man who had gone deeper into the pit of sin, but a man who simply had been looking into God's mirror and saw the depravity of his heart—even as he was still being conformed into the image of Christ.

If you are a true believer, if you are truly a spiritual person, if you are really growing in your faith, then you will be humble and open, always realizing there is so much to learn. This is the mark of a person who really wants to know God. A truly spiritual person will always say there is so much more to learn, there is so much more in his or her life that needs to change.

In contrast, the self-deceived person, the person who thinks they are spiritual, will really not be open to counsel. They will not be open to teaching. They think they know it all, which only shows how little they know.

# TRUE FAITH

*Thus also faith by itself, if it does not have works, is dead.*
*(James 2:17)*

The Great Blondin, probably the Evel Knievel of his day, was notorious for his incredible, death-defying acts. On one occasion, he strung a tightrope across the Niagara Falls. As a crowd gathered, he stood before them and said, "How many of you believe that I, the Great Blondin, can walk across this tightrope to the other side?"

They all said, "We believe! We believe!" So he walked across the tightrope and came back again. The people applauded, thrilled by his tremendous feat,

Then he said, "How many of you believe that I, the Great Blondin, can not only walk back across that tightrope, but this time do it while I push a wheelbarrow?"

"We believe!" they yelled louder, wanting to see him do this.

Then he said, "How many of you *really* believe it?"

"Oh, we really believe it!" they shouted back. One man was yelling a little bit louder than all the others, so the Great Blondin pointed to him and said, "Then get in the wheelbarrow." The man quickly disappeared.

That is how a lot of people are today. A lot of us will say, "I believe! I believe!" But how many are truly willing to get into God's wheelbarrow, so to speak? Some people have a pseudo-faith, but not real belief as the Bible would require. Therefore, it is of the greatest importance that we know what true faith is. The Book of James points out that there is such thing as a phony faith, a dead faith. And any declaration of faith that does not result in a changed life and good works is a false declaration. It is faith alone that justifies. But faith that justifies can never be alone.

# *Thursday*

# TRUE BELIEF

*You believe that there is one God. You do well.*
*Even the demons believe—and tremble!*
*(James 2:19)*

It may surprise you to know that the demons and the devil himself are neither atheists nor agnostics. The devil and the demons believe in the existence of God. The devil and his demons believe in the deity of Jesus Christ. The devil and his demons believe that the Bible is the very Word of God. And the devil and his demons believe Jesus is coming back again. So you could say, in a very limited sense, that the devil and his demons are orthodox in their beliefs. By that I mean they are orthodox in that they do believe the right things about God. But it is a devil's faith.

James used this shocking analogy to point out that even correct belief, as important as it is, is in itself not enough. After all, not only do the demons believe, but they also tremble. In fact, it is an interesting word that James used. "Tremble" means "to bristle," and speaks of the type of horror that would cause your hair to stand on end. The devil and his demons tremble before the Lord, because they know His power. They know His authority. But do they believe in the sense that James is describing? Do they trust in Him? Do they cling to Him? No, they do not.

So you see, you can know the right things about God and not necessarily believe, in the biblical sense, in God. True belief in Jesus Christ is the quality of faith that will bring you to Him to commit yourself to Him, to rest completely on Him, and to trust Him fully, which will result in a radical change in your attitudes and lifestyle.

# WHERE'S THE EVIDENCE?

*For as the body without the spirit is dead, so faith without works is dead also.*
*(James 2:26)*

The Book of Acts records the story of a man named Simon, who had been misleading people in Samaria with his cultic practices. But one day Philip, a follower of Christ, showed up and began to do miracles by the hand of God. The people turned from Simon and began to follow the God whom Philip proclaimed.

Simon could see that Jesus was bad for business. He needed to do something. So we read that Simon believed and was baptized (see Acts 8:13). But it would appear that this was not a genuine conversion, because later the apostle Peter said to Simon, "Your heart is not right in the sight of God. Repent therefore of this your wickedness" (Acts 8:21–22).

This shows us that you can believe in the power of God, that Jesus Christ is the Son of God, that the Bible is God's Word, that Jesus is coming again, and can even be baptized, yet not really know God in a personal way. So what does it mean to believe? The word "believe" is made up of two words: "be" and "live." Faith helps us to "be" spiritually. But then it is expressed in Christian works and deeds. "Be" and "live." I put my faith in Christ, but then I live it out.

Some might argue there is a conflict between faith and works, even pitting the teachings of Paul against the teachings of James. But that is not the case. James was addressing those who claimed to be believers, but didn't show any real evidence of it in their lives. He was saying that if it is real faith, then there will be evidence.

# *Weekend*

# REAL FAITH, REAL RESULTS

*But someone will say, "You have faith, and I have works."*
*Show me your faith without your works, and I will show you*
*my faith by my works. (James 2:18)*

If you were in a rowboat and wanted to move forward, which would better: the right oar or the left oar? You actually need both, because if you only use one oar, you will go in circles. But when both oars are working together in harmony, they will get you to the shore.

The same goes for faith and works. Faith in God, resulting in works, will result in a balanced Christian life. They are essentially inseparable. The apostle Paul put it all together when he said, "For by grace you have been saved through faith, and that not of yourselves; it is the gift of God, not of works, lest anyone should boast" (Eph. 2:8–9). Then he continued, "For we are His workmanship, created in Christ Jesus for good works" (v. 10). Paul was saying that if you really have faith, then it will result in works in your life.

In his epistle, James chose two very different examples to illustrate the kind of faith that God desires: Abraham and Rahab (see James 2:21–25). He could not have chosen two people more different in character or background. But he did so to clearly show that no one, whatever his or her condition, nation, or class in society, has ever had a real faith without results. Abraham was known as the father of faith and of the Jewish nation. Rahab, on the other hand, was a Gentile and a sinner. Yet both of them had faith that produced results in their lives.

If you have a genuine faith, then it will show itself in works.

*Monday*

# SMALL, BUT DEADLY

> *For every kind of beast and bird, of reptile and creature of the sea,*
> *is tamed and has been tamed by mankind. But no man can tame the tongue.*
> *It is an unruly evil, full of deadly poison.*
> *(James 3:7–8)*

Some years ago I went to the Rose Parade. One of the most memorable sights of this impressive parade is when I saw a man riding down Colorado Boulevard on the back of a buffalo. I had never seen anything quite like it. I have seen buffaloes in the wild, but I had never seen anyone actually ride one. With nothing more than a bit and a bridle, the rider came galloping down the street on this beast. It was unbelievable. It just shows you what a little bit can do.

A horse controlled by a bit can render a great service. But uncontrolled, it can do much harm. In the same way, a tongue controlled by Jesus Christ can be a great blessing. But uncontrolled, it can do much damage. Just as a horse is controlled by a bit, we are controlled by our words. Think about it: one word or one statement can determine the course of our lives. For example, saying "I will" to the claims of Christ can change our eternal destiny. Our words so dramatically affect the course that our lives will take.

James says the tongue is "a little member" (James 3:5), which simply means that it is a small part of our body. But it can do so much damage. We may see someone with bulging biceps and muscular legs and feel intimidated. But what we ought to be worried about is that little two-ounce slab of mucus membrane in his mouth—the tongue. That can do more damage than anything else.

# *Tuesday*

## SUBTLE DAMAGE

*He who goes about as a talebearer reveals secrets;*
*therefore do not associate with one who flatters with his lips.*
*(Proverbs 20:19)*

Among the many ways we can use our words to hurt others, three of them are backbiting, gossip, and flattery.

The word used for "backbite" in Hebrew means "to play the spy." It is a picture of someone who collects clues and scraps of information regarding a person's character and then relates the information to anyone who will listen.

Gossip is more subtle, because it can veil itself in "acceptable" language. People will say, "Have you heard?" or "I personally don't believe it's true, but I did hear that. ... " Or one of my personal favorites: "I wouldn't normally share this, but I know it won't go any further. Keep this to yourself." Of course, we Christians like to wrap gossip in spiritual language: "I need to tell you this about so-and-so so you can pray for them. ... " But how often do we really make it a matter of prayer?

A more subtle misuse of the tongue is in flattery. Flattery is just a fancy lie. It is when you say something that is really not true to win a person's favor, their attention, or their approval when you don't mean what you said about them at all. A good definition of gossip and flattery is this: Gossip is saying behind a person's back what you would never say to his or her face. Flattery is saying to a person's face what you would never say behind his or her back.

That is why James tells us, "If anyone does not stumble in word, he is a perfect man, able also to bridle the whole body" (James 3:2). That is a mark of true spirituality.

# A DEADLY POISON

*For we all stumble in many things. If anyone does not stumble in word,*
*he is a perfect man, able also to bridle the whole body.*
*(James 3:2)*

Some of the greatest people God has used have had a problem with their tongues. God called Job "blameless" and "upright." But Job had trouble controlling his tongue, as revealed when he said, "Behold, I am vile; what shall I answer You? I lay my hand over my mouth" (Job 40:4).

Isaiah was one of God's choice servants. But isn't it interesting that when he came into the presence of God, he said, "Woe is me, for I am undone! Because I am a man of unclean lips" (Isa. 6:5). It's worth noting that when Isaiah, a man of God, stood in the presence of a perfect and holy God, the first thing he became aware of was that he had misused his words.

Without question, Moses was one of the greatest men ever used by God. But he, too, had trouble with his tongue at times. It is written about him, "He spoke rashly with his lips" (Ps. 106:33). So he struggled with it as well.

Even the silver-tongued orator of the Christian church, the apostle Paul, had trouble with his tongue. On one occasion as he stood before the high priest Ananias, Ananias commanded that Paul be hit in the face, which he was. Paul quickly retorted, "God will strike you, you whitewashed wall!" (Acts 23:3).

Of course, the one who would probably receive the foot-in-mouth award would be Simon Peter. The Bible records many occasions in which Peter said things that he regretted. We see how easily it can happen. The tongue is a deadly poison. And this is why we must dedicate it to God.

# Thursday

# THE ULTIMATE CHOICE

*You will show me the path of life; in Your presence is fullness of joy;*
*at Your right hand are pleasures forevermore.*
*(Psalm 16:11)*

I n the 1990s, we found a new scapegoat, something we could blame practically everything on. It was called El Niño. No matter what happened, that is what we could blame it on. I think that is because, as a society, we love a scapegoat. We love someone or something to blame things on, because we are living in a time when no one wants to take responsibility for their actions anymore.

But in James 4, we find the real source of our problems. James says it comes from us—from our desire for pleasure: "Where do wars and fights come from among you? Do they not come from your desires for pleasure that war in your members?" (James 4:1). When you get down to it, this is the source of all conflict in life for the most part.

First, let's understand that the Bible is not saying it is wrong to desire pleasure in life overall, because certainly there is pleasure that comes from many good things in life, from many things that God can bless. And pleasure comes from our relationship with God himself. What gets to the heart of the matter is the word that James used: "desires." In Greek, it is the word *hedone*, from which our English word hedonism comes from. Hedonism, of course, is the basic belief that pleasure is the chief good in life, and that one should essentially live for pleasure.

The Bible speaks often of the joy of the Lord and the true happiness that comes from God. So here is what it comes down to. The ultimate choice in life is between pleasing ourselves and pleasing God.

# THE NEVER-ENDING PURSUIT

*All the labor of man is for his mouth, and yet the soul is not satisfied.*
*(Ecclesiastes 6:7)*

Years ago I was visiting the home of Billy and Ruth Graham when I noticed a strange dog that would chase his tail all day long. At one point, he came to a little embankment, still chasing his tail. I watched him, wanting to see how far this dog would go. He fell down the embankment, which was pretty steep. Then he scurried back up and started chasing his tail again. So I asked Mrs. Graham, "What's wrong with your dog?"

"He always does that," she told me.

I returned six months later and didn't see the dog. So I asked Mrs. Graham about the dog that chases his tail.

"He got it," she said. "He's dead."

A lot of people today are like that dog, chasing after things that will never satisfy. They go around in circles, never making any progress. James 4:2 says, "You lust and do not have. You murder and covet and cannot obtain. You fight and war. Yet you do not have because you do not ask." Note the words, "cannot obtain." If this verse tells us anything at all, it reminds us three times that the natural human heart is never content. This awful craving for the pleasures of life never stops. It just goes on and on and on. Trying to find satisfaction in the things of this life is like chasing after a mirage. It is always out of your reach. It always will elude you. James was essentially saying, "You lust. You kill. You fight. You are always reaching. You are always groping. But you are never going to quite have it."

It is a never-ending pursuit, like the dog chasing his tail.

# Weekend

# THE PURPOSE OF PRAYER

*You ask and do not receive, because you ask amiss,*
*that you may spend it on your pleasures.*
*(James 4:3)*

Why do we pray for certain things? What is the purpose of prayer? Perhaps if we didn't first think about it, if we just said what came to mind, we would say that it is to get things from God. Then there are some who would tell us that if we name it and claim it and ask for it in Jesus' name, then God must give it to us. But this is nonsense. It distorts the purpose of prayer.

It comes down to our motives in prayer. When James warned, "You ask and do not receive, because you ask amiss, that you may spend it on your pleasures" (James 4:3), he was saying, "Because of your lust for pleasure, because of your obsession with self, it can even affect your prayer life." If I pray about something and yet my motive is wrong, then my prayer will go unanswered.

Prayer is not getting my will in heaven; prayer is getting God's will on Earth. Prayer is not trying to convince God to do what I want Him to do; prayer is a process that I go through in which I learn the will of God and live accordingly. Am I suggesting that God will not answer a prayer that is outside of His will? Yes. Does this mean that God will inspire us in what to pray for and that is all we should pray for? In a nutshell, yes. God wants us to get into alignment with Him and start praying for the things that will bring glory to His name. And when we start praying like that, we will start seeing our prayers answered in the affirmative.

*Monday*

# A FOUNDATIONAL TRUTH

*If mortals die, can they live again? This thought would give me hope,*
*and through my struggle I would eagerly wait for release.*
*(Job 14:14 NLT)*

In one of the oldest books of the Bible, the Book of Job, the question is asked, "If mortals die, can they live again?" That is something everyone should ask in life: "What's going to happen to me when I die? What is there beyond this place called Earth?"

Before I became a Christian, I thought about this quite often. I was only a teenager, and it was sort of a heavy subject to be contemplating. But I did find myself thinking about death on semi-regular basis. It isn't that I was obsessed with death or that I wanted to die. My belief at the time was that once people stopped living, they simply ceased to exist. I was not certain there was a place called heaven. I was definitely hoping there wasn't a place called hell. My conclusion was that when you're gone, you're gone. It's all over with.

We all know that death is coming, but what happens beyond the grave? According to the Bible, there is life beyond the grave. And because of what Jesus Christ did on the cross, and because He rose from the dead three days later, we as Christians have the hope that when we die, we will immediately go into the presence of God into a wonderful place called heaven.

That is why the resurrection of Jesus from the dead is one of the most important biblical truths there is. The resurrection of Christ from the dead, next to the Crucifixion itself, is the most significant event in church history. It is not a peripheral issue. It is foundational. It is bedrock. It is the bottom line.

# Tuesday

# HOPE BEYOND THIS LIFE

*But if there is no resurrection of the dead, then Christ is not risen.*
*And if Christ is not risen, then our preaching is empty and your faith is also empty.*
*(1 Corinthians 15:13–14)*

Not only does the Bible tell us we will live beyond the grave, but it also tells us there is hope beyond this life. The resurrection of Jesus from the dead proves there is life beyond the grave for the believer. The Bible says, "He has appointed a day on which He will judge the world in righteousness by the Man whom He has ordained. He has given assurance of this to all by raising Him from the dead" (Acts 17:31).

No doubt this is why the devil has tried to discredit the Resurrection over the years. This is why, ever since the first century, he has been spreading his rumors about what happened to the body of Christ. And one of the oldest rumors of all was that His body was stolen by the disciples.

But claiming that the body of Jesus was stolen actually proves the resurrection of the Lord. His friends could not have taken it, because they left the scene and were convinced He was dead. The apostles had no reason to counterfeit a Resurrection they did not even believe in themselves.

And as we look at church history, we know that with the exception of John (who survived an execution attempt and was banished to the island of Patmos), all the apostles were martyred for what they believed. Don't you think at least one of them would have suddenly exposed such a lie if it were a lie? But they didn't, because none of them could deny what was true: Christ *was* risen, Christ *is* risen, and He is alive.

# CERTAIN OF HIS DEATH

*Christ died for our sins according to the Scriptures. (1 Corinthians 15:3)*

An advice columnist received this letter about the Resurrection: "Dear Uticus, Our preacher said on Easter that Jesus just swooned on the cross and the disciples nurtured Him back to health. What do you think? Sincerely, Bewildered."

Here was the response: "Dear Bewildered, Beat your preacher with a cat of nine tails with 39 heavy strokes. Nail him to a cross. Hang him in the sun for three hours. Run a spear through his heart. Embalm him. Put him in an airless tomb for 36 hours, and see what happens. Sincerely, Uticus."

Inevitably, unbelievers will offer their own concepts regarding the crucifixion and resurrection of Jesus in an attempt to discredit the Bible and its message. Among the most commonly held theories is "the swoon theory," proposing that Jesus didn't actually die on the cross, but went into a deep coma, or swoon. It further proposes that He was revived in the cool atmosphere of the tomb, was somehow able to get out of the tightly-wrapped strips of cloth, and appeared to His disciples. Yet the Roman guards were the first to report the death of Jesus. They were experts at execution, and they would be put to death themselves if they allowed a condemned man to escape death. These soldiers were so certain Jesus was dead, they did not bother to break His legs. They thrust a spear into His body and out came blood and water (which occurs when the heart stops beating), giving them the final proof they needed.

We can either believe or hang our doubts on some flimsy theory. But the death and resurrection of Jesus means that one day, we all will stand before God and be held accountable.

# *Thursday*

# WHOLEHEARTED DEVOTION

*Now when He rose early on the first day of the week,*
*He appeared first to Mary Magdalene.*
*(Mark 16:9)*

Of all the people Jesus could have first appeared to after His resurrection, He appeared to Mary Magdalene. It is interesting to think about, because among the Jews of the day, the testimony of a woman was not held in high regard. In fact, some of the rabbis falsely taught that it was better for the words of the Law to be burned than to be delivered by a woman. Yet Jesus chose a woman to be the first herald of His resurrection.

It is also worth noting that women were the last at the cross and the first at the tomb. Mary had courage that many of the men did not have when Jesus was crucified. She stood by Him through it all. In fact, the Bible tells us that after He was crucified, Mary "observed where He was laid" (Mark 15:47). She watched as they took His crucified body from the cross and wrapped it and placed it in a tomb that belonged to Joseph of Arimathea. And while the guards were deciding to post a soldier by that tomb, she spent an entire night there all alone, before the guards were there ... before the disciples were there.

And her love was rewarded. God said, "And you will seek Me and find Me, when you search for Me with all your heart" (Jer. 29:13). God rewards the person who is diligent. And for those who will take time in their day to seek the Lord, for those who will take time to read His Word, for those who will take time to wait upon Him, He will reveal His truths to them.

# A New Relationship

*Jesus said to her, "Do not cling to Me, for I have not yet ascended to My Father; but go to My brethren and say to them, 'I am ascending to My Father and your Father, and to My God and your God.'"*

*(John 20:17)*

On the morning of the Resurrection, Jesus didn't allow Mary to touch Him. He was essentially saying, "It's not going to be the way it used to be. You can't hold on to Me in the old way. It's a new covenant."

Then He made a radical statement: "Go to My brethren and say to them, 'I am ascending to My Father and your Father, and to My God and your God'" (John 20:17). For Jesus to call God His Father was one thing. But He said, "I am ascending to My Father and your Father. ... " In other words, "He is your Father now too."

If you came from a fatherless home, God can be the Father you never had. Jesus opened up a new relationship for us through His death on the cross and His resurrection from the dead. No longer must we go through a high priest to seek atonement for our sin, because Jesus became the final sacrifice for our sins. And He has given us free access to God the Father, to whom we can come in times of need.

Do you know God as your Father? Or does He seem like some distant force? If that is the case, I have good news for you: God is not some mere force or distant power somewhere in the universe. He is personal, He is caring, and He loves you. And that is why He sent His Son to die on the cross in our place.

# *Weekend*

# MUCH FORGIVEN

*"Therefore I say to you, her sins, which are many, are forgiven,
for she loved much. But to whom little is forgiven, the same loves little."
(Luke 7:47)*

I t is often those who realize just how much they deserve hell who are the most devoted followers of Jesus. Think of Saul of Tarsus, later to become the apostle Paul. Here was a man who went out of his way to hunt down Christians, arrest them, and have them executed. Here was a man who presided over the execution of an innocent man named Stephen. But after he met the living Jesus on the Damascus Road, he dedicated himself to God with the same fervor he had dedicated himself to the devil.

I wish more Christians would serve the Lord with as much as energy as they once served the devil. Granted, there are some believers today who were once into a life of crime. Some were drug addicts, but were transformed by Christ and are serving Him. But there are others who lived a relatively moral life.

The bottom line is that we were all sinners. We were all separated from God and on our way to hell. When Jesus died on the cross, He shed His blood for our sins. And when we put our faith in Him as our Savior and Lord, we were forgiven. The forgiveness that God extends to the most hardened criminal is just as significant as the forgiveness He extends to the most moral person. All of us need Jesus. All of us were separated from Him. But it is often those who have come from the lowest pit who want to do the most for the Lord.

Maybe we all need to think more about all that He has really done for us.

*Monday*

# THE PRIVILEGE OF GIVING

*But this I say: He who sows sparingly will also reap sparingly, and he who sows bountifully will also reap bountifully. (2 Corinthians 9:6)*

I heard the story of a Southern preacher who was speaking to his congregation and said, "We have to crawl before we can walk."

The congregation responded in unison, "Let us crawl, Preacher. Let us crawl."

Then the preacher said, "We have to walk before we can jog."

"We have to walk, Preacher, then. Let us walk," came the reply.

The preacher continued, "We have to jog before we can run."

"Let us jog, Preacher. Let us jog," they answered.

"But before we can run," he told them, "we have to learn how to give."

There was a moment of silence, followed by, "Let us crawl, Preacher. Let us crawl."

Any time a pastor raises the topic of finances, some people get a little uncomfortable. But the Bible certainly has a lot to say about money. It is the main subject of nearly half the parables Jesus told. In addition, one out of every seven verses in the New Testament deals with this topic. Scripture offers five hundred verses on prayer, fewer than five hundred on faith, and more than two thousand verses dealing with the subject of money. One of the reasons we are uncomfortable with this topic is because of the abuse in this area on the part of some Christian leaders. This misrepresentation of God puts sort of a bad taste in our mouths. But let's not go too far the other way and fail to recognize that the Bible does have a lot to say about giving, and there are many wonderful promises attached to it. Yes, it is a responsibility. But it is more than that. It is a privilege as well.

# Tuesday

# THE BLESSING OF GIVING

*"Wherever your treasure is, there your heart and thoughts will also be."*
*(Matthew 6:21 NLT)*

It was Martin Luther who said there are three conversions necessary: the conversion of the heart, the conversion of the mind, and the conversion of the purse (or wallet, as we would say today). But for many of us, this is often the last thing to change.

You can tell a lot about a person by their giving or lack thereof. You can tell a lot about someone by taking a tour of his or her checkbook, because it will reveal their real value system. Why? Because Jesus said, "Wherever your treasure is, there your heart and thoughts will also be" (Matt. 6:21 NLT).

It has been said that we should give until it hurts, but in reality, it should hurt when we cease to give. We should realize what a great privilege giving is. It is also a test of our faithfulness to God. Jesus said, "And if you are untrustworthy about worldly wealth, who will trust you with the true riches of heaven?" (Luke 16:11). Before God entrusts us with spiritual responsibility, He wants to see how we do with the temporal, financial resources and assets He has placed in our care.

As we give generously, God will return generously to us. As we give to Him from what we have received, He will meet our needs. This doesn't mean we are striking some kind of deal with God that stipulates as we give to Him, He must give back to us in a multiplied way. Then our motives are wrong. The right motive is to say, "Lord, because You have given to me, I am gladly giving back to You." The fringe benefit is that God promises to give to you in return.

# The Joy of Giving

*You must each make up your own mind as to how much you should give.*
*Don't give reluctantly or in response to pressure.*
*For God loves the person who gives cheerfully.*
*(2 Corinthians 9:7 NLT)*

A family went to church one Sunday morning, and after the service, the father began to complain about everything. He said, "You know, I didn't like anything about that church. The music was too loud. The sermon was too long. The announcements were unclear. The building was hot. The people were unfriendly." He went on and on, complaining about virtually everything.

His son, who was very observant, finally said, "Dad, you have got to admit that it wasn't a bad show for a dollar."

And that is how it can be for us sometimes. We don't fully understand the joy of giving. Yet the Bible talks a lot about money, and it talks a lot about the *giving* of money. Why? Because, as Jesus said, "Wherever your treasure is, there your heart and thoughts will also be" (Matt. 6:21). Also, the apostle Paul talked to the churches quite a bit about giving. In fact, wherever he would go and establish a church, he taught the believers the importance of giving. In 2 Corinthians, we read of him urging the Corinthians to learn to be generous people, citing as an example the generosity of the believers in Macedonia who gave to the poor saints in Jerusalem.

It is not about the money; it is about our hearts. Giving— or the lack thereof—is just an indication of where we are spiritually. To be a true follower of Jesus Christ means that God will have control over every area of our lives. A person isn't totally following Jesus if he or she hasn't learned how to give.

# *Thursday*

# THE BALANCE OF GIVING

*For the love of money is a root of all kinds of evil, for which some*
*have strayed from the faith in their greediness, and pierced themselves*
*through with many sorrows.*
*(1 Timothy 6:10)*

It has been wrongly said that the Bible teaches that money
is the root of all evil. The Bible teaches no such thing.
Rather, it teaches that "the *love* of money is a root of
all kinds of evil" (1 Tim. 6:10, emphasis mine). There is
a difference. The issue is not money, but the love of it. Verse
10 continues, "For which some have strayed from the faith
in their greediness, and pierced themselves through with
many sorrows." So we see that as a result of coveting money,
some actually have strayed from the faith.

You might look at someone who has been blessed financially
and think, "That person is obviously very worldly and money-
oriented." Then you look at those who have very little and
conclude they aren't materialistic. But the fact of the matter
is that just the opposite may be true. It may be that the person
who has been blessed gives more than you will ever know, but
just doesn't tell anyone about it. It also may be that the person
who has very little is obsessed with money. The point is that if
you are obsessed with money, it can destroy your life spiritually. For some people, having a lot could result in their spiritual ruin.

We need to find the right balance, just as one writer in
Proverbs observed: "Feed me with the food allotted to me;
lest I be full and deny You, and say, 'Who is the Lord?'
or lest I be poor and steal, and profane the name of my
God" (Prov. 30:8–9).

# The Discipline of Giving

*"On the first day of the week let each one of you lay something aside, storing up as he may prosper, that there be no collections when I come."*
(1 Corinthians 16:2)

Years ago, when I was in military school, we were given five cents each week to spend at the canteen (that is where they had the candy). I tried to stretch that five cents as far as I could, but I really wanted to buy more. We also were given a dime to put in the offering every Sunday at chapel. But one Sunday when the offering came, I started thinking about how much candy a dime would buy. So I kept the dime. Then I bought a bunch of candy. I also got a stomachache, and I felt guilty all week long. Even as a small child, I understood that dime belonged to the Lord, and that I had taken something that was God's.

Giving is a personal act, and every one of us should set aside an amount of money to give. Even children ought to be taught this. It might be a few pennies, a nickel, or even a dime. But they should be taught that they should give to the Lord.

Some people might say, "I think that is legalistic. I like to just give as it comes to me. I like to give in the moment." Yet Paul instructed the believers to set something aside ahead of time (see 1 Cor. 16:2). In reality, is it legalistic to say, "I am going to take a portion of my income and set it aside to be invested in the work of the kingdom of God"? That is not legalism, friend. That is good planning and obedience. And it is a good way to live.

# Weekend

# OUR MOTIVE IN GIVING

*But I want it to be a willing gift, not one given under pressure.*
*(2 Corinthians 9:5 NLT)*

The story is told of Billy and Ruth Graham and an experience they had in church one Sunday. As the offering was being taken, Billy Graham reached into his pocket and meant to pull out a five-dollar bill. Instead, he pulled out a fifty-dollar bill and didn't discover it until he already had placed it in the offering plate. He was a little horrified by what he had done and turned to his wife Ruth and said, "Well, at least I will get a reward in heaven for giving fifty dollars."

"No," Ruth said, "you are going to get a reward for five dollars, because that is all you meant to give."

Motive is everything, because God looks on the heart. The Bible tells us that "God loves a cheerful giver" (2 Cor. 9:7). The word used for "cheerful" could be translated "hilarious." This suggests a joy in giving that leaps over all restraints. Amazingly, as Paul urged the Corinthians to give, he cited the Macedonian believers who were relatively impoverished in comparison to the Corinthian believers. In speaking of them in 2 Corinthians 8:2, he said, "Though they have been going through much trouble and hard times, their wonderful joy and deep poverty overflowed in rich generosity" (NLT). How do the terms "much trouble," "hard times," "deep poverty," and "rich generosity" fit together in one verse? They fit when people have discovered the joy of giving. Giving is not a luxury of the rich. It is a privilege of the poor and of everyone, not just for people who have disposable income.

Giving is a responsibility. It is an opportunity. And it is a blessing for every follower of Jesus Christ.

*Monday*

# THE PROBLEM WITH SELF-ESTEEM

*" 'And the second, like it, is this: 'You shall love your neighbor as yourself.'*
*There is no other commandment greater than these."*
*(Mark 12:30–31)*

When Scripture says, "Love your neighbor as yourself," it is not saying, "First learn to love yourself, and then love your neighbor." Rather, it is saying, "It is obvious you already love yourself. Love your neighbor in the same way." It is this love of self, this obsession with self, which gets us into trouble. We don't need a better self-image. We don't need greater self-esteem. And we certainly don't need more self-love.

But here is what we do need. Jesus said "If anyone desires to come after Me, let him deny himself, and take up his cross daily, and follow Me" (Luke 9:23). Notice that He did not say, "If anyone desires to come after Me, let him *esteem* himself" or "let him *love* himself." Rather, Jesus said, "Let him deny himself, and take up his cross daily, and follow Me." In the original language, the word "deny" means "to repudiate, to disdain, to disown, to forfeit, to totally disregard." That is not an easy thing to do.

So in reality, the basic problem in our lives is not our spouse. It is not our boss. It is not our neighbors. It is not our upbringing. It is not low self-esteem. And it is not a poor self-image. It is the overt love of ourselves. Jesus said, "But those things which proceed out of the mouth come from the heart, and they defile a man. For out of the heart proceed evil thoughts, murders, adulteries, fornications, thefts, false witness, blasphemies" (Matt. 15:18–19).

So here is what it comes down to. The ultimate choice in life is between pleasing ourselves and pleasing God.

# Tuesday

# GOD'S TRADE-IN PLAN

*"He who finds his life will lose it, and he who loses his life for My sake will find it."*
*(Matthew 10:39)*

I am amazed when people say, "I'm trying to find myself," usually followed by the statement that they are abandoning their marriage or making a significant change in their lives. But Jesus said that if you want to find yourself, then you must lose yourself. This means taking advantage of God's trade-in plan. It's a really good deal. You come with what you have and trade it in. You say, "Lord, here is my life. I give it to You. I dedicate it to You. I give You my plans, my future, and my resources. I want Your will more than my own."

It is not a depressing thing to dedicate our lives to God; it is a liberating thing. In exchange, He gives us His life. In exchange, He gives us His grace. In exchange, He gives us His power to be the people we want to be.

So we come to the Lord and recognize the problem is with ourselves. We recognize the answer is taking up the cross daily and following Him. The things so many people chase after endlessly in life—pleasure, happiness, fulfillment, and meaning in life—do not come so much from seeking them. Rather, they are the beautiful end products of knowing and walking with God.

In a nutshell, the Christ-centered life must take the place of the self-centered life. God and others must come before our own desires. It seems simple, but it is profound. And if we will practice it, it will change our lives. Ultimately, we will find the pleasure, the fulfillment, and the happiness we have been seeking—not from seeking these things, but from seeking Him.

# THE ROLE OF FAITH

*Now He could do no mighty work there, except that He laid His hands on
a few sick people and healed them. And He marveled because of their unbelief.*
*(Mark 6:5–6)*

There is no question that faith is a key element in effective prayer. On one occasion, Jesus could not do many miracles in a certain place because of the unbelief of the people there. That place was Nazareth, which happened to be His hometown. He had done miracles in other places, but not in Nazareth. And it was because of their unbelief.

Our faith does play a part in the work of God. Sadly, there has been a distortion of this truth by false teachers who say that we make things happen, that faith is a type of force we just need to use. In an effort to counter this extreme teaching, we may swing too far the other way and end up with no faith at all.

There is a place for having faith and believing the promises in God's Word. When people ask me to pray for them to be healed, I do. But I always add, "Lord, if You have another purpose that we don't know about, then not our will, but Yours, be done." I think we need as much faith as we can muster when come before God with our requests. But I appreciate the honesty of the man who said, "Lord, I believe; help my unbelief!" (Mark 9:24). I believe God will honor that.

When you pray, "Lord, this seems to be Your will from my understanding of Scripture. ... I believe, Lord, but help my unbelief. ... and if You have another plan, then just overrule it," that is a proper way to bring something before the throne of God.

# *Thursday*

# FORGET SOMETHING?

*For I am not ashamed of the gospel of Christ, for it is the power*
*of God to salvation for everyone who believes.*
*(Romans 1:16)*

A woman went to a doctor with both ears severely burned. The doctor said, "In all of my years of practice, I have never seen anything quite like this. How did you burn your ears?"

"Well," she said, "I was ironing and watching television. Suddenly, the telephone rang. I answered the iron instead of the phone and burned my ear."

"That is horrible," the doctor said. "But how did you burn your other ear?"

"Can you believe it?" she said. "The idiot called back!"

It seems to me that, like this woman, some people in the church today are preoccupied as well. In many ways, we have lost our focus and have missed what our priorities should be. For one, I think we have lost sight of who our real enemies are. Is it Hollywood? Is it the government? According to the Bible, our enemies are the world, the flesh, and the devil.

I think we also have forgotten what we are really for, as well as the real weapons of our warfare. Are our real weapons boycotts and protesting? No. Primarily, they are prayer and the Word of God.

Lastly, I think we have forgotten what our real message is. Is our primary message that we are against homosexuality or that we are against abortion? Rather, our primary message should be the gospel, which is the story of the life, death, and resurrection of Jesus.

My fear is that more people know what we as Christians are against than what we are for. Do they know what we believe? Do they know what we think about Jesus Christ?

# SPIRITUAL ADULTERY

> *You adulterers! Don't you realize that friendship with this world*
> *makes you an enemy of God? I say it again, that if your aim is to*
> *enjoy this world, you can't be a friend of God.*
> *(James 4:4 NLT)*

When the devil uses this world to appeal to the sinful bent inside us, all hell can break loose in our lives. James 4 likens this flirting with the world as unfaithfulness, or spiritual adultery.

This analogy of unfaithfulness is used often in Scripture. The Bible likens the church to the bride of Christ. We are to be loyal to Him. We are to be faithful to Him. And to have another god would be the same as leaving one's spouse for someone else.

God used this analogy to describe the wayward wanderings of His own people, Israel. He said, "For My people have committed two evils: They have forsaken Me, the fountain of living waters, and hewn themselves cisterns—broken cisterns that can hold no water" (Jer. 2:13). A broken cistern was like having a well with holes in it. And when we lose our passion for Jesus and go after other things, the same can happen to us.

Remember when you first gave your heart to Jesus Christ? Remember how excited you were to come to church and hear a Bible study and worship with God's people? Remember the first time you prayed and actually had God answer your prayer in the affirmative? The problem is that as time passes, you can leave your first love. Sure, you still come to church, unless something more interesting comes along. Something has changed.

Whenever we leave our first-love relationship with Jesus Christ, it is only a matter of time until someone or something will take His place.

# *Weekend*

# FORGETTING GOD

*Whereas you do not know what will happen tomorrow.*
*For what is your life? It is even a vapor that appears for a little time*
*and then vanishes away.*
*(James 4:14)*

There was a time in my life when I could remember every week and month and year. Now I remember decades more easily than I remember individual years. Time seems to go by so quickly.

When Billy Graham was asked what had been his greatest surprise in life, he answered, "The brevity of it." That is so true. Time marches on.

Scripture certainly echoes this idea of the shortness of human life. Job said, "Now my days are swifter than a runner; they flee away, they see no good" (Job 9:25). David said, "Indeed, You have made my days as handbreadths, and my age is as nothing before You; certainly every man at his best state is but vapor" (Psalm 39:5).

And James posed this question: "For what is your life? It is even a vapor that appears for a little time and then vanishes away" (James 4:4). James wasn't asking a philosophical question, but a more descriptive one. A better way to translate it would be, "What sort of life do you have?"

It is also important to note that he was speaking to Christians who were involved in the world of commerce, those who seemed to be taking credit where credit was not due. They were boasting of their ability to make money and be successful, and in the process, they were forgetting all about God. It is always dangerous for us to take credit for what God has given us the ability to do. God warns that He will not share His glory with another. So let's be careful to not forget God in our lives.

*Monday*

# IF HE WILLS

*Instead you ought to say, "If the Lord wills, we shall live and do this or that."*
*(James 4:15)*

The Book of Acts tells the story of Philip and how the Lord was blessing him in Samaria as he preached the gospel. Everything was going well. People were coming to faith. Miracles were taking place.

Then God told him to go to the desert. And not only did God tell him to go to the desert, but He told him to go to Gaza, to a road that was rarely used. And not only did He tell him to go to this rarely used road, but He told him to go at the hottest time of the day. Essentially God said, "Go out to the middle of the desert to a deserted road in the middle of the afternoon, and I will show you what to do next."

Sometimes the will of God doesn't make sense. We may plan to do a certain thing, but God may intervene. He might have another plan. The idea is that we should remember God in our plans, and we should also remember He may change our plans.

Often in his writings, the apostle Paul would refer to the will of God for his life. He told the believers at Ephesus he would return to them for renewed ministry if God willed. And he wrote to the Corinthians that he planned to visit them if the Lord willed. That is important for us to factor into our plans as well. We always should remember, "If the Lord wills."

Sometimes the Lord will lead us differently than we would like to go. But what we must come to recognize is that the will of God is perfect, and we should never be afraid of it.

# Tuesday

# WHERE CREDIT IS DUE

*And you shall remember the Lord your God, for it is He who gives
you power to get wealth, that He may establish His covenant which
He swore to your fathers, as it is this day.*
*(Deuteronomy 8:18)*

The Bible is filled with stories of people who took
credit for something God gave them the ability
to do. A classic example is someone who, at one
point, was the most powerful man on Earth. His name
was Nebuchadnezzar, and he was the king of Babylon.
One day, he strolled across his royal balcony and surveyed
his surroundings. Before him were the hanging gardens,
which were one of the Seven Wonders of the Ancient World.
Below stretched Babylon's busy canals and tiled walls. All
around he could see the massive city walls and its 250
watchtowers placed in strategic locations.

Nebuchadnezzar walked out and looked at this incredible
city. Then he said, "Is not this great Babylon, that I have
built for a royal dwelling by my mighty power and for the
honor of my majesty?" (Dan. 4:30). The Bible says that
while these words were still on the king's lips, a voice came
from heaven and God said, "King Nebuchadnezzar, to
you it is spoken: the kingdom has departed from you!" (v. 31).
Then God struck this once-mighty king with madness,
and he remained in that state for a number of years. God
eventually restored Nebuchadnezzar's sanity, and ultimately,
he put his faith in the true God.

How easily we can do the same thing as King
Nebuchadnezzar. But Scripture reminds us that it is
God who gives us the ability to succeed. Never take credit
for your success in whatever area it may be, whether in
business, in your family, or in your marriage. Give God
the glory instead.

# THE CLOCK IS TICKING

*"Yes, a person is a fool to store up earthly wealth
but not have a rich relationship with God."*
*(Luke 12:21* NLT*)*

A watchmaker who built grandfather clocks inscribed these words on every clock he built: "Lo, here I stand by thee upright to give thee warning day and night, for every tick that I do click cuts short the time thou hast to live." It reminds us that our life is like a vapor of smoke that appears for a moment and then vanishes away.

Jesus told the story of a rich man who enjoyed great success. Reflecting on his accomplishments, he said, "I know! I'll tear down my barns and build bigger ones. Then I'll have room enough to store everything. And I'll sit back and say to myself, 'My friend, you have enough stored away for years to come. Now take it easy! Eat, drink, and be merry!'" (Luke 12:18–19 NLT). But God told him, "You fool! You will die this very night. Then who will get it all?" (v. 20 NLT).

We can find some commendable things about this rich man. He was a hardworking farmer. He probably would have had to work longer and get up earlier and expend more energy than the other farmers of his day to achieve such success. But his mistake was not being successful in his work. His mistake was not even acquiring possessions. His mistake was failing to make plans for eternity. He was living large. But he forgot the clock was ticking, that life was passing by.

And this man who died, leaving all his possessions behind, is like many people today. They just want to enjoy the moment. "Take it easy!" they say. "Eat, drink, and be merry!" Yet God says that is not the way to live.

# Thursday

# COMMISSION AND OMISSION

*Therefore, to him who knows to do good and does not do it, to him it is sin.*
*(James 4:17)*

Sin can be defined in many ways. There is the sin of commission, which is doing that which is wrong—crossing the line, disobeying God, and breaking a commandment. But then there is a sin that James mentions, which is omission. This is failing to do what is right. We may boast of the things we no longer do. We might say, "Since I gave my life to Jesus Christ, I've changed …"; "I don't do drugs"; "I don't drink"; "I don't lie"; "I don't cheat"; "I don't use profanity. … "

These things are commendable—and they should be part of the life of a Christian. But sin is not only doing the wrong thing; it is also failing to do the right thing. You might be priding yourself in all of the things you no longer do, but the question is are you doing the right things? The Bible says, "Therefore, to him who knows to do good and does not do it, to him it is sin" (James 4:17). Many of us do well in avoiding certain sins, but we may fall short in doing the things that God is calling us to do.

James says the source of our problems is ourselves and our desire for self-gratification. So instead of thinking about ourselves, we should put the will of God at the forefront of our lives. The beautiful thing is that when we seek God, happiness comes as a by-product. It comes as a result of having our lives in order as we seek first the kingdom of God.

Are you doing what God is calling you to do today?

# *Friday*

# OUR RESPONSE TO HIS RETURN

*Yes, dear friends, we are already God's children, and we can't even imagine what we will be like when Christ returns. But we do know that when he comes we will be like him, for we will see him as he really is. (1 John 3:2 NLT)*

It's worth noting that whenever the subject of the Lord's return comes up in Scripture, it is usually connected to an exhortation or admonition to take action as a result.

For instance, 2 Peter 3:10 tells us, "But the day of the Lord will come as unexpectedly as a thief. Then the heavens will pass away with a terrible noise, and everything in them will disappear in fire, and the earth and everything on it will be exposed to judgment" (NLT).

We might ask, "So what? What does that mean to me?" Peter continues, "Since everything around us is going to melt away, what holy, godly lives you should be living!" (v. 11). You see, it should affect us.

But nowhere in the Bible are we told to quit our jobs and sit on a rooftop or hide out in the mountains as we wait for the Lord's return. Rather, the Bible constantly exhorts believers to live godly lives. We read in 1 Thessalonians 5, "But you aren't in the dark about these things, dear brothers and sisters, and you won't be surprised when the day of the Lord comes like a thief. … So be on your guard, not asleep like the others. Stay alert and be sober" (vv. 4, 6 NLT).

In speaking of Christ's return, John tells us in his epistle, "And all who believe this will keep themselves pure, just as Christ is pure" (1 John 3:3 NLT). Yes, Jesus is coming. And if we believe that, it should impact the way we live.

# Weekend

# A PURIFYING EFFECT

*So I turned to the Lord God and pleaded with him in prayer and fasting.*
*(Daniel 9:3 NLT)*

When we study Bible prophecy (and we should), there ought to be a reason. There are some who love to consider the developments that are taking place globally, technologically, and militarily today. Bible prophecy is sort of a hobby to them. But it should not be studied for mere entertainment.

Rather, the study of Bible prophecy should be undertaken to motivate us toward personal godliness and bold evangelism. The Bible tells us that as the prophet Daniel studied the Book of Jeremiah, he realized God's impending judgment was coming upon the nation of Israel and that Jerusalem would lie desolate for seventy years.

How did that affect him? Daniel said, "So I turned to the Lord God and pleaded with him in prayer and fasting. I wore rough sackcloth and sprinkled myself with ashes. I prayed to the Lord my God and confessed" (Dan. 9:3–4 NLT).

Interestingly, when you read the Book of Daniel, you really won't find any criticism of him. That is not to say Daniel was perfect, but it is to say that he was very godly. In spite of that, as he studied prophecy, instead of being merely entertained by it, he was personally moved. He confessed, "We have sinned and done wrong" (v. 5 NLT).

Is that how you are affected when you realize that God's judgment is coming? Instead of saying, "Yes, Lord, come and judge the world, because they deserve it," would you say, "Lord, is there any sin in my life that would displease You?" Our study of Bible prophecy should motivate us to live holy lives. It should have a purifying effect on us.

*Monday*

# HOW TO WAIT

*Therefore He said: "A certain nobleman went into a far country to receive for himself a kingdom and to return. So he called ten of his servants, delivered to them ten minas, and said to them, 'Do business till I come.'"*
*(Luke 19:12–13)*

L ike children on Christmas Eve who can't wait for morning to come to open their presents, we should be looking for the Lord's return in the same way. Yet a lot of believers are not doing this at all. They are not watching and waiting. Instead, they are simply biding their time.

James tells us in his epistle, "Therefore be patient, brethren, until the coming of the Lord. See how the farmer waits for the precious fruit of the earth, waiting patiently for it until it receives the early and latter rain" (James 5:7). The word James used for "patient" is not speaking of a passive resignation, but of a patient, expectant waiting on the Lord. James was not saying we should have a *laissez-faire* attitude that says, "I suppose the Lord will show up one of these days. It might be in my lifetime. … I don't know." Rather, we should be waiting in expectancy and excitement, even joy.

And in Romans 13, we are reminded that as we understand the present time, the hour has come for Christians to "awake out of sleep; for now our salvation is nearer than when we first believed" (v. 11). The passage continues, "Let us walk properly, as in the day, not in revelry and drunkenness, not in lewdness and lust, not in strife and envy. But put on the Lord Jesus Christ, and make no provision for the flesh, to fulfill its lusts" (vv. 13–14).

This is the way we are to live.

# Tuesday

# RIGHT ON TIME

*But you must not forget, dear friends, that a day is like a thousand years to the Lord, and a thousand years is like a day. (2 Peter 3:8 NLT)*

We live in a culture in which every thing happens fast. We don't have to wait for much of anything anymore. So when we are told to wait for the Lord's return, it can be hard for us. We look around at our world and say, "Lord, come on. Have You forgotten? When are You coming back?"

But we must understand that God has His own schedule. He is not bound by ours. He came the first time at the appointed hour, and He will come the second time in the same way. The Bible tells us, "But when the right time came, God sent his Son, born of a woman, subject to the law God sent him to buy freedom for us who were slaves to the law, so that he could adopt us as his very own children" (Gal. 4:4–5 NLT). God watched this little world of ours, and He knew when the right moment in time had come.

When Jesus arrived on the scene, the people were ready. The Romans were ruling Israel. Taxes were high, morale was low, and morals were even lower. It had been four hundred years since Israel had heard from God ... since a prophet had come ... since an angel appeared ... since a miracle had been performed. Then John the Baptist burst on the scene, announcing that the Messiah had indeed arrived.

When the time was just right, God sent His Son. And when the time is just right, the Son will return again to this earth. He will come when the time is just right.

# GET ROOTED

*You also be patient. Establish your hearts, for the coming of the Lord is at hand.*
*(James 5:8)*

A number of years ago, we held a Harvest Crusade in Colorado. When we arrived, it was around seventy degrees, and the sun was shining. Our crusade was to begin the next evening. But as we watched the news that night, we learned that a cold front was moving in. The next morning, there was snow on the ground. That is how quickly the weather can change in a place like Colorado. The sun is shining, and the next thing you know, there's a blizzard.

That is how life can be as well. Everything is looking great, when all of a sudden, a storm cloud appears. Something horrible happens. That is why the Bible tells us, "Establish your hearts ... " (James 5:8). Another way to translate this verse is, "Strengthen and make firm your inner life." The same word is used to describe Jesus' attitudes and actions when He headed for Jerusalem, knowing what awaited Him there: "When the time had come for Him to be received up, that He steadfastly set His face to go to Jerusalem" (Luke 9:51). Jesus, being God, had full knowledge of all that was about to unfold, yet He resolutely set out for Jerusalem. That is the same meaning behind the word "establish" in James 5:8.

God wants us to be rooted and grounded, yet many Christians are not. They have not taken the time to develop the habit of personal Bible study or the discipline of prayer or even regular church attendance. But God is saying we need to get rooted, because our faith will be challenged. We will face hardship. And a storm can come, just when we're least expecting it.

# Thursday

# WHEN TO PRAY

*Is anyone among you suffering? Let him pray.*
*Is anyone cheerful? Let him sing psalms.*
*(James 5:13)*

When we find ourselves in trying circumstances, often the temptation is to strike out at the person who helped bring those circumstances upon us. Or, we want to blame someone for our state of affairs. We may even become mad at God for allowing this in our lives. Or, we might wallow in self-pity.

But when we are afflicted, when we are suffering, or when we are in trouble, God tells us what we should do: pray. Why? For one thing, it just may be that God might remove that problem because of our prayers. That is not to say that God will always take our afflictions, suffering, or troubles away. But it is to say that sometimes He will.

By simply bringing our circumstances before the Lord and acknowledging our need and dependence upon Him, we can see God intervene in the situation we are presently facing. Prayer can also give us the grace we need to endure trouble and be brought much closer to God.

James 5:13 tells us, "Is anyone among you suffering? Let him pray." The word "suffering" used here could also be translated "in trouble" or "in distress." Is anyone among you in trouble? Are you distressed? Then you should pray.

So when the bottom drops out, when you feel you are just hanging by a thread, when circumstances have become incredibly difficult, or when they have grown worse by the minute, what should you do? You should pray. You should pray when you are afflicted. You should pray when you are sick. You should pray when you are corrupted by sin. And you should pray when specific needs occur. Pray, and don't give up.

*Friday*

# WHEN TROUBLE COMES

*From the end of the earth I will cry to You, when my heart is overwhelmed;*
*lead me to the rock that is higher than I.*
*(Psalm 61:2)*

I have come to realize that when I am seeking to walk in the will of God and when I am engaging in the things of God, then I can expect opposition from the enemy of God, the devil. Sometimes afflictions do not come into our lives because of our disobedience, but quite the opposite. Our afflictions, our troubles, and our hardships can come because we are obedient to God.

Remember Job and all of the hardship that came upon him because he was a perfect and an upright man, a man who feared God and turned away evil?

Then there was Nehemiah, who went out to rebuild the walls of Jerusalem that had been torn down and were lying in rubble. God had directed him to do this, but as soon as he undertook this great work for the Lord, a man named Sanballat opposed him and threatened him. What did Nehemiah do? Did he get a restraining order against Sanballat? Did he immediately stop what he was doing and run and hide? No. Instead, Nehemiah did what James says we should do when we are afflicted or when we are in trouble. He prayed. He said, "Hear, O our God, for we are despised; turn their reproach on their own heads, ... for they have provoked You to anger before the builders" (Neh. 4:4–5). Nehemiah cried out to God and brought his problems to Him.

As 1 Peter 5:7 reminds us, "Casting all your care upon Him, for He cares for you." So when trouble comes, pray. Bring your troubles, your problems, and your cares to God.

# *Weekend*

# SONGS IN THE NIGHT

*The Lord will command His lovingkindness in the daytime, and in the night His song shall be with me—a prayer to the God of my life.*
*(Psalm 42:8)*

The great British preacher C. H. Spurgeon said, "Any fool can sing in the day. ... It is easy to sing when we can read the notes by daylight; but the skillful singer is he who can sing when there is not a ray of light to read by. ... Songs in the night come only from God; they are not the power of man."[3]

When Paul and Silas were imprisoned for preaching the gospel, it was a hot and horrible environment. Prisons back then were far more primitive than they are today. Archaeologists have discovered what they believe was the actual prison where Paul and Silas were imprisoned as recorded in Acts. It was nothing more than a dark hole, without ventilation.

But instead of cursing God and questioning how a God of love could do this to them, Paul and Silas realized it was time to pray. The Bible tells us, "But at midnight Paul and Silas were praying and singing hymns to God, and the prisoners were listening to them" (Acts 16:25). Songs—not groans—came from their mouths. And instead of cursing men, they were blessing God. No wonder the other prisoners were listening.

When we are in pain, the midnight hour is not the easiest time to hold a worship service. There are times when we don't feel like singing to the Lord or praising Him. But Hebrews 13:15 reminds us, "Therefore by Him let us continually offer the sacrifice of praise to God, that is, the fruit of our lips, giving thanks to His name."

Are you facing a hardship today? God can give you songs in the night.

*Monday*

# A PATTERN FOR HEALING

*Is anyone among you sick? Let him call for the elders of the church,
and let them pray over him, anointing him with oil in the name of the Lord.*
*(James 5:14)*

I believe that God heals today. We know He has miraculously built into the human body a natural process in which it heals over time. But I believe God can quicken the healing process. I also believe that He can do a miracle when we have been told there is no hope. I have seen so many of these miracles myself. God promises His healing touch and tells us that by His stripes we are healed. So we should ask God to heal us when we are facing sickness.

In James 5, we are given the scriptural pattern for healing: "Is anyone among you sick? Let him call for the elders of the church, and let them pray over him, anointing him with oil in the name of the Lord."

It is interesting that Bible *does not* say, "Is anyone among you sick? Then go find a faith healer." I am not suggesting that miracles didn't take place in the early church, because indeed they did. I am not saying that healing was not done by faith, because it was. My point is that it was never the focus of the apostles. The early church did not follow signs and wonders; signs and wonders followed them. This is an important distinction.

We can go to God and ask Him to heal. I thank God that healing is available to us today. But we make a mistake when we focus on phenomenon. Instead, we should focus on the proclamation of God's Word and leave the miracles, the healings, and the rest up to God to do as He sovereignly chooses.

# Tuesday

# JUST LIKE US

*"The effective, fervent prayer of a righteous man avails much."*
*(James 5:16)*

When we read the words of James 5:16, which says, "The effective, fervent prayer of a righteous man avails much," we might think, *That counts me out. I am not a righteous person.* In a technical sense, this is true of all of us. None of us are flawless. But in another sense, those of us who have put their faith in Christ are righteous, because He has deposited His righteousness into our account. And without a doubt, His credit is good in the bank of heaven.

The Bible says, "But of Him you are in Christ Jesus, who became for us wisdom from God—and righteousness and sanctification and redemption" (1 Cor. 1:30). Christ has become our righteousness. And the effective, fervent prayer of a righteous man or woman avails much.

James then cites the example of a greatly admired righteous man: "Elijah was a man with a nature like ours, and he prayed earnestly that it would not rain; and it did not rain on the land for three years and six months. And he prayed again, and the heaven gave rain, and the earth produced its fruit" (vv. 17–18).

When we think of Elijah, we often remember his outrunning chariots, raising the dead, calling fire down from heaven, and stopping the rain with his prayers. He seemed almost superhuman. What we forget is that after his great contest with the prophets of Baal on Mount Carmel, he ran when he heard that Queen Jezebel was so outraged that she wanted him killed.

He was a man just like us, with the same vulnerability. So if Elijah could still muster up the faith to believe God for great things, surely we can do the same.

# *Wednesday*

# THE ONE BOOK

*As for God, His way is perfect; the word of the Lord is proven;*
*He is a shield to all who trust in Him.*
*(Psalm 18:30)*

In spite of our breathtaking advances in science and technology, we have only seen the human condition get worse and worse. It seems like things get darker every day. And in these anxious and critical days in which we are living, people are wondering what this world is coming to.

Many, in desperation, will grasp at straws. We see evidence of this in our bookstores today. When someone comes up with a new belief system, others will quickly accept it. In fact, I am absolutely amazed at the things people will believe without ever looking at the claims of Christ or the teaching of Scripture. They will reject it wholesale, without giving it even a cursory glance. They will believe in just about anything but the right thing.

That is because there is a sense of desperation, a sense of uncertainty. We're searching for answers to questions like, "Why are we here?"; "What is the meaning of life?"; and "What is going to happen next?" Some will put their faith in world leaders if they promise peace and tell us they will be able to resolve the conflicts in the world. Others will reach out to psychics, fortune-tellers, and astrology, trying to find some kind of meaning or the latest prediction by tabloid prophets.

Yet all the while, there is someone who knows exactly what the future holds. And He tells us all about it in His book, the Bible. The Bible is the one book that predicts the future with absolute accuracy. That comes down to the basic test of the true God, the true faith, the true prophets, and the true belief.

# *Thursday*

## SIGNS OF THE TIMES

*"Now when these things begin to happen, look up and
lift up your heads, because your redemption draws near."*
*(Luke 21:28)*

Sometimes I think I can predict the weather as precisely as
most weather forecasters today. Doesn't it seem like they
can be incredibly inaccurate? It seems that whatever they
say, the opposite will happen. On the other hand, I can just
walk outside and look up. If it's sunny and warm, it probably
will be a pleasant day. If I see some grey clouds, then I know it
might rain.

Jesus rebuked the Pharisees and Sadducees for their
inability to interpret the signs of the times (see Matt. 16:
1–4). Yet we see the same reminders today. They scream at
us from the front pages of our newspapers, from our television screen, and in events that take place around the world.
There are signs that are being fulfilled, signs that are saying
to us repeatedly, "Jesus is coming again." And we need to
wake up and pay attention.

All of the signs Jesus spoke of are to remind us to be ready.
Jesus said that prior to His return, the conditions on Earth
would be like they were in the days of Lot and Noah (see Luke
17:26–30).

As we look at Lot's time, he was, of course, an inhabitant
of the cities of Sodom and Gomorrah, places that were known
for their excessive wickedness, and specifically for their sexual
perversion. Noah's time was characterized by exceedingly
wicked violence and crime. Describing the time of Noah,
Genesis 6:5 says, "Then the Lord saw that the wickedness
of man was great in the earth, and that every intent of the
thoughts of his heart was only evil continually."

Is that not an accurate description of our time right now?

# LIKE NOAH'S DAY

*"In those days before the Flood, the people were enjoying banquets and parties and weddings right up to the time Noah entered his boat. People didn't realize what was going to happen until the Flood came and swept them all away. That is the way it will be when the Son of Man comes."*
*(Matthew 24:38–39 NLT)*

The people in Noah's day mocked his beliefs. They laughed at the old man who was building his huge boat when there was no body of water around. But when those first drops of rain started coming down, they changed their tune.

This mockery like Noah experienced, that is, the mockery of the things of God, will also be a sign of the last days. The Bible says in 2 Peter 3:3, "First, I want to remind you that in the last days there will be scoffers who will laugh at the truth and do every evil thing they desire. This will be their argument: 'Jesus promised to come back, did he? Then where is he? Why, as far back as anyone can remember, everything has remained exactly the same since the world was first created'" (NLT). How accurate this description is. It's the same argument being used today. The writing is on the wall for all to see. And it isn't hard to read that writing if you're paying attention.

According to the Bible, there is a generation that will not see death. Instead, they will be removed from the face of the earth. And if you believe in the Rapture, you are not alone. According to one study done by a news magazine, 61 percent of Americans believe that Jesus Christ will return to the earth, and 44 percent believe in the Rapture.

Judgment is coming. There is no doubt about it.

# *Weekend*

# Not How, But Where

*With the Lord one day is as a thousand years, and a thousand years as one day.*
*The Lord is not slack concerning His promise, as some count slackness,*
*but is longsuffering toward us, not willing that any should perish but that*
*all should come to repentance.*
*(2 Peter 3:8—9)*

I am glad God didn't answer my prayer back in 1972 when I was praying with many other believers, "Lord, come soon." Here's why: A lot of people have become Christians since 1972. The Bible says, "The Lord is not slack concerning His promise, as some count slackness, but is longsuffering toward us, not willing that any should perish but that all should come to repentance" (2 Peter 3:9).

For believers, the Rapture means no death; it doesn't mean that some will not die. But it does mean there is a generation that will not die, a generation that will not have to go into the grave, a generation that will be caught up into the presence of the Lord. Now the question often arises, "Are we that generation?" I don't know. We could be. I think I could make a fairly good case for it. But no one can say with complete certainty. The Lord may not come in our lifetime.

But I want you to know if that does not happen, if the Lord does not return, then I won't be disappointed, because my hope is not in the coming of the Lord. My hope is in the Lord that is coming. I hope yours is too. That is what is important. I know that I am going to heaven one day. And what is exciting to me is not *how* I get there as much as *where* I am going. I have that hope. Do you?

*Monday*

# FAILING FORWARD

> *Then I looked on all the works that my hands had done and on the labor in which I had toiled; and indeed all was vanity and grasping for the wind. There was no profit under the sun.*
> *(Ecclesiastes 2:11)*

D id you know that success can be a form of failure? Some may argue that success is the most important thing in life. After all, there is so much emphasis on it today. But is success the most important thing in life? That all depends on whose definition of success you choose.

Many people achieve their goals, but my question is what did it cost to achieve them? Was it by using deception and betrayal? By abandoning their principles and sacrificing integrity? By neglecting their family and friends? By forgetting about, and in some cases, outright abandoning God?" If so, they may be successful by certain definitions, but ultimately, they're failures.

We can do worse than fail. We can succeed and be personally proud of our success. We can succeed and worship the accomplishment rather the One who helped us to reach it. We can succeed and forget whose hand it is that gives and withholds.

Sometimes failure can be good, because we can learn from our mistakes. And failure can be good, even when we do something that is wrong ... if we learn from it, that is, and if we learn to fail forward.

By failing forward, I mean that after we have done something wrong and have tasted the bitter results of it, we say, "I really don't want to do that again." So we put safeguards around our lives and take precautionary steps to never fall into that same trap. If that is the case, then we have learned something from our failures.

# Tuesday

## THE GREATEST SUCCESS

*[He] made Himself of no reputation, taking the form of a bondservant,*
*and coming in the likeness of men. And being found in appearance as a man,*
*He humbled Himself and became obedient to the point of death, even the death*
*of the cross. (Philippians 2:7–8)*

What do we consider success? If we were to classify a successful person, what would be the earmarks? Power? Wealth? Popularity? Respect?

If that is our criteria for success, then apparently Jesus was a horrible failure. Was He popular? Not for long. The fickle multitudes sang His praises for awhile, but they turned on Him a short time later. So in a sense, He was not popular. In fact, after one of His sermons, all of His followers deserted Him except for the twelve disciples.

Was He politically powerful? No. He was a political failure. All levels of government first rejected Him and then conspired to kill Him.

Did Jesus have lots of friends? Not really. He had a lot of fair-weather friends. He had a lot of people who claimed to be His friends, but when it came to the end, He had only a handful.

Did He have money and possessions? Not really. He said, "The Son of Man has nowhere to lay His head" (Matt. 8:20; Luke 9:58). He had one garment that we know of, for which the soldiers gambled at the foot of the cross.

Was Jesus respected by His peers? If you consider the religious leaders His peers, then the answer would be no. They rejected His work.

But despite His failure by these standards, Jesus Christ was the greatest success that anyone ever could have been. Why? Because He came with a purpose: to die for the sins of the world. And He accomplished that task.

# MORE IMPORTANT THAN SUCCESS

*"We had thought he was the Messiah who had come to rescue Israel."*
*(Luke 24:21 NLT)*

Sometimes we think we are failures, because what we do isn't as big as we had hoped it would be, or we don't have the worldly earmarks of success.

But more important than how successful we have been is how faithful we are. We may not know how successful we have been in this life, especially in our spiritual endeavors, until we get to heaven. Those whom we thought were great successes may not have been as successful as we thought they were. And those whom we deemed failures may have been the greatest successes of all. We just don't know.

Before Jesus' disciples saw Him again after His death on the cross, they probably felt He had failed. I think the two disciples on the Emmaus road summed it up well when they were joined by the risen Lord, not knowing it was Him. They said, "We had thought he was the Messiah who had come to rescue Israel. That all happened three days ago" (Luke 24:21 NLT). These guys were so depressed that they left Jerusalem. They wanted to get as far away as possible from the scene of the crucifixion. Probably in their minds, Jesus had failed them. The others probably felt that way too. But when they saw the risen Lord, they found the opposite to be true. What seemed to be the end was really a new beginning.

Life can work that way too. Maybe something in your life right now seems like the end. But it might be a new beginning for you. God might be doing something above and beyond what you could ever imagine. So be faithful, learn from your mistakes, and keep moving forward.

# *Thursday*

# ADMITTING FAILURE

*They went out and immediately got into the boat,*
*and that night they caught nothing.*
*(John 21:3)*

It was a familiar scene. The disciples had been fishing all night, but caught nothing. Then they heard a voice from the shore call out, "Children, have you any food?" (John 21:5). The word "children" used here could also be translated "boys." Both terms would normally be used by a parent or an authority figure. I wonder if Peter thought, *Who is he calling boys? We are men. Why is he even talking to us? It's not his business.*

But John, always the perceptive one, recognized that it was Jesus. But why did the Lord ask them this question? The point was to show them their own need. He wanted them to admit their failure: "We caught nothing." It isn't that this was the biggest failure you could ever have. After all, we have all had this happen when we have gone fishing. But Jesus was using their empty nets to illustrate a larger point.

God will do the same with us. Before we can find restoration, before we can find forgiveness, we have to admit our failure. That is really hard for some people. We don't like to admit we have failed. It seems like more people are willing to say, "I'm sick" than "I'm sorry" or "I have sinned." We have become a nation of dysfunctional victims with all kinds of imaginary diseases. It seems like no one wants to take responsibility for their actions anymore.

So to the disciples, the Lord said, "Did you catch anything?" Before we can find God's forgiveness, and indeed, His restoration, we must first admit our need. No excuses. No blaming others. Instead, just honest confession as we take responsibility for our own actions.

# OBEYING THE CAPTAIN

*And He said to them, "Cast the net on the right side of the boat, and you will find some." So they cast, and now they were not able to draw it in because of the multitude of fish. (John 21:6)*

It sounded a little illogical. The disciples had been out fishing all this time and hadn't caught anything. Now Jesus was telling them to move the net to the other side of the boat. Was that really going to matter? But the technique wasn't important. What was important was Who told them to do what. So the disciples threw their net to the other side.

This would remind them of an earlier encounter with the Lord, when Peter loaned his boat to Jesus, because Jesus wanted to speak to the multitudes gathered on the shore. When He had finished speaking from His floating pulpit, Jesus said to Peter, "Launch out into the deep and let down your nets for a catch" (Luke 5:4).

Peter responded, "Master, we have toiled all night and caught nothing ... " (v. 5). But then he made an interesting statement: "Nevertheless at Your word I will let down the net" (v. 5). In the original language, this was a unique nautical phrase that could be translated, "Nevertheless, captain of this boat, we will do it." Whatever Peter's tone might have been in answering the Lord, he caught a lot of fish that day.

Sometimes God's commands don't always make sense to us. But it's important that we obey them whether we like them or not, whether we agree with them or not. When Jesus is the captain of your boat, things will always go much better. Let Him on board. Give Him the wheel. Let Him take control. And don't be afraid to obey His Word.

# *Weekend*

## GIVING TO GOD AND OTHERS

*For you know the grace of our Lord Jesus Christ, that though He was rich, yet for your sakes He became poor, that you through His poverty might become rich. (2 Corinthians 8:9)*

In the Book of Acts, we see how the early church turned their world upside down. The Bible says of them, "And they continued steadfastly in the apostles' doctrine and fellowship, in the breaking of bread, and in prayers. ... Now all who believed were together, and had all things in common, and sold their possessions and goods, and divided them among all, as anyone had need. ... And the Lord added to the church daily those who were being saved" (Acts 2:42, 44–45, 47).

The early church was a healthy church, or a W-E-L-L church. They were a *worshipping* church, they were an *evangelistic* church, they were a *learning* church, and finally, they were a *loving* church. These were people who cared about each other and looked out for one another. And that is what needs to happen in our lives and in our church. We must grow past that phase in which we are coming to church only to receive. We must learn the joy and blessing of giving to God and others.

You may think that happiness and joy will come from being served. But the greatest joy and happiness comes from giving and serving. Jesus said, "For even the Son of Man did not come to be served, but to serve, and to give His life a ransom for many" (Mark 10:45). Jesus not only came to save us from our sin, but to make us like himself. He came not to be served, but to serve. And as we grow spiritually, we should do the same.

# *Monday*

## SOMETHING'S MISSING

*For I am hard-pressed between the two,*
*having a desire to depart and be with Christ, which is far better.*
*(Philippians 1:23)*

I read a story about a little dog named Mugsy who was walking across the street one day and, tragically, was hit by a truck. His sad owners took Mugsy down to the pet cemetery and buried him. They were so sorry they would never see their precious little dog again.

But three days later, much to their surprise, they found Mugsy scratching at the back door. They could hardly believe their eyes as they opened the door and let little Mugsy in. He was covered with dirt but alive. It turns out their little dog wasn't dead after all. They had buried him alive, but the industrious little pooch clawed his way out and found his way home.

There is no place like home. And I want you to know there is a home waiting for every child of God, a future destination for all believers. It's called heaven. We need to be homesick for heaven. Though we have never been there, we still have something God has built within us that gives us a certain homesickness, a desire to be there. I love the way the apostle Paul put it when he said, "For I am hard-pressed between the two, having a desire to depart and be with Christ. ... Nevertheless to remain in the flesh is more needful for you" (Phil. 1:23–24).

God has put a homing instinct inside every man and woman, a sense there is something more to life. In fact, Ecclesiastes 3:11 says, "He has put eternity in their hearts." Because of this, we will never be fully satisfied in this life. There is always going to be something missing.

# Tuesday

# WHERE IT'S AT

*We grow weary in our present bodies, and we long for the day*
*when we will put on our heavenly bodies like new clothing.*
*(2 Corinthians 5:2 NLT)*

I remember when my son Jonathan turned eleven, I asked
him, "What age are you really looking forward to?"
"Sixteen," he replied. "I want to be sixteen."

That is so typical. When you are young, sixteen is where it's
at. Then you hit sixteen, and you say, "Eighteen—that's the age
to be!" Then you hit eighteen, and you want to be twenty-one,
because you can do so much when you're twenty-one. Then
you hit twenty-one, and you say, "No one takes me seriously
yet. They think I'm still a kid. Wait until I hit my thirties.
Those are the earning years." You hit your thirties and say,
"If I could just be in my forties, then I will have arrived." Then
you hit forty, and you say, "I wish I were a teenager again. I wish
I could have that carefree life I used to have." That's when the
so-called midlife crisis kicks in for a lot of people. Next come
the fifties, and then the sixties . . . the golden years. You look
back, and you have many memories and regrets.

One could almost look back on life and come to the same
conclusion that Benjamin Disraeli, former Prime Minister
of England came to: "Youth is a blunder; manhood a struggle;
old age a regret." That's a pretty accurate assessment of life
without Christ.

But when Jesus Christ is at the forefront of your life, you
don't have to feel that way. You can live a life that is rich and
full on this earth and know that beyond the grave, there is
something better: that wonderful place called heaven.

# THE NUT IS GONE

*But the fact is that Christ has been raised from the dead.*
*He has become the first of a great harvest of those who will be raised to life again.*
*(1 Corinthians 15:20 NLT)*

A minister who was conducting a funeral service wanted to speak of some of the wonderful things about the deceased. But this poor guy said the wrong thing. He boldly proclaimed, "What we have here is only the shell," gesturing toward the coffin." Then he added, "But the nut has gone." He didn't want it to come out that way. But that is a pretty accurate statement of what happens when we die.

God will give us new bodies one day—resurrection bodies. And we will need these new bodies because we will be in a new place called heaven. Of course, we wouldn't think of sending astronauts into space dressed like they are going to the beach. They must have special suits that are designed to allow them to breathe and function in their new environment. Our earthly bodies suit us fine for life on Earth. But in heaven, we will need new bodies.

We will need new bodies for our new environment because, to begin with, if we were to see God in the bodies were are living in right now, we would disintegrate on the spot. Why? Because we are not perfect people. Our bodies are limited by the effects of sin. The very fact that we age, can get sick, and will one day die (if the Lord does not come back for us first) means that we have bodies that are tainted by sin. We need new bodies, made into the image of Jesus.

You will leave the shell, but the "nut," the real you, will go into the presence of the Lord.

# *Thursday*

# READY FOR YOUR REWARD?

*"But when you do a charitable deed, do not let your left hand know what your right hand is doing, that your charitable deed may be in secret; and your Father who sees in secret will Himself reward you openly."*
*(Matthew 6:3–4)*

Maybe you were a great achiever academically. As a young boy or girl, you were winning the spelling bees. You always got A's on your report cards. Maybe you were given some special honor, such as a scholarship to attend a great college, because of your incredible abilities. Or perhaps you were a big sports star. You always excelled in sports, and you have plenty of trophies and ribbons to prove it.

Me? I always had those honorable mention ribbons. Do you know what those are? They are the ribbons they give you when you really do poorly, but they don't want you to feel too bad for yourself. You know, after first, second, third, fourth, and fifth have crossed the finish line, and an hour later, someone comes across, they say, "Give him an honorable mention ribbon." They were usually purple, although I don't know why that was. I had a room filled with purple ribbons. I was never quite that achiever.

But in heaven, there will be many rewards for those who have been faithful to God over the years. Even the smallest and most insignificant gesture on behalf of God's kingdom will not be overlooked by our Heavenly Father. Jesus spoke of our service to God, pointing out that even though it may not be seen by people, it is indeed seen by Him: "Your Father who sees in secret will Himself reward you openly."

One day in our future, when we stand before the Judgment Seat of Christ, the Lord will reward us openly.

*Friday*

# GOOD FOR NOTHING?

*For we must all appear before the judgment seat of Christ, that each one may
receive the things done in the body, according to what he has done, whether good
or bad. (2 Corinthians 5:10)*

The Bible tells us that we must all appear before the
Judgment Seat of Christ. This word "appear" can be
translated, "to make manifest." This suggests that the
purpose of the Judgment Seat of Christ is a public manifesta-
tion, or demonstration, of the essential characters and motives
of an individual.

This judgment is not about whether we will get to heaven,
because it takes place in heaven. Rather, it is about the rewards
believers will receive. Jesus said, "And behold, I am coming
quickly, and My reward is with Me, to give to every one
according to his work" (Rev. 22:12). God has a reward for
those who have faithfully served Him.

What will be judged, according to 2 Corinthians 5:10, is
what we have done, whether good or bad. The word used for
"bad" in this verse is not speaking of something ethically or
morally evil, because Christ paid the price for our sins at the
cross of Calvary.

Rather, the word used for "bad" speaks of evil of another
kind. Another way to translate it would be "good-for-noth-
ingness," or "worthlessness." The idea of good or bad is not
of someone who has done something outwardly and blatantly
wrong. The idea is of someone who wasted his or her life, a life
that was good for nothing. It is someone who has thrown away
his or her time, energy, and life in general.

What are you doing with your life for Christ's sake? I
know what He has done for you. What are you doing for
Him? Are you wasting your life on nothingness?

# Weekend

# MAKE IT COUNT

*Therefore, whether you eat or drink, or whatever you do,*
*do all to the glory of God. (1 Corinthians 10:31)*

I remember when, as a young Christian, I would sit in the pews at Calvary Chapel of Costa Mesa and listen to Senior Pastor Chuck Smith speak. I would think to myself, *I wonder if God would ever use me. I wonder if the Lord would ever speak through me.* Never in my wildest dreams did I ever think that God would allow me to be a pastor and someone who has the privilege of proclaiming the gospel. It was beyond my own dreams, beyond my own aspirations, even.

If you are planning your future right now, if you are thinking about what course you want to follow in life, ask God for His direction. Say, "Lord, I want to be the person that You want me to be. I want to marry the person You want me to marry. I want to be in the center of Your will. I don't want to go out there and blow it. Help me to do Your will." God's plans for you are better than anything you have ever planned for yourself.

God has given each of us certain abilities, talents, and resources. The question is what are you doing with them? Are you seeking to use them for His glory? Are you offering your resources and future to Him?

I'm not saying that you have to be a pastor. But whatever you do, whether you are a doctor, an architect, a secretary, a computer programmer, a builder, a musician, or something else, you should want to serve the Lord and do it for the glory of God. That's what matters. Your life can be a testimony and a witness for Jesus.

# *Monday*

# HEAVEN'S AWARDS CEREMONY

*For no other foundation can anyone lay than
that which is laid, which is Jesus Christ.*
*(1 Corinthians 3:11)*

Each year, millions of people watch the Academy
Awards. They tune in to see what the celebrities are
wearing and who will win the Oscars.

Now when it comes to that future day of rewards in heaven
called the Judgment Seat of Christ, it is not going to be quite
like the Academy Awards. We think the names of certain
people will be called out, great men and women of the faith
that we have heard of, and that they will get all the awards. But
it depends on what their motives were. It depends on why they
did what they did. We don't really know who will receive what.

But I do know this: God will judge us on the quality of what
we did rather than on the quantity. He will look at the motive.
That is what matters.

Paul said of this judgment, "Now if anyone builds on this
foundation with gold, silver, precious stones, wood, hay, straw,
each one's work will become clear; for the Day will declare it,
because it will be revealed by fire; and the fire will test each
one's work, of what sort it is. If anyone's work which he has built
on it endures, he will receive a reward" (1 Cor. 3:12–13).

The wood, hay, or straw that burns quickly does not speak of
gross sin as much as it does speak of putting more importance
on the passing things of this life than on the things of God.

But if you have built your life on the right foundation, if
you have done the things of God with the right motive for His
glory, then you will receive a reward.

# Tuesday

## HIDDEN VALUE

*Now he who plants and he who waters are one,*
*and each one will receive his own reward according to his own labor.*
*(1 Corinthians 3:8)*

A man who was doing a little cleaning went up to his attic and was throwing away a bunch of old junk. Then he came across an old vase that he thought might be worth something. So, he brought it to an antique dealer who knew a little bit about these things. He was shocked when he walked out with a check for $324,000. It turns out that the vase was a piece of fifteenth-century art from the Ming dynasty. And all that time it had been sitting there in his attic.

There are people who faithfully labor behind the scenes for the Lord whom we don't know of. But their Heavenly Father who sees them in secret will one day reward them openly. In fact, you might be one of those people. No one knows your name. No one knows what you do. But you are faithful to what the Lord has asked you to do, trying to do the best with what He has given you.

So don't be jealous of what someone else has. Don't worry about what God has called someone else to do, because you won't be judged for that. And they won't be judged for what He has called you to do. Be faithful with what God has put before you. Be thankful you have a life to use for God's glory, and use it for Him.

You may think that what you do for the Lord doesn't have any real value. But what is so valuable here will be worthless there. And what may not seem valuable here may be priceless there when we stand before God.

# WORTH WAITING FOR

*"Blessed are you when they revile and persecute you, and say all kinds of evil against you falsely for My sake. Rejoice and be exceedingly glad, for great is your reward in heaven, for so they persecuted the prophets who were before you."*
(Matthew 5:11–12)

You may have given up many things to follow Jesus Christ. You may have lost friends, even family, to be His servant. You may have resisted many temptations. Perhaps there have been hardships that you have endured because of your faith. God promises you a special reward in heaven.

There are many who have suffered much worse, those throughout church history who have laid down their lives—men and women who were put to death for their faith in Christ, men and women who, if they would have denied the Lord, could have walked away but would not make that compromise. They have a special reward waiting for them in heaven.

James 1:12 says, "Blessed is the man who endures temptation; for when he has been approved, he will receive the crown of life which the Lord has promised to those who love Him." If you have suffered the loss of something like a friendship, if you have taken ridicule and persecution, know that God will reward you (see Matt, 5:11–12). Whatever you gave up, He will make it up to you.

Sure, we give up a few things to follow Christ. Sometimes we may think, *I know it's wrong, but it looks kind of fun. I kind of wish I could do it.* But we know we shouldn't. So we resist. As time passes, you will look back at the fallout, the repercussions, and say, "I'm glad I avoided that." And ultimately, in that final day, God will give you a reward.

# Thursday

# A GREAT REUNION

*He chose to share the oppression of God's people instead of enjoying the fleeting pleasures of sin. (Hebrews 11:25 NLT)*

A Christian father who was terminally ill called his three sons to his bedside. To his two sons who were believers, he said, "Good-bye, my sons. I will see you in the morning." Turning to his third son, he simply and sadly said, "Good-bye, my son."

The young man was deeply disturbed. He said, "Father, why is it you said to my brothers, 'I will see you in the morning,' and you only said to me, 'Good-bye my son'? Why didn't you say you would see me in the morning too?"

His father replied, "Son, you have never asked Jesus Christ into your heart to be your Savior and Lord. And that is what breaks my heart the most. I will never see you again." That son began to ask his father how he could be saved, how he could see his father again. His father told him how. And so he prayed and received Christ into his life. Then his father said, "Now our family will be together in eternity."

That can happen for everyone who has put their faith in Christ. It will be a great reunion one day in the future. But what does the unbeliever have to look forward to? Judgment after death and a miserable, empty life on Earth. There might be some fun in sin—for awhile. But payday comes. "The wages of sin is death" (Rom. 6:23). Sin can be thrilling. But payday is coming.

If you do not commit your life to Christ, ultimately you will look back on your life and realize you wasted it. But don't wait until the end of your life to figure that out. Figure it out now.

# SEND IT AHEAD

*"But lay up for yourselves treasures in heaven, where neither
moth nor rust destroys and where thieves do not break in and steal."*
*(Matthew 6:20)*

P eople employ different strategies in the game of
Monopoly. Some buy every piece of property on the
board in hopes of putting their opponents out of
business. Others save up, hoping they will land specifically
on the blue spaces so they can buy up Boardwalk and Park
Place and put hotels on them. You can make a lot of money
when you play Monopoly, but that money isn't going to do
a thing for you in the real world, because when the game is
over, so are your winnings.

In the same way, when we get to heaven, all that we have on
this earth will have no value at all if we do not invest it properly.
That is why it is important to think about what we are spending
our money on. It has been said that you can't take it with you,
but you can send it on ahead. How? By investing in the work
of the kingdom of God. In doing so, you are laying up for
yourself treasures in heaven.

Money is neither good nor evil. Money is neutral. The Bible
does not say that money is the root of all evil. Rather, it says,
"The *love* of money is a root of all kinds of evil" (1 Tim. 6:10,
emphasis mine). So it isn't money itself that is the problem;
it is the love of it. If money is the most important thing to you,
then it can be the root of all kinds of evil in your life. But if
you can get it into the proper perspective, it can be a force
for good to help and touch people.

## Weekend

# WHERE YOUR TREASURE IS

*"Do not lay up for yourselves treasures on earth, where moth and*
*rust destroy and where thieves break in and steal. ...*
*For where your treasure is, there your heart will be also."*
*(Matthew 6:19, 21)*

How accurate is the statement in Proverbs 23:5, which says, "For riches certainly make themselves wings; they fly away like an eagle toward heaven." Haven't you found that to be true? Have you ever wondered, "Where did that money go? Is there a hole in my pocket?" It is amazing how quickly money can leave, especially if you are well-invested in the stock market.

Jesus said, "Do not lay up for yourselves treasures on earth, where moth and rust destroy and where thieves break in and steal; but lay up for yourselves treasures in heaven, where neither moth nor rust destroys and where thieves do not break in and steal. For where your treasure is, there your heart will be also" (Matthew 6:19–21). Was Jesus condemning those who are financially prosperous? No. Was He saying that it is wrong to make and save money? Absolutely not. What He was saying is that it is wrong to put all of our hope in earthly treasures and have nothing waiting for us on the other side. Why? Because these earthly treasures simply will not last.

Jesus did not say this because wealth might be lost—it is because wealth always will be lost. In other words, we are going to leave it behind. As I have often said, you have never seen a hearse pulling a U-Haul. We leave everything behind. Either it leaves us while we live, or we leave it when we die. There are no exceptions.

*Monday*

# PHILADELPHIA?
# OR LAODICEA?

*"He who has an ear, let him hear what the Spirit says to the churches."*
*(Revelation 3:6)*

I f you feel that the history of the church is dark at worst and checkered at best, then you are not alone in that assessment. In Revelation, Jesus has given us His view of the Christian church and its progression—or, in many ways, regression—beginning with the first century.

The church of Ephesus was in danger of leaving its first love and ending up like the lukewarm church of Laodicea. After the church of Ephesus, as the church was beginning to leave its first love, the church of Pergamos is mentioned. This was a time we know as the Dark Ages, when Christianity essentially became the state religion. This weakened the church, and many unscriptural and idolatrous practices entered in.

Then, like a breath of fresh air, a great spiritual awakening known as the Protestant Reformation took place, as represented by the church of Sardis. A much-needed revival swept the church, but it was only a matter of time until it, too, had grown cold, causing Jesus to say, "You have a name that you are alive, but you are dead" (Rev. 3:1). Flowing out of Sardis we have two streams, each representative of the last-days church: the church of Philadelphia, which would be the awakened church that is coming back to spiritual life; and the church of Laodicea, a lukewarm, ineffective church.

I believe we are living in the last days, and we are either members of the church of Laodicea or members of the church of Philadelphia. Either we are awakened, living, functioning believers, living as God wants us to live, or we are lukewarm, ineffective Christians. To which group do you belong? The choice is up to you.

# Tuesday

# WHAT'S YOUR TEMPERATURE?

*So then, because you are lukewarm, and neither cold nor hot,*
*I will vomit you out of My mouth.*
*(Revelation 3: 16)*

When you are feeling a little under the weather, one of the first things your doctor will want to know is your body temperature. Why? Because a drop or a rise in your temperature is an indication that something is wrong. Your temperature is an assessment of your health.

We can apply the same principle in the spiritual life. What is your spiritual temperature right now? That, too, is an indicator of your health—your spiritual health. According to Scripture, there are only three possible answers, because there are only three possible spiritual temperatures.

The first is burning hot, which means you have a heart that is on fire for God. Remember the story of the two disciples who, although they didn't know it at the time, encountered the risen Lord on the Emmaus road? They said, "Did not our heart burn within us while He talked with us on the road, and while He opened the Scriptures to us?" (Luke 24:32). A burning heart is the best spiritual temperature of all.

The second temperature is cold. Jesus said, "And because lawlessness will abound, the love of many will grow cold" (Matt. 24:12). This would describe someone who is just going through the motions and, for all practical purposes, is spiritually lifeless.

Then there is lukewarm. It may surprise you to know that of the three spiritual temperatures, this is the most offensive to Jesus. In fact, lukewarm is even more offensive to Him than being icy cold.

# LUKEWARM LAODICEA

> *"I know all the things you do, that you are neither hot nor cold.*
> *I wish you were one or the other!"*
> *(Revelation 3:15 NLT)*

A re you an awakened believer? An on-fire believer? Are you using the gifts and resources that God has given you? I hope so, because we find the sad alternative in the church of Laodicea in Revelation 3.

This church, in contrast to the church in Philadelphia (see Rev. 3:7–12), was not reviving. It was not keeping God's Word. This was a complacent, apathetic, half-hearted, yet very religious church that was hiding behind the veneer of prosperity and wealth and accomplishment. But Jesus gave His diagnosis of their true spiritual condition: "I know all the things you do, that you are neither hot nor cold." (Rev. 3:15 NLT). While the church of Sardis was a cold, dead church, and the church of Philadelphia was hot, alive, and vital, Laodicea was neither cold nor hot. It was merely lukewarm.

Archeologists have made an interesting discovery at Laodicea. They found that it had no local water supply. The city obtained its water through an aqueduct from the hot springs of Hierapolis some six miles away. So let's say, for example, that you were staying in a hotel in ancient Laodicea. If you turned on the faucet, you wouldn't get hot water. You wouldn't get cold water. You would get lukewarm water. Jesus basically told them, "Speaking of that, I think your spiritual condition is lukewarm." He was saying these people were in the middle. They were halfhearted. The lukewarm person has no passion, no enthusiasm, and no urgency for the things of the Spirit. It is a condition in which conviction does not affect the conscience, heart, or will. And it is religion in its worst form.

# *Thursday*

# WILL HE FIND FAITH?

*"Nevertheless, when the Son of Man comes, will He really find faith on the earth?" (Luke 18:8)*

I don't know about you, but I hate to be sick. Some people seem to like it, such as hypochondriacs who are always talking about their illnesses. They love to go on and on about their aches and pains and groans and moans. They almost seem to enjoy it in a strange sort of way.

Personally, I don't like being cooped up. I don't want to be lying on my back somewhere. As soon as I feel my energy coming back, I get up and go do things. Then I usually prolong my sickness, because I can't sit still. Have you ever done that? You felt like you were getting better, but you were a little wobbly. You were not as bad as you once were, but you are not as good as you need to be. You are sort of in that in-between stage.

That is like the church of Philadelphia that Jesus spoke of in Revelation 3. This church was getting back to its roots, to its foundation, and to the things that made it strong. But it was not as powerful as it once was. It had a little strength.

But what kind of spiritual condition will the church be in when Christ returns? Jesus said, "When the Son of Man comes, will He really find faith on the earth?" (Luke 18:8). It was more of a statement than a question, really. He was saying there will not be the level of faith there ought to be. And as we look at the church today, we can clearly see that the further the modern church has strayed from the New Testament model, the weaker and more ineffective it has become.

# A LACK OF KNOWLEDGE

*"For you have a little strength, have kept My word, and have not denied My name." (Revelation 3:8)*

In Revelation 3, we see that Jesus commended the awakened church of Philadelphia because they kept His Word. How important that is in these days in which we are living. The Bible warns us that some of the signs of the last days, among other things, will be the presence of false prophets, false apostles, false teachers, and even lying wonders.

If that is not a description of the time we are living in, then I don't know what is. In my entire life as a Christian, I have never seen more false teaching than I do today. What's more, I have never seen a greater biblical illiteracy among Christians than I am seeing right now. I am amazed at how many believers lack the very basics of Christian theology. Hosea's cry for his day rings true for ours as well: "My people are destroyed for lack of knowledge" (Hos. 4:6).

C. S. Lewis warned, "If you do not listen to Theology, that will not mean that you have no ideas about God. It will mean that you have a lot of wrong ones."[4] How we need the Word of God. How we need *to know* the Word of God. And the only way we ever will know the true from the false is by having a good knowledge of the Scripture.

Are you keeping His Word today? I believe the church has, in many ways, strayed from this to its own peril. We have placed entertainment, politics, activism, and psychology at the forefront, and we have pushed the Bible to the back. We are missing it. And as a result, we are not making the difference we ought to be making.

# HOLD ON TO YOUR CROWN

*"Behold, I am coming quickly! Hold fast what you have,*
*that no one may take your crown."*
*(Revelation 3:11)*

As the times get more difficult, as hostility increases and the world becomes more and more secular and casts aside even the trappings of Christianity that it formerly practiced, we as Christians living in the last days must be careful not to give up and go along with these worldly attitudes and pursuits.

When Jesus said, "Hold fast what you have, that no one may take your crown" (Rev. 3:11), it is not referring to losing our salvation. In the Bible, the concept of a crown is something that is given to a believer for his or her faithfulness. Various crowns are promised to believers, depending on how they lived. Paul said, "Finally, there is laid up for me the crown of righteousness, which the Lord, the righteous Judge, will give to me on that Day, and not to me only but also to all who have loved His appearing" (2 Tim. 4:8). If you look forward with great anticipation to the return of Christ, then you will have a crown of righteousness waiting for you.

The crown Jesus spoke of in Revelation 3 represents the opportunities God has given to us. There is a reward promised to every believer who faithfully serves the Lord. Don't lose that opportunity. Don't squander it, because by missing it, you will forfeit the crown that Jesus has for you.

If you do not faithfully serve the Lord with the right motives and do what God has set before you, you will still get to heaven, but there won't be a crown waiting for you. But if you take hold of those opportunities God has given to you, then He will give you that crown.

# *Monday*

# LIGHT YEARS AHEAD

*The heavens declare the glory of God and the firmament shows His handiwork.*
*(Psalm 19:1)*

On Christmas Eve 1968, astronauts Frank Borman, James Lovell, and William Anders were orbiting the moon in Apollo 8. They were so moved by what they saw that they publicly read Genesis 1:1–10, much to the chagrin of many people, I might add.

Over the years, people have scoffed at the Bible and have pointed out how unscientific it supposedly is. This is not unique to our times. Since the earliest days of history, people have laughed at the Bible. There were those who mocked the Bible because it says the stars are uncountable. They said the Bible cannot be true, because although there are a lot of stars, you can count them. But as time has passed and technology has improved, we have developed more powerful telescopes. We have come to the conclusion that the stars are indeed innumerable.

It was the Bible that said the Earth hung upon nothing (see Job 26:7), describing gravity. It was the Bible that said, "Things which are seen were not made of things which are visible" (Heb. 11:3), predating, by centuries, the discoveries of modern science that eventually realized that all matter is made up of invisible energy. It was the Bible that said the Earth was round (see Isa. 40:22), but for years people laughed at the absurdity of such a statement. Everyone knew the Earth was flat. Or so they thought.

Let's understand, however, that it is not the purpose of the Bible to tell us how the heavens go, but rather how to go to heaven, how to know God, and how to live in this troubled and confused human race. It is the only book that speaks with authority in this realm.

# Tuesday

# THE ALPHA AND OMEGA

*In the beginning God created the heavens and the earth. (Genesis 1:1)*

Every child eventually gets around to asking, "Where did God come from? Who created God?" That is not an easy question to answer, because clearly the Bible teaches that God is eternal. He did not have a beginning, nor does He have an end. No one created God. He always was.

When we read the first four words of Genesis 1:1, "In the beginning God," we see that the whole universe is not here by just an accidental compression of gasses and explosions. Did it just happen that the Earth was ninety-three million miles away from the sun? Did it just happen that the atmosphere became a combination of nitrogen and oxygen in a balance of seventy-nine to twenty, with one percent variance gasses? Did it just happen that there is a blanket of ozone around our planet? Did it just happen that there is a ratio of two-thirds water to one-third land mass? Did it just happen that in this water, there was an unusual combination of molecules, of proteins, that just happened to come together at the right time, in the right proportions, at the right pressure, temperature, and so forth, and that these spontaneously grafted into a cell that became a human being?

What are the chances of all of this happening by coincidence, as some would say? I think it takes far more faith to believe in evolutionary theory than it takes to believe in the concept that God created the heavens and Earth.

As an artist, I know that it takes work to produce a work of art. And when I look at this incredible planet that God has made, I can only rationally conclude there is a Master Designer behind it all.

# THINKING OF YOU

*When I consider Your heavens, the work of Your fingers, the moon
and the stars, which You have ordained, what is man that You are
mindful of him, and the son of man that You visit him?*
*(Psalm 8:3–4)*

One night, probably when David was watching over his
sheep, he looked up at the incredible stars and made
this statement: "When I consider Your heavens, the
work of Your fingers, the moon and the stars, which You have
ordained, what is man that You are mindful of him, and the
son of man that You visit him?" (Ps. 8:3–4).

It is incredible to think that the Creator of the universe,
the Almighty God who knows every star by name, would care
about us. And not only does He care about humanity as a
whole, but He also cares about us as individuals. Not only
does He care about us as individuals, but He also knows
about every detail of our lives. God even knows the very
thoughts that we think. Jesus said, "Your Father knows the
things you have
need of before you ask Him" (Matt. 6:8).

Psalm 40:5 tells us, "Many, O Lord my God, are Your
wonderful works which You have done; and Your thoughts
toward us cannot be recounted to You in order. If I would
declare and speak of them, they are more than can be num-
bered." Psalm 115:12 says, "The Lord has been mindful of
us. He will bless us."

So, even when family and friends have forgotten about
you, know this: the Lord is thinking about you. The Lord
cares about you. He is interested in even the smallest details
of your life. They might seem trivial to someone else, but
not to God. If it concerns you, then it concerns Him.

# Thursday

## Chosen

*His unchanging plan has always been to adopt us into his own*
*family by bringing us to himself through Jesus Christ.*
*And this gave him great pleasure.*
*(Ephesians 1:5 NLT)*

Have you ever met someone that you thought was the greatest person you had ever met? Maybe it was someone you fell in love with, or a new friend you made. You thought, *This is the greatest friend I have ever had.*

But as the years, or even weeks, pass, do you still feel that way? Maybe you started to think, *I don't want this person as a friend anymore.* Why? Because you learned more about him or her.

It was C. H. Spurgeon who said, "It's a good thing God chose me before I was born, because he surely would not have afterwards."

God created you, and yes, even before you were born, He knew exactly how you would turn out. He knew you would have your flaws and shortcomings. But He chose you to be adopted into His family. This means He knew there would come a day when we would put our faith in Jesus Christ and God would us me His children. The Bible says, "He made us accepted in the Beloved" (Eph. 1:6). It doesn't teach that if we try to live a really good life and live by certain standards and work really hard, then we might just find God's approval.

Rather, the Bible teaches that before we were even born, before we were even known, we were chosen by God and selected by Him to be His children. Now He has "made us accepted in the Beloved," meaning that our righteousness today is not based on what we have done for Him, but on what He has done for us.

# *Friday*

# God's Masterpiece

*Then God said, "Let Us make man in Our image, according to Our likeness."*
*(Genesis 1:26)*

A little girl climbed up on the lap of her great-grand-mother and studied her white hair and wrinkles. She said, "Grandma, did God make you?"

Her grandmother said, "Yes, He sure did."

The little girl looked at her for a moment and said, "Did God make me too?"

"Yes, He sure did. He made you too."

Then the little girl said, "Don't you think He is doing a better job now than He used to?"

As David wrote in Psalm 139, the human body, created by God, is a masterpiece of exquisite design. He said, "I will praise You, for I am fearfully and wonderfully made" (v. 14). The human body is incredibly engineered, governed by several hundred systems of control, each interacting and affecting the other.

For example, the brain has ten billion nerve cells to record what we see and hear. Our skin has more than two million tiny sweat glands, about three thousand per square inch, all part of an intricate system that keeps our body at an even temperature. God has put this pump in our chest known as a heart that makes our blood travel 168 million miles per day, equivalent to going around the world 6,725 times. The lining of our stomach contains thirty-five million glands secreting juices, which aid the process of digestion.

These are just a few of the involved processes and chemical wonders that God has built into our bodies to sustain human life. There is nothing like a man or woman made in the image of God. We are not highly evolved forms of animal life; we are clearly made in the image of God himself and stand apart from all other creation.

# Weekend

# CREATED FOR A PURPOSE

*"He himself gives life and breath to everything,
and he satisfies every need there is."*
(*Acts 17:25* NLT)

Why did God put us on this earth? Was it because He needed us? Was it because, after all that He had made, even the animal life, there was a sense of loneliness and He wanted companionship? Some would suggest that.

But God did not create man because He needed Him. In Acts 17, Paul said, "God, who made the world and everything in it, since He is Lord of heaven and earth, does not dwell in temples made with hands. Nor is He worshiped with men's hands, as though He needed anything, since He gives to all life, breath, and all things" (vv. 24–25). The implication is that God does not need anything from humanity.

God asked Job, "Who has preceded Me, that I should pay him? Everything under heaven is Mine" (Job 41:11). No one has ever contributed to God that which did not first come from God, who created all things.

Though it is true that God did not make us because He needed us, it is also true that He loves us and, amazingly, He desires a relationship with us. But first and foremost, God created us for His own glory. God said, "Everyone who is called by My name, whom I have created for My glory; I have formed him, yes, I have made him" (Isa. 43:7). Therefore, we are to glorify Him in everything we say or do with our lives.

Paul summed up his life in this way: "For to me, to live is Christ, and to die is gain" (Phil. 1:21). This should be the motto of every Christian. You are here to bring glory to God—through your career, through your marriage, and through your family. Through every achievement, you are capable of bringing glory and honor to the Lord.

*Monday*

# THE CHOICE
# WE ALL MUST MAKE

*We love Him because He first loved us. (1 John 4:19)*

Man, who was created uniquely in the very image of God, was placed in a literal paradise on Earth—heaven on Earth, if you will. He had every legitimate comfort that this world could offer. There was nothing that Adam lacked. He was surrounded by unparalleled beauty. It was a perfect climate. The animal kingdom was subdued. There was no crime, no violence, no perversion—just absolute perfection. Not only that, but God brought a companion for Adam named Eve. And the best feature of all: Adam was able to walk in undisturbed fellowship and communion with God, twenty-four hours a day.

But God gave Adam another wonderful treasure, something that we all have. It is called free will. God loved Adam and wanted to have fellowship with him. But God wanted Adam to love Him not out of fear, but out of love, because love, by its very nature, must be voluntary.

If we are going to really love God, then we need to be able to choose to do so out of our own free will. Involuntary love is a contradiction in terms, and there really is no such thing. If Adam was free to love God on his own initiative, then he also was free not to love God. If he was able to make the right moral choice, then he was, by necessity, also able to make the wrong moral choice. And we all know the choice that he made.

God's creation of morally free beings in His own image clearly ran the risk of having them reject Him and His love. Tragically for Adam and Eve, the wrong choice was made, and we have been feeling the repercussions of it to this very day.

# Tuesday

# IN HIS IMAGE

*And the Lord God formed man of the dust of the ground, and breathed into his nostrils the breath of life; and man became a living being. (Genesis 2:7)*

When God made man, it was a combination of that which is very low and that which is very high. On one hand, man is described as being formed out of "the dust of the ground" (Gen. 3:7). But on the other hand, he was made in the image of God. God breathed into man and made him a living soul.

It is worth noting that the same, basic chemical elements of the earth—nitrogen, oxygen and calcium—are also the basic physical elements of the human body. But I think the real intention of pointing out that we were formed from dust is to remind us of our humble origins. This is often mentioned in the Bible to describe how small we really are. In fact, people in Scripture mentioned this fact to describe their own fallen state. Abraham, when pleading with God over the future of Sodom, said, "Indeed now, I who am but dust and ashes have taken it upon myself to speak to the Lord" (Gen. 18:27). Hannah, who was praising the Lord for hearing her prayers for a son, said, "He raises the poor from the dust and lifts the beggar from the ash heap" (I Sam. 2:8). Scripture also reminds us that from dust we came and to dust we will return (see Gen. 3:19; Job 34:15; Eccl. 3:20).

Yet we were made in the image of God. Although we are made of the most humble and lowly of materials, God Almighty breathed into us and gave us life, lifting us above all other created beings. Why? Because we were made in His very image.

# SOW A THOUGHT ...
# REAP A DESTINY

*By the word of Your lips, I have kept away from the paths of the destroyer.*
*(Psalm 17:4)*

When the devil wanted to lead the first man and woman into sin, he started by attacking their minds. And he still uses that tactic to this day. Paul warned of this when he said, "But I fear, lest somehow, as the serpent deceived Eve by his craftiness, so your minds may be corrupted from the simplicity that is in Christ" (2 Cor. 11:3). The devil attacks our minds, because our brain, our thoughts, our imagination—these are command central. With the mind you can reach into the past through memories, and you can reach into the future through imagination. The devil knows that if he can get us to think about something, to contemplate it, to consider it, then he is halfway there.

The Bible tells us, "For the weapons of our warfare are not carnal but mighty in God for pulling down strongholds, casting down arguments and every high thing that exalts itself against the knowledge of God, bringing every thought into captivity to the obedience of Christ" (2 Cor. 10:4–5).

It has been said, "Sow a thought; reap an act. Sow an act; reap a character. Sow a character; reap a destiny." It starts with a thought, but it can lead to a destiny. The devil knows that if he can get us to think about something, to consider something, then he almost has us.

Eve's mind certainly was not filled with the things of God when the devil approached her. Had it been, she could have effectively resisted his temptations. When we have the Word of God hidden in our hearts, it will give us an important resource that we can call upon to effectively resist temptation.

# *Thursday*

# THE FATHER KNOWS BEST

*Now the serpent was more cunning than any beast of the field which the Lord God had made. ... (Genesis 3:1)*

I find it interesting that the devil didn't deny that God had spoken to Eve. He said to her, "Has God indeed said, 'You shall not eat of every tree of the garden'?" (Gen. 3:1). He simply questioned whether God had really said what Eve thought He said. Essentially, he was questioning God's fairness and love for Eve: *If God really loved you, He would let you eat of this tree too. He is holding out on you. It's not fair. God must not love you to keep something from you.*

Maybe you have felt that way before. Or maybe you feel that way now. Maybe you feel God is holding something back from you that you really think you need. Just remember, if God says no, then it is for your own good. That is hard for us to understand sometimes. But consider the way you would deal with young children. You wouldn't let them live entirely on sugar, watch cartoons all day, or stay up all night, even though they think they need to do these things. Instead, you set certain limits, because you know what is good for them.

God does the same with us. He says no to certain things. But if God says no, then it is the right thing. Psalm 84:11 says, "No good thing will He withhold from those who walk uprightly." There is nothing God tells me to avoid that is good. If He tells me to avoid it, then it is because it would harm me. If He says, "Don't do this. It is not good," then take His word for it.

No good thing will He withhold from you.

# ENTERTAINING DOUBT

*Then the serpent said to the woman, "You will not surely die."*
*(Genesis 3:4)*

A woman who was married to a very miserly husband told him one morning that she was going shopping. "No," he said, "You're not going shopping. I don't want you to buy anything."

"OK. I'll go window shopping," she said.

"Go ahead," he told her. "You can look, but you cannot buy."

When she came home that evening with a beautiful, expensive new dress, he was so angry. He said, "I thought you were going window shopping. You came back with this expensive dress!"

"I know," she said. "I was just looking. I tried this dress on. Then the devil appeared. He said, 'That's a cute dress. It sure looks good on you.'"

"Right then, you should have said, 'Get behind me, Satan!'" her husband told her.

"I did! Then he got behind me and said, 'It looks good from the back too.'"

There is a big difference between dealing with doubt and entertaining it. Entertaining is something you do when you want to spend time with someone. You invite them dinner and entertain them for the evening. But we don't want to entertain doubt.

We all will be faced with doubts, and doubt and skepticism are not necessarily in themselves bad things. They can challenge us to really dig in deeper and know why we believe. But it is a short step from questioning God's Word to denying it. If Eve had not listened to the devil's questioning God's Word, she never would have fallen into the trap of denying God's Word. Eve was at the wrong place, listening to the wrong voice, which led her to do the wrong thing.

# Weekend

# CONVICTION VS. CONDEMNATION

*Now Joshua was clothed with filthy garments,
and was standing before the Angel.
(Zechariah 3:3)*

After the devil tempts you, if you take the bait, then he has another tactic he uses with great effect: he will condemn you. This is vividly illustrated in Zechariah 3:1–5, which gives us a rare, behind-the-scenes look at what happens in heaven. The scene could be compared to a courtroom, in which God is the judge, Joshua the high priest is the defendant, and Satan is the prosecuting attorney. He is trying to prove that Joshua is guilty. First the devil will get you to sin. Then he will accuse you and condemn you for having given in to his temptation. Revelation 12:1 describes him as "the accuser of our brethren, who accused them before our God day and night."

When we have disobeyed God, Satan moves in for the final blow. He attacks us in our hearts and minds: *You call yourself a Christian? How could a Christian do what you just did?* He is an accuser. He is a liar. And when Satan talks to you about God, he lies.

But sometimes when he talks to God about you, he tells the truth. For example, he points out that you have done the wrong thing. But we need to distinguish between the devil's accusations and the Spirit's conviction. When you sin, the Holy Spirit convicts you. He uses God's Word in love and seeks to bring you back into fellowship with the Father. But when the devil accuses you, he uses your sin in a hateful way and seeks to make you feel helpless and hopeless. He wants you to experience regret and remorse, but not repentance. But true conviction from the Holy Spirit will always draw you closer to God.

*Monday*

# ENGAGING OUR HEARTS

> *"These people draw near to Me with their mouth, and honor Me with their lips, but their heart is far from Me. And in vain they worship Me."*
> *(Matthew 15:8–9)*

Cain and Abel both came from the same home, both had the example of Adam and Eve to follow (which I would assume was a relatively good example of people who loved God), and both were probably taught to pray from their youth. Yet one became a true worshipper, offering an acceptable gift to the Lord. The other became a false worshipper, offering an unacceptable act of worship.

It comes down to motive. Motive is so important in what we do. Hebrews 11:4 gives us this insight: "By faith Abel offered to God a more excellent sacrifice than Cain." Abel exercised faith in his worship; Cain did not. Hebrews further says, "Without faith it is impossible to please Him" (Heb. 11:6). Abel's heart was moved toward God, as his actions demonstrated. This reminds us that worship is really a form of prayer.

The sad and amazing thing is that we can sing worship songs to God without a single thought about the God we are singing to. God said, "These people draw near to Me with their mouth, and honor Me with their lips, but their heart is far from Me" (Matt. 15:8). It is possible to be singing and not have any thought of God whatsoever. We can be in a worship service, and as we are singing, we are thinking things like, *I don't really like this song. ... I'm hungry. ... It's cold in here. ... When is this service going to be over?* When we worship, our hearts need to engage. Otherwise, we are just going through the motions. And that is not real worship.

# Tuesday

# RECEIVING FROM GIVING

*There is one who scatters, yet increases more; and there is*
*one who withholds more than is right, but it leads to poverty.*
*(Proverbs 11:24)*

A mother who wanted to teach her daughter the joy
of giving gave her both a quarter and a dollar to take
to church one Sunday morning. She told her daughter that she could put in either one; the choice was hers. As
they were leaving church, the mother asked her daughter
what she ended up giving to the Lord.

The little girl replied, "I was going to give the dollar, but
just before the offering, the man in the pulpit said we should
be cheerful givers. I knew I would be a lot more cheerful if I
just gave the quarter." That is how a lot of us are. We think,
*I am not cheerful about giving, so I suppose I had better keep it for myself.* But
we need to understand that God wants to change our hearts.
We need to discover the joy of giving. And if we haven't yet
discovered it, then we need to ask God to change our hearts,
because giving is a blessing. We can experience joy in it.

Jesus said, "It is more blessed to give than to receive" (Acts
20:35). It is hard for children to wrap their minds around
that truth. But as we get older, and especially if we become
parents, we discover the joy of giving. We actually find more
pleasure in giving than receiving. The word Jesus used for
"blessed" is a word that could be translated "happy." In other
words, the Bible is saying that if you want to be a happy person,
then be a generous person. If you want to be a happy person,
then be a giving person.

# IT'S AT THE DOOR

*If you do well, will you not be accepted?*
*And if you do not do well, sin lies at the door.*
*And its desire is for you, but you should rule over it.*
*(Genesis 4:7)*

Years ago, my son Christopher was lying out in the sun at our house when he woke up to find a huge gopher snake, coiled up and hissing at him, poised to strike. It must have been six or seven feet long. Terrified, he ran into the house and shut the door behind him.

That is a picture of how sin can be: ready to strike. It is at the door—for all of us. It is potentially there at all times, and for some of us, it has already slithered across the threshold.

When Cain saw that the Lord accepted Abel's offering, but not his, he was angry. So God gives him a warning. He essentially told Cain what was going to happen to him if he didn't get himself under control: "Sin lies at the door. And its desire is for you, but you should rule over it" (Gen. 4:7). Another way to translate it would be, "Sin is crouching at the door like a beast. ..." What a vivid picture that is of sin crouching, ready to pounce like a wild animal.

So the next time sin is knocking at your door, you might say, "Lord, would You mind getting that? I'm going to stand in Your strength. I'm going to trust in You. You are the only one who can give me the strength to overpower sin." If we will master sin, then we must first be mastered by Him who mastered it.

Tragically, Cain did not allow himself to be mastered by God, but instead became enslaved by the devil.

# *Thursday*

# THE DANGERS OF JEALOUSY

*"And whoever exalts himself will be humbled,*
*and he who humbles himself will be exalted."*
*(Matthew 23:12)*

A fisherman who caught crabs would keep them in a little bucket without a lid. Someone noticed this and asked him, "Don't you have to keep a lid on that bucket?"

He said, "No, they never get out."

"Why? Because they can't get out?"

"No," he said, "When one crab tries to go over the side, the others reach up and pull him back down again."

That is just like human beings as well. As one person begins to climb, others are thinking, *How dare you succeed? ... How dare you do better than me? ... How dare you get that promotion? ... How dare you get that attention? ... How dare you do well when I am not doing just as well? ...You get back down here with me.*

It has been said that envy shoots at another and wounds itself. This is so true. Envy can eat us up inside. We need to recognize it as sin and repent of it. We may try and rationalize our jealousy, but we need to realize it is wrong and ask God to forgive us. God wants us to put the needs of others above our own, love one another, and care for one another. This is so very important.

Instead of worrying about what other people have, let's be thankful we are even drawing breath in our lungs. It is a gift from God. And if God lifts you to an exalted position, then that is His grace. If He lifts up someone else, that also is His grace. None of us deserve it; it is all the grace of God. Just be faithful to what God has called you to do.

# ABEL'S WAY

*Woe to them! For they have gone in the way of Cain.*
*(Jude 1:11)*

The Bible warns us of the way of Cain. But what is it? The way of Cain is when we try to come to God apart from His sacrifice. The way of Cain is to worship with impure motives. The way of Cain is to have a heart and life full of jealousy, envy, and hatred. The way of Cain is to lie about what we have done. The way of Cain is to reject all responsibility for our actions.

If we live in the way of Cain, then we will experience the curse of Cain. God said to him, "What have you done? The voice of your brother's blood cries out to Me from the ground" (Gen. 4:10). If God would have killed Cain on the spot, it would have been just. Yet God spared him. But instead of thanking God for this reprieve, Cain was upset. He said, "My punishment *is* greater than I can bear!" (v. 13). This is typical of the unrepentant. They blame everyone but themselves.

Don't let that happen to you. Don't go in the way of Cain. Don't let jealousy and envy control and ruin your life. Don't let sin master you. Don't let impure motives hinder your worship of God. Don't come to God with self-righteousness.

Walk instead in the way of Abel. Hebrews says of him, "By faith Abel offered to God a more excellent sacrifice than Cain, through which he obtained witness that he was righteous, God testifying of his gifts; and through it he being dead still speaks" (Heb. 11:4). Abel's way is the way of faith. It is the way of trust. It is the way of the cross. It is the only way.

# Weekend

# THE GENEROSITY PRINCIPLE

*The generous prosper and are satisfied;*
*those who refresh others will themselves be refreshed.*
*(Proverbs 11:25 NLT)*

A famous pirate named Juan Carlos was known for his theft and was rumored to have buried treasure hidden somewhere. A man approached Juan Carlos one day in Mexico, pushed him to the ground, and said, "Tell me where all your money is buried, or I will kill you right here on the spot!"

Juan Carlos didn't speak a word of English and needed an interpreter, so he saw a boy nearby and called him over. The boy relayed the man's message to Juan Carlos, and fearing for his life, Juan Carlos said to the boy, "Tell this man I don't want to die. Tell him the money is located thirty paces north of the city water tower, under a large rock."

The boy turned to the man and replied, "Juan Carlos says he is an honorable man and that he will never tell you where the money is. Juan Carlos says kill him now."

There are some people who, once they have something, don't ever want to let it go. But the Bible tells us that as we give, God will give to us. In 2 Corinthians 9:8, we read, "And God will generously provide all you need. Then you will always have everything you need and plenty left over to share with others" (NLT).

This goes along with the principle Jesus gave us: "If you give, you will receive. Your gift will return to you in full measure, pressed down, shaken together to make room for more, and running over. Whatever measure you use in giving—large or small—it will be used to measure what is given back to you" (Luke 6:38 NLT). As God blesses you, you can bless others.

*Monday*

# Unwavering Faith

*I know how to be abased, and I know how to abound.
Everywhere and in all things I have learned both to be full
and to be hungry, both to abound and to suffer need.
(Philippians 4:12)*

Have you ever been sorely mistreated through no fault of your own? Perhaps you were the victim of an orchestrated campaign of slander and lies. Maybe you were falsely accused of things that, ironically, you had gone to great lengths to avoid. Maybe you have been a victim of another kind of injustice. It may seem that God has somehow forgotten you.

Most of us live by a code of ethics, and within this code, we believe that if people do what is right, they should be rewarded. And if people do what is wrong, they should ultimately face some sort of punishment. A good part of life happens to work out that way. But sometimes it doesn't, and we want to know why. I do not have any easy answers to this dilemma. But in the Book in Genesis, we see how one man named Joseph dealt with this very issue. He suffered not for doing wrong, but for doing right. He experienced mistreatment, misunderstanding, and downright hostility.

If anyone had a good reason to question God, it was Joseph. If anyone could have claimed he was a victim, and the world was against him, it was Joseph. If anyone could have felt that God had possibly forgotten him, it was Joseph. Yet amazingly, as far as we know, he never did any of those things.

The single greatest characteristic of Joseph's life was his unwavering faithfulness to God in all circumstances. No matter what came his way, Joseph trusted God. He is an amazing example for all of us to emulate.

# Tuesday

# Wait Training

*Now godliness with contentment is great gain.*
*(1 Timothy 6:6)*

Have you learned the secret of contentment? Many of us are content when things are going our way. When life is going the way we want it to, we are content, relatively speaking. But when life deals us a hard blow, when the bottom drops out, when we face a conflict, suddenly we are no longer content.

Maybe you are in a situation like that right now. Maybe you have been the victim of accusations that are untrue. Maybe someone you love has abandoned you. Maybe you have helped someone out who was really in a miserable situation, only to have that person turn on you. Maybe someone made promises to you they did not keep. Maybe something like this has happened to you and you feel abandoned.

Even though it may seem everyone else has deserted you, God has not. God never forgets about His children. Sometimes God will allow us to experience hardship because He is teaching us to walk by faith, not by sight and not by feeling, just as He did with Joseph in the Book of Genesis. In that case, the Lord wanted to whip young Joseph into shape, because he had some formidable tasks ahead, like running a world empire. There would be no time for pity parties. You could say that Joseph was in wait training.

Maybe you are in wait training too. You wonder why the Lord is not doing anything in your life, why no doors are opening for you. Just hang in there. There are some lessons that God may want to teach you. The Bible says, "Godliness with contentment is great gain" (1 Tim. 6:6). That contentment will come not from your circumstances, but from your relationship with God.

# BITTER? OR BETTER?

*And I am sure that God, who began the good work within you, will continue his work until it is finally finished on that day when Christ Jesus comes back again.*
*(Philippians 1:6 NLT)*

When we experience a time of difficulty, a time of hardship, a time in which we have been misrepresented or misunderstood, we have two options. The first is that we can become disillusioned and bitter. We can become so burned because of what others have done that we withdraw. We become cynical. We are angry. And in some cases, we can even become angry at God. Tragically, many go this route. The double tragedy is that bitter people are rarely content to keep their bitterness to themselves. They usually want to pull others into their web of misery. That is why Hebrews 12:15 says, "Look after each other so that none of you will miss out on the special favor of God. Watch out that no bitter root of unbelief rises up among you, for whenever it springs up, many are corrupted by its poison" (NLT).

The second option is that we can use our difficulty as a platform for putting our trust in God. The cause of all of the disillusionment that we face in life is because we put our trust in people. Yet God warns us time and time again not to trust in people. People are going to let you down—even the best people. Psalm 118:8 says, "It is better to trust in the Lord than to put confidence in man."

The dealings of God, the trials that come your way, will make you either bitter or better. The choice is yours. You decide. Are you going to become a bitter person? Or are you going to become a better person?

# *Thursday*

# IN THE POTTER'S HANDS

*Shall the potter be esteemed as the clay; for shall the thing made*
*say of him who made it, "He did not make me"?*
*Or shall the thing formed say of him who formed it,*
*"He has no understanding"?*
*(Isaiah 29:16)*

I haven't had a lot of experience with clay—it goes only as far as high school. I remember that when we would make things out of clay, if the clay wasn't pliable and moldable, it would end up as an ashtray.

A great illustration of this is given to us in the Book of Jeremiah. God instructed Jeremiah to go down to a potter's house, where Jeremiah saw him working at his wheel, on a pot he was shaping. Jeremiah tells us, "But the jar he was making did not turn out as he had hoped, so the potter squashed the jar into a lump of clay and started again. Then the Lord gave me this message: 'O Israel, can I not do to you as this potter has done to his clay? As the clay is in the potter's hand, so are you in my hand'" (Jer. 18:4–5 NLT).

We are like clay on the potter's wheel. We see in the wheel an instrument with which the Potter accomplishes His definite purposes. We see in the Potter an intelligent, capable Artist with a purpose. We see in the clay a moldable material. The Potter has a thought in mind for the clay. We have a choice: we can let God mold away, or we can be like the piece of clay that Jeremiah described.

God has a plan for you. Do you want to be what He wants you to be? If you are smart, you will yield and allow Him to do His work.

# God's Specialty

*Nor has the eye seen any God besides You,*
*who acts for the one who waits for Him.*
*(Isaiah 64:4)*

I know it is hard to imagine sometimes what God is up to in your life. You see a blank canvas, but God sees a finished painting. You see a piece of coal, but God sees a refined diamond. You see an untalented person, but God sees a mighty man or woman of God. This is also true of those we see in Scripture. We see an impetuous, impulsive Simon, but God sees a strong, decisive apostle named Peter. We see a conniving, manipulative Jacob, but God sees a godly, trusting man named Israel. We see a young, naïve Joseph, but the Lord sees a brilliant, wise world leader. And when it was all said and done, Joseph was able to look back and say to his brothers, "You meant evil against me; but God meant it for good" (Gen. 50:20). He recognized God used the things that happened to him to mold him into a compassionate, forgiving leader of many. He was clay in the Potter's hand. He trusted in the Lord.

God specializes in making something out of nothing. I wonder what He is doing with you right now. You are a work in progress. He is not finished yet. Any good artist usually doesn't like someone looking over his shoulder, trying to second-guess what he is about do. He will say, "Wait until I am done, and then you will see."

So trust in the Lord during those times when it is hard to see what He is doing. Don't allow hardships you face to make you a bitter person. It is time to let go of that. Rather, allow them to make you a better person.

# Weekend

## THE BAD NEWS IN THE GOOD NEWS

*For I have not shunned to declare to you the whole counsel of God.*
*(Acts 20:27)*

Sometimes people cannot fully appreciate the good news unless they have first heard the bad news. And this can be true when we share the gospel. We delight in the wonderful, life-changing message of God's Word that promises forgiveness and peace and fulfillment and best of all, the hope of heaven beyond the grave. We deliver that aspect of the message with relish.

But then there is that pesky part about hell. The Scriptures reminds us that the wages of sin are death (Rom. 6:23), that we are separated from God, and no matter what we do, we cannot bridge the gap. That is why God sent His Son to die for us and why we must turn from our sin, put our complete faith in Christ, and follow Him. If we do, then we will go to heaven. But if we reject His offer of forgiveness, we ultimately will face judgment and go to hell.

We want to soften that part, maybe not even mention it. But know this: hell is as much a part of the message of the gospel as heaven. And one of the great joys of the gospel is knowing, as a Christian, where I don't have to go as well as knowing where I am going to go.

Sometimes we are reluctant to share that. But it is the truth. Paul said, "Therefore I testify to you this day that I am innocent of the blood of all men. For I have not shunned to declare to you the whole counsel of God" (Acts 20:26–27). That should be true of each one of us. We should declare the truth, the whole truth, and nothing but the truth.

# *Monday*

## THROUGH THE FIRE

*But He knows the way that I take;*
*when He has tested me, I shall come forth as gold.*
*(Job 23:10)*

God specializes in bringing certain situations about in which only He can get us out of them. That way, we can't thank our lucky stars or compliment ourselves on our own cleverness or resourcefulness. Rather, we must say, "Only God could have done this." The Lord wants to receive the glory for what He does. And He clearly says in Scripture that He will not give His glory to another (see Isa. 42:8).

It reminds us of a man who knew something about suffering, whose very name, in fact, is synonymous with the word. I am speaking, of course, of Job. Here was a man who lost his children, the destruction of his home, and the loss of everything he owned, including his health.

Job had a lot of questions, the same questions that many of us have. He said, "Oh, that I knew where I might find Him, that I might come to His seat! I would present my case before Him, and fill my mouth with arguments. I would know the words which He would answer me, and understand what He would say to me" (Job 23:3–5).

Job honestly admitted what he was struggling with. Then he added what would become a classic statement of faith: "But He knows the way that I take; when He has tested me, I shall come forth as gold" (Job 23:10). Job was saying, "I don't know what is going on. I don't know why God has allowed these things to happen. But I know this: when I am tested, I will come forth as gold." That was God's objective for Job. And it is His objective for you too.

# Tuesday

# TAKING THE BAD WITH THE GOOD

*But Job replied, "You talk like a godless woman. Should we accept only good things from the hand of God and never anything bad?" So in all this, Job said nothing wrong. (Job 2:10 NLT)*

Sudden reversals in our lives can be difficult to take, especially if they are for the worse. And sometimes when we face a sudden reversal for the worse, we can be despondent. We may think God has abandoned us.

But interestingly, when we experience a reversal for the better, we are sometimes arrogant. Instead of thinking God has abandoned us, we sometimes abandon God. Prosperity often can be a harder test to pass than adversity. After all, when you are experiencing adversity, you are dependent upon God for whatever it is you need. You need food, clothing, your health, and existence. But when you are enjoying prosperity, when things are going reasonably well, you can forget the Lord. Even worse, you can start taking personal credit for what you have accomplished.

Let's say, for example, that you are working away in business. You are barely making it. Then all of a sudden, everything comes together. You are making sales left and right. You are on the top of the heap. But instead of giving the glory to God, you say to yourself, *I'm pretty good, aren't I?* Or let's say you're in school, and all of a sudden, you find yourself doing better than the other students are. You are getting straight A's. You think, "I am a little smarter than the rest of these idiots, I suppose." Or maybe you are achieving in some other area of life. Remember that it was God who brought that success to you.

The question is will you remember God in adversity, but also remember Him in prosperity?

# NOTEWORTHY LIVING

*Now when they saw the boldness of Peter and John,
and perceived that they were uneducated and untrained men,
they marveled. And they realized that they had been with Jesus."*
*(Acts 4:13)*

In Acts 3 we read about how, when Peter and John went up to the temple to pray, they passed by a man who had been lame from birth. On that particular day, the Lord instructed Peter to say to him, "Silver and gold I do not have, but what I do have I give you: In the name of Jesus Christ of Nazareth, rise up and walk" (v. 6). The Bible tells us that after Peter and John pulled this man to his feet, he was walking, leaping, and praising God.

The religious leaders, who basically thought their problems were eliminated when Christ was crucified, heard about this. Here were Peter and John, in the power of Jesus Christ, impacting lives. Acts 4:13 tells us, "Now when they saw the boldness of Peter and John, and perceived that they were uneducated and untrained men, they marveled. And they realized that they had been with Jesus." What a great statement: "They realized they had been with Jesus." In the same way, Pharaoh looked at Joseph and realized God was in him. He noticed that Joseph was discerning and wise (see Gen. 41:39). Joseph's diligence, hard work, and integrity got people noticing and asking.

I wonder if people can see those qualities in us. Can they tell there is something different about us? I think this is the greatest compliment that can be paid to a Christian. But far too often, it is the opposite. We contradict what we believe by the way we live.

Have you been with Jesus? Can people see evidence of that in your life?

# *Thursday*

# THE BY-PRODUCT OF HOLINESS

*For whom He foreknew, He also predestined to be conformed to the image of His Son, that He might be the firstborn among many brethren.*
*(Romans 8:29)*

We must remember that God is more interested in the eternal than the external. In other words, He is doing a work inside of us. But we tend to concentrate on the externals. We ask ourselves, *Is it making my life happier?* Somehow in our minds, we have the idea that Jesus came to Earth for the express purpose of just making our lives a little bit better.

I am not disputing the fact that if you are a committed Christian, then you will have an abundant life. I am not disagreeing with the fact that Christ will give you joy and peace and purpose and fulfillment. But having said that, let me also point out that God is more interested in our holiness than our happiness. And if you are a holy person, then you will also be a happy person. If you chase after happiness, you will never really find it. But if you pursue holiness, then happiness will be the by-product.

And here is a revolutionary thought: After Romans 8:28 comes Romans 8:29. We all love to quote Romans 8:28: "And we know that all things work together for good to those who love God, to those who are the called according to His purpose." But verse 29 says, "For whom He foreknew, He also predestined to be conformed to the image of His Son. ..."

God crushes in order to create. He bruises in order to bless. He tears down in order to build. He uproots in order to plant. Everything that He does in our lives is for a reason. God wants to make you a holy person.

# THE VALUE OF A CONSCIENCE

*Cling tightly to your faith in Christ, and always keep your conscience clear.*
*For some people have deliberately violated their consciences;*
*as a result, their faith has been shipwrecked.*
*(1 Timothy 1:19 NLT)*

My son Jonathan once asked me, "Dad, what is a conscience?" That is a pretty good question, because defining a conscience is not as easy as it may seem.

So I tried to illustrate it for him. I said, "A conscience is a lot like our ability to feel pain, like when you are walking barefoot, and you start to step on a piece of glass. You sense pain, which is a signal from the brain saying, "Red alert! Red alert! Stop! Don't step down any harder!" It is a warning of something that could be far worse. Though you may not enjoy the temporary discomfort, it beats the alternative, which is completely stepping down, puncturing your foot, bleeding, and possibly risking infection and other complications. There is pain involved, but it warns of something that could be far worse. Pain tells us there is a physical problem that must be dealt with, or the body will suffer harm. I told Jonathan that conscience can be a lot like that.

I added that you could also compare a conscience to a fire alarm. We had a fire alarm in our house that was a little too sensitive. Every time my wife would cook something, the silly thing would go off. It was one of those very loud, high-pitched-type alarms that was almost deafening. On a couple of occasions, I had to climb up on a ladder and yank it out of the ceiling.

Our conscience can be this way as well. It alerts us to danger. It warns us of something that is wrong in our lives.

# *Weekend*

# THE COWORKER
# OF CONSCIENCE

*The purpose of my instruction is that all the Christians there
would be filled with love that comes from a pure heart,
a clear conscience, and sincere faith.*
(1 Timothy 1:5 NLT)

When we rationalize sin or an ungodly lifestyle, our hearts just get harder and harder. We have learned to live with it, but with no real pangs of conscience and no real guilt to speak of. Then one day, a crisis hits. The bottom drops out. Something dramatic happens that awakens us to what we have really done. And we come to our senses.

It reminds me of the New Testament story of the prodigal son. He had to somehow rationalize in his mind that was okay for him to demand that his father divide up the estate and give him his portion of the inheritance. Then off he went, spending it all on prostitutes and prodigal living. But when the money was gone and his friends with it, he came to his senses. He said, "How many of my father's hired servants have bread enough and to spare, and I perish with hunger! I will arise and go to my father … " (Luke 15:17–18). It came to him at a time when he hit rock bottom, when he reaped the consequences of his actions.

Maybe that has been happening to you. Maybe you have been rationalizing a certain sin, but something has happened recently that made you realize you need to do something about it. Guilt, working in conjunction with our conscience, is a spiritual pain that tells us something is wrong and needs to be confronted and cleansed. So eliminating the guilt should not be the objective; getting to the source of it should be. Guilt is but the symptom of a deeper problem.

# HOW GOD USES GUILT

*Beloved, if our heart does not condemn us, we have confidence toward God.*
*(1 John 3:21)*

Columnist Ann Landers once made this statement about guilt: "One of the most painful, self-mutilating, time and energy consuming exercises in the human experience is guilt. It can ruin your day or your week or your life if you let it." Landers concluded, "Remember, guilt is a pollutant and we don't need any more of it in the world."

But I have to disagree with Ann Landers on that point. I think guilt has an important part to play in our lives. I think God can use guilt. Guilt can remind us that we have crossed the line, that we have done something wrong. And God can work with guilt in the human conscience to bring us to our senses.

The word "conscience" is a combination of Latin words that mean "to know" and "together." In fact, the Greek word for conscience is found more than thirty times in the New Testament and means "co-knowledge," "knowing together with you," or "knowledge together with oneself." That is, conscience knows our inner motives and our true thoughts.

The Hebrew word for "conscience" is usually translated "heart" in the Old Testament. So when we read in the Old Testament about having a tender heart toward God, it is speaking of having a sensitive conscience. When read about being upright in heart, it is speaking of having a pure conscience. This is not to equate the conscience with the voice of God, because our conscience can, at times, be wrong. That is why you must saturate your heart and mind with the Word of God to essentially educate it. And when your conscience is educated by the Word of God, it can, in fact, serve an important purpose.

# Tuesday

# KEEPING YOUR
# CONSCIENCE PURE

*For our boasting is this: the testimony of our conscience that we conducted our-*
*selves in the world in simplicity and godly sincerity, not with fleshly wisdom but*
*by the grace of God. (2 Corinthians 1:12)*

The question arises, "How can I keep a pure conscience?" Here are four principles that can help: *First, confess and forsake all known sin.* Examine your feelings of guilt in light of God's Word. Is there anything you are doing that Scripture warns about? Martin Luther said, "My conscience is captive to the Word of God." The Bible says, "For if our heart condemns us, God is greater than our heart, and knows all things" (1 John 3:20). We need to educate our conscience so that it is acting on the right information.

*Second, ask forgiveness and be reconciled to anyone you have wronged, if possible.* Jesus said, "Therefore if you bring your gift to the altar, and there remember that your brother has something against you, ... first be reconciled to your brother, and then come and offer your gift" (Matt. 5:23–24). Seek reconciliation. It is not always possible, but you need to make the effort.

*Third, make restitution, if possible.* Try to undo the wrong you have done. Saying you are sorry is enough to be forgiven by God, but you also should try and undo any damage you have done. This is part of what it means to repent.

*Fourth, don't procrastinate in clearing your conscience.* Some people think they can put off dealing with their guilt, believing their conscience will somehow clear itself in time. It won't.

Maybe your conscience has been troubling you lately. If there is something that you have done, God is only awakening you to it so that you can acknowledge your sin and turn from it.

# THE THIRD CONVERSION

*But as you abound in everything—in faith, in speech, in knowledge,*
*in all diligence, and in your love for us—see that you abound in this grace also.*
*(2 Corinthians 8:7)*

The story is told of Sam Houston, hero of Texas history, who gave his life to the Lord in the later years of life and asked to be baptized. He was taken down to a little country stream and the pastor said, "General Houston, you should take your glasses off, because I am going to immerse you in water." There were also some papers in General Houston's pocket, so he took those out as well.

Then, just as he was getting ready to go into the water, the pastor noticed that General Houston still had his wallet in his pants. He said, "Well, General, you might want to take that wallet out of your pants. It is going to get wet."

Houston responded, "If there is any part of me that needs baptizing, it is my wallet." So Houston was baptized, wallet and all.

Maybe some of us need our wallet or checkbook baptized. As Martin Luther said, "There are three conversions necessary: the conversion of the heart, mind, and the purse."

Jesus said, "Give, and it will be given to you: good measure, pressed down, shaken together, and running over. ... For with the same measure that you use, it will be measured back to you" (Luke 6:38).

You might say, "Well, if I had a million dollars, then I would give more to the Lord." But that is not necessarily true. It's all relative. Maybe you feel that you can't afford to give. But in reality, you can't afford *not* to. It is a joy. It is a privilege. And it is an opportunity.

# *Thursday*

# FORGIVEN PEOPLE

*Stop judging others, and you will not be judged.*
*Stop criticizing others, or it will all come back on you.*
*If you forgive others, you will be forgiven.*
*(Luke 6:37 NLT)*

J esus taught us to pray, "And forgive us our debts, as we forgive our debtors" (Matt. 6:12). This is part of what we call the Lord's Prayer, which is essentially a model prayer. The word "debt" used in this verse could be translated "trespasses," "shortcomings," "resentments," or "what we owe to You and the wrong we have done." Jesus was essentially saying, "Every day, you should ask God to forgive you of your sins."

Any Christian who is walking with God is acutely aware of the fact that he or she needs daily cleansing from God. It has been said the greater the saint, the greater the sense of sin and the awareness of sin within. The more you walk with the Lord, the more you will be aware of how far short you fall. After years of walking with the Lord, the apostle Paul described himself as the chief of sinners (see 1 Tim. 1:15).

Jesus not only taught us that we should pray for our own forgiveness, but He also spoke of forgiving our debtors. According to Jesus, our generous and constant forgiveness of others should be the natural result of our understanding of the forgiveness that God has extended to us. Forgiven people should be forgiving people. If you know anything about the forgiveness of God, then you should forgive others. In other words, if you are not a forgiving person, then I have to wonder how much you know of God's forgiveness. He has given it to you unconditionally. He has extended it to you in great generosity. We should do the same for others.

# BEWARE OF BITTERNESS

*People with good sense restrain their anger;*
*they earn esteem by overlooking wrongs.*
*(Proverbs 19:11* NLT*)*

In many ways, forgiveness is the key to all relationships that are healthy, strong and lasting. Why? Because as flawed people, we sin. Husbands offend wives. Wives offend husbands. Parents offend children. Children offend parents. Friends offend friends. Sometimes it is intentional; sometimes it is not. Because we are human, we will hurt and be hurt. Therefore, we must learn to forgive. Where there is no forgiveness, a root of bitterness grows. And when it does, that is the end of the relationship.

Hebrews 12:15 warns us that we should be "looking carefully lest anyone fall short of the grace of God; lest any root of bitterness springing up cause trouble, and by this many become defiled." Of course, we are living in a time when forgiveness is not very popular. In fact, it is looked down upon to a large degree. We don't exalt forgiveness in our society; we exalt vengeance. Our culture operates by the old adage, "Don't get mad. Get even."

In the days after April 20, 1999, when experts were scratching their heads and asking, "Why this violence at Columbine?", my response was, "Why not? What did we expect in a culture drenched in violence, from video games to music to television to movies to the Internet?" The two teens who carried out their horrendous act said they were tired of being picked on. They were operating by what are so often exalted as virtues in our culture: violence and revenge.

Yet the Bible tells us again and again to forgive. If you want to have lasting and successful relationships, then you had better learn how to forgive. And you had better learn how to forget. Inevitably, conflict will come.

# *Weekend*

# A Test of Our Character

*Rejoice with those who rejoice, and weep with those who weep.*
*(Romans 12:15)*

The Bible tells us, "Rejoice with those who rejoice, and weep with those who weep" (Romans 12:15). It is not so hard to weep with someone who is weeping. When someone is hurting, when a crisis hits and he calls you, it is not so hard to pray with him and encourage him. But what about when he calls back a week later and says, "Guess what? I just got a raise. A really big raise"?

Or maybe the Lord opened up a ministry opportunity for someone else, when you felt you were deserving of it. You think, *It isn't fair. That should have been mine.*

We can weep with those who weep. But can we rejoice with those who rejoice? It is a good test of our character.

Everything that we have in our lives has been given to us by the mercy and grace of God. Who are we to say what is and is not fair? God has been gracious to each of us.

Many of us are familiar with the story of the prodigal son, who took his portion of his father's estate, wasted it on prodigal living, and then came to his senses and returned home. But we often forget the other prodigal: the older brother who was angry with his father for throwing a party for his long-lost sibling. His father told him, "Son, you are always with me, and all that I have is yours. It was right that we should make merry and be glad, for your brother was dead and is alive again, and was lost and is found." (Luke 15:31)

We can be the same way. Instead, let's just be thankful for what God has given us.

*Monday*

# SET A PRISONER FREE

*"But as for you, you meant evil against me; but God meant it for good, in order to bring it about as it is this day, to save many people alive."*
*(Genesis 50:20)*

The word "oops" is not in God's vocabulary. Isn't that great to know? God is in control. We, on the other hand, cannot control everything that happens in our lives, even though we sure try. But there is one thing we can do, and that is forgive. We can forgive those who have wronged us. We can forgive those who have taken advantage of us. We can forgive those who have slandered us and made fun of us. We can forgive those who have betrayed us.

You may think they don't deserve it. But remember, you have been forgiven. Therefore, you should be forgiving. Of course, you are not going to feel like it at times. You may see him or her and feel your blood begin to boil. That is when you need to say, "As an act of faith, as a step of obedience to Jesus Christ, I forgive this person."

Corrie ten Boom, a Nazi concentration camp survivor, once said, "To forgive is to set a prisoner free and discover the prisoner was you." You should not only forgive to help that person, but you also need to forgive for your own mental and spiritual health. Just let it go. Put it in the hands of God and determine not to be tormented by it one day longer.

Is there someone you need to forgive today? Are you harboring a grudge toward someone? Forgive. Forgive whoever it is that has hurt you. As Ephesians 4:32 tells us, "And be kind to one another, tenderhearted, forgiving one another, even as God in Christ forgave you."

# Tuesday

## MORE LIKE GOD

*And the Lord passed before him and proclaimed, "The Lord, the Lord God, merciful and gracious, longsuffering, and abounding in goodness and truth, keeping mercy for thousands, forgiving iniquity and transgression and sin ... " (Exodus 34:6–7).*

An unforgiving Christian is a contradiction in terms, an oxymoron. To say you are a follower of Jesus Christ and yet harbor unforgivingness in your heart is simply wrong.

Jesus touched on the issue of forgiveness time after time. It was a theme of so many of His parables. It was a part of His prayers. He hammered this issue again and again in His private talks He had with His disciples.

You are never more like God than when you forgive. Alexander Pope said, "To err is human, to forgive is divine." We reflect the nature of God in such a dramatic way when we are willing to forgive. If you really want to be like the Lord, then you need to be a forgiving person, because He is a forgiving God.

Exodus 34 gives us this description of God, "The Lord, the Lord God, merciful and gracious, longsuffering, and abounding in goodness and truth, keeping mercy for thousands, forgiving iniquity and transgression and sin ..." (vv. 6–7). Therefore, if we want to be like Him, we should do the same.

Jesus taught us to pray, "And forgive us our debts, as we forgive our debtors" (Matt. 6:12), but He also taught us to pray, "Your kingdom come. Your will be done on earth as it is in heaven" (v. 10). What is going on in heaven? The worship of God, the exaltation of Christ, and the granting of forgiveness. Therefore, we should be worshiping God. We should be exalting Jesus Christ. And we should be forgiving one another.

# WHY WE MUST FORGIVE

*Dear friends, never avenge yourselves. Leave that to God. For it is written,*
*"I will take vengeance; I will repay those who deserve it," says the Lord.*
*(Romans 12:19 NLT)*

On one occasion, Peter came to the Lord and asked, "Lord, how often shall my brother sin against me, and I forgive him? Up to seven times?" (Matt. 18:21). According to rabbinical teaching of that day, you were to forgive an offender three times. So Peter thought he would take it even further: "What about seven times, Lord? I will double it and throw one in for good measure." He probably thought the Lord would commend him and say, "Very good, Peter. Thank you for bringing that up. All of you should follow the example of Peter. Forgive seven times."

But that is not what Jesus said. Rather, He answered, "I do not say to you, up to seven times, but up to seventy times seven" (v. 22). Of course, Jesus wasn't saying that if someone sins against us more than 490 times, then we are no longer obligated to forgive. He was really advocating unlimited forgiveness. We are to forgive again and again. Keeping count has nothing to do with true forgiveness. Jesus was eliminating any limits on it and saying that we should be forgiving people. It is only reasonable that those who are forgiven should forgive.

Not only that, but our failure to forgive will result in our divine chastening, because it displeases God. To refuse to forgive is to usurp God's authority. If you are a Christian, then unforgivingness is not your right. And when you don't forgive, you not only are disobeying Scripture, but you are taking the place of God himself. A Christian is to forgive and leave vengeance in the hands of God.

# *Thursday*

# The Ultimate Family Reunion

*But I do not want you to be ignorant, brethren, concerning those who have fallen asleep, lest you sorrow as others who have no hope. (1 Thessalonians 4:13)*

Have you ever had a significant reunion with a member of your family? Maybe it was someone you thought you would never see again or someone you had been separated from for many years.

But then again, maybe there is someone who was taken from you quickly and unexpectedly. There are things you wish you had said to that person, regrets that you now have. There is something to learn from that. If there is anyone in your life you need to say something to, say it now while you can. Tell that person you love him or her. Let that person know what he or she means to you. Do something to communicate with them, because you never know when their time may come. Then again, you never know when your time may come either.

The good news is there will be a family reunion for every child of God, a day when we will see those believers who have died and are in heaven.

When his young child died, David said, "I shall go to him, but he shall not return to me" (2 Samuel 12:23). That is the hope of every Christian. Our friends and loved ones cannot come to us, but we will go to them someday.

You can join them one day in the great reunion when the Lord comes for His church, as described in 1 Thessalonians 4:17: "Then we who are alive and remain shall be caught up together with them in the clouds to meet the Lord in the air. And thus we shall always be with the Lord." It is the ultimate family reunion.

# GOD'S SAFETY NET

*For all have sinned and fall short of the glory of God.*
*(Romans 3:23)*

Visitors to San Francisco can't help but be amazed at that architectural wonder called the Golden Gate Bridge. During its initial phases of construction, a number of workers lost their grip and fell to their deaths in the San Francisco Bay. Needless to say, this slowed down the construction process quite dramatically. The builders were trying to think of a way to remedy this, so they did something that had never been done before. A giant net was installed under the construction area. The workers knew that if they did fall, the net would catch them. It wouldn't be a pleasant experience, but they would live to tell about it. The result was they could work without the fear of dying. They were able to move quickly and finish the project.

Did you know that God has put a safety net under you? By that I mean, when you slip, when you fall, when you make a mistake, it does not mean that your name has been blotted out of the Book of Life and that you are now *persona non grata* with God. Because He came into your heart, forgave you, and committed himself to you, He now protects you. He seals you. He has justified you as a result of that commitment.

The fact is that we as Christians will sin and fall short. The Scriptures, as well as our own experiences in life, tell us this is true. According to 1 John 1:8, "If we say that we have no sin, we deceive ourselves, and the truth is not in us." This is not an excuse for ungodly living. Nor is it a license for sin. It is a simple acknowledgement of reality.

# *Weekend*

# WHAT GOD
# HAS CHOSEN TO FORGET

*As far as the east is from the west, so far has He removed our transgressions from us. (Psalm 103:12)*

Many times, sins that we have committed years ago come back to haunt us. You would think that, as time passes, our former sins would no longer bother us. But sometimes they bother us even more, because we have witnessed the repercussions of them.

Sometimes I will see evidence of this in our services at Harvest Christian Fellowship, the church where I pastor. During our invitations to receive Christ, some people will come forward week after week. The counselors instruct them that they don't need to keep doing this, because those who have received Christ into their lives are forgiven.

We dishonor Jesus Christ when we come to Him time after time, asking forgiveness for sins that He has not only forgiven, but also forgotten. We don't need to get saved again and again. I am not suggesting that we do not need to go to God for the regular forgiveness of sin, because the Bible tells us, "If we confess our sins, He is faithful and just to forgive us our sins and to cleanse us from all unrighteousness" (1 John 1:9). I am speaking of a person who doubts his or her salvation and repeatedly wants to be born again. We only need to be born again once—not twice, not three times, and not four times. Why? Because God has not only forgiven us of our sins, but He has also forgotten them.

Often we confess our sins to God and then continue to drag them up and spread them out, forgetting that God has not only forgiven them, but He has forgotten them. Therefore, we should not choose to remember what God has chosen to forget.

*Monday*

# GOD'S WORD ON IT

*And we know that all things work together for good to those who love God,*
*to those who are the called according to His purpose.*
*(Romans 8:28)*

Without a doubt, Romans 8:28 is one of the greatest verses in the Bible. It is one that is claimed quite often by believers, especially during times of hardship. And so it should be.

But let's make sure we meet the criteria of the text: "And we know that all things work together for good *to those who love God, to those who are the called according to His purpose*" (emphasis mine). Do you love God? Are you the called according to His purpose? Romans 8:28 does not apply to you if you do not love God.

There are times in our lives when things seem to be falling apart, when they don't make any sense. Some people will say, "It is the fickle finger of fate." Or, "*Que sera, sera*. Whatever will be will be. The future's not ours to see. ... "

True, the future is not ours to see. But the Christian can be confident that God is in control and has a master plan for his or her life. We can know that we serve a sovereign God who is good. As I have often said, we may not know what the future holds, but we know who holds the future.

The word used here for "good" does not necessarily mean that the event in and of itself is good, but that its long-term effect will be useful and helpful. It is hard for us to imagine certain things working for good. The Bible isn't saying tragedy is good. Rather, it is saying that God can take a horrible thing and make good come as a result of it.

# Tuesday

## ALL THINGS

*It is good for me that I have been afflicted, that I may learn Your statutes.*
*(Psalm 119:71)*

**D**id you know that everything you have experienced up to this point in life can be used for good? That is not to say you haven't experienced hardship. That is not to say bad things haven't happened to you. But it is to say that God can work them out for good.

That includes the experiences of your childhood, whether good or bad. That includes your parents, whoever they may be. That includes your education, your present employment, or your lack of it. He will work all things together for good.

I went through hardship as a kid. I came from a home that was broken many, many times over, a home of alcoholism. I wouldn't wish my childhood on anyone. But God used it to make me the person that I am.

In the same way, God has used what you have gone through to make you the person that you are. So let it be worked together for good and accept God's promise to you: "All things work together for good to those who love God, to those who are the called according to His purpose" (Rom. 8:28). The phrase, "work together" also could be translated, "working together." In other words, it isn't over yet. Maybe you are going through a process right now in which God is working things together for good. You don't see it yet. But you are a work in progress. Be patient. You have God's word on it: He will work all things together for good to those who love Him and are the called according to His purpose. God is ultimately working all things for good—not just the good things, but *all* things.

# A Whopper of a Catch

*The Lord is not slack concerning His promise,*
*as some count slackness, but is longsuffering toward us,*
*not willing that any should perish but that all should come to repentance.*
*(2 Peter 3:9)*

S ometimes the question arises, "Why does God take
some people before their time?" That is hard to answer.
When a young person dies, it is very difficult to deal
with, because we assume that we all are somehow given the
privilege of living long lives. But no one has that guarantee.
Yet I have seen so many instances in which the lives of people
impacted others, and when their deaths came about, many
came to faith as a result.

A great biblical example of this is young Stephen, the first
martyr of the church. The Bible tells us that "Stephen, full
of faith and power, did great wonders and signs among the
people" (Acts 6:8). But when Stephen was wrongfully accused
of blasphemy and brought before the Jewish leaders, he was
put to death under the leadership of a man named Saul.
One could look at that and say, "It is so tragic! Stephen had
so much life ahead of him. He could have impacted so many."
While Stephen did not impact thousands and thousands, he
did impact one, who reached untold multitudes. The one he
reached was the notoriously wicked Saul of Tarsus, later to
become the apostle Paul. So while it may be true that Stephen
did not reach many, when he reached Saul, he got himself
one whopper of a catch.

Maybe you haven't reached thousands with the gospel.
Maybe you haven't reached hundreds. But how do you know
that the one person you are witnessing to could not be the
next Billy Graham or the next man or woman to impact
our culture?

# *Thursday*

# THE CURE FOR
# SPIRITUAL BLINDNESS

*"Satan, the god of this evil world, has blinded the minds of those who don't believe, so they are unable to see the glorious light of the Good News. ... "*
*(2 Corinthians 4:4 NLT)*

People have said to me, "Greg, what is the one thing that I could say to an unbeliever that would cause him or her to get saved?", as if I would actually know that. There is no such thing. While the message of the gospel plays an important part, a person's spiritual eyes must be opened. And that is the work of the Spirit of God.

When Paul was standing before King Agrippa, he told him that God had called him to preach the gospel. Then Paul broke down what the gospel was and what the process of conversion was. He said that people needed to have their eyes opened, "to turn them from darkness to light, and from the power of Satan to God" (Acts 26:18 NLT). Why? Because according to 2 Corinthians 4:4, "Satan, the god of this evil world, has blinded the minds of those who don't believe, so they are unable to see the glorious light of the Good News that is shining upon them. They don't understand the message we preach about the glory of Christ, who is the exact likeness of God" (NLT).

This means there is nothing we can do or say that will make a person believe if his or her eyes are not opened spiritually. So what should we do? We need to pray that God would open their eyes and help them see their need for Him. God wants people to come into His kingdom (see 2 Peter 3:9). Yet we need to recognize that He has given everyone a free will. So we need to pray.

# EMPOWERED

*For the weapons of our warfare are not carnal*
*but mighty in God for pulling down strongholds.*
*(2 Corinthians 10:4)*

On the day of Pentecost, approximately 120 believers were gathered together when the Holy Spirit was poured out. Their world was not too much different than ours in some ways. In other ways, it was even worse, because they lived under the jurisdiction of the godless Roman Empire. Immorality was rampant. Their religious establishment, for all practical purposes, was corrupt. Idolatry, spiritism, and even demon worship were practiced openly. Everywhere the first-century Christians went, they faced ridicule, harassment, and persecution for their faith.

Yet within a period of approximately thirty years, the original 120 and their converts came to be known as "these who have turned the world upside down" (Acts 17:6). They didn't do it with a lot of the technology that we utilize today. They didn't have fax machines, satellite technology, the Internet, television, or even a printing press. They didn't have all the surveys that could be done to canvas an area and figure out what kind of church to put together that would meet the needs of that community. They just went out, armed with the Word of God and energized by the Holy Spirit. They made a difference.

Nowadays, it seems like the world is turning the church upside down. What has happened? As A. W. Tozer once said, "If the Holy Spirit were taken away from the New Testament church, 90 percent of what they did would come to halt. If the Holy Spirit were taken away from today's church, only 10 percent of what it does would cease." That is because we have gotten away from our dependence on the Holy Spirit. Instead, we have turned to the techniques and strategies of man.

# *Weekend*

# WHILE WE WAIT

*"I must work the works of Him who sent Me while it is day;
the night is coming when no one can work."
(John 9:4)*

As we look at how dark our culture is today, we wonder if we can ever really make a difference. It seems so overwhelming. It seems as though darkness is spreading and light is receding. It is like the time Isaiah described when he said, "Destruction is certain for those who say that evil is good and good is evil; that dark is light and light is dark; that bitter is sweet and sweet is bitter" (Isa. 5:20).

To illustrate that very point, I could cite movies that are popular right now. We celebrate that which the Bible says is wrong and offensive to God, and we laugh at that which the Bible holds forth as standards we should live by. The good news is that the same Holy Spirit who set the early church in motion can use us if we are willing.

It is interesting to note that in the first century, the question on the disciples' minds was, "Is the end of the world near?" That same question is on the minds of many today. What Jesus essentially said to His disciples was, "This isn't the time for that. My purpose is to rule and reign in the hearts of people. Don't be so concerned about when I am going to do that. Rather, be concerned about what you should be doing while you wait.

The same principle holds true for us. Don't worry about when. He will return when the time is right. What we should be committing ourselves to, what we should be interested in, is what we are supposed to be doing as we await the Lord's return.

# *Monday*

## START HERE

> *"But you shall receive power when the Holy Spirit has come upon you; and you shall be witnesses to Me in Jerusalem, and in all Judea and Samaria, and to the end of the earth."*
> *(Acts 1:8)*

E vangelism starts at home. This is exactly what we at Harvest Christian Fellowship found through the Harvest Crusades. We started reaching out as a church in our own community. Then God opened up doors for us to reach out in different places in Southern California. Then He opened doors for us to reach out across the nation. Finally, He opened doors for us to reach out in Australia and New Zealand—a long way from our church in Riverside, California. But as we sought to be faithful where we were, God opened more doors of ministry.

I have met many people who have told me, "I want to get into the ministry." I will ask what they mean by that.

"I want to be in the ministry," they tell me, "meaning I want to preach to people. I want to reach people."

"That's great," I say. "There are ministry opportunities all around you. Maybe you ought to start by crossing the street. Talk to your neighbor. Or talk to your family members. Or talk to your friends whom you know are not believers. Ministry opportunities are everywhere." Jesus said, "Lift up your eyes and look at the fields, for they are already white for harvest!" (John 4:35).

He wants you to go first to your family ... first to your neighbors ... first to your coworkers ... first to your friends ... first to your sphere of influence. Then He will open up other opportunities for you. Wherever you look, if you simply will say, "Lord, use me," then you will find opportunities.

# *Tuesday*

# JUST ASK FOR A REFILL

*And do not be drunk with wine, in which is dissipation; but be filled with the Spirit, speaking to one another in psalms and hymns and spiritual songs, singing and making melody in your heart to the Lord.*
*(Ephesians 5:18–19)*

In Acts 4, we read about how the believers prayed that God would give them even more boldness to share the gospel. The Bible says the room was shaken, and they were filled with the Spirit. God gave them a refill. And He will give you a refill.

Ephesians 5:18 tells us, "And do not be drunk with wine, in which is dissipation; but be filled with the Spirit." In the original language, this could be translated as being directed to all people, everyone. In other words, this applies not only to pastors and evangelists, but also to businessmen and women, homemakers, and so forth. Whatever you do, you need this power.

Second, the original language indicates that this state-ment is a command—not a suggestion. God is not saying, "If you have time in your busy schedule, please be filled with the Spirit." God is essentially saying, "You need this. I order you to be filled with the Spirit."

Third, it is something that is continuous. The phrase also could be translated, "*Being* filled with the Spirit." In other words, it is being filled over and over again.

Isn't it great to know that God gives refills? I must admit that I am not a big fan of restaurants that charge for refills, especially when you get your bill and see that you've spent thirty dollars for iced tea. So when I'm in a restaurant, I will often ask first before I order a refill.

Thankfully, God doesn't charge for refills. He will refill you with His Spirit.

# POWER WITH A PURPOSE

*"And this gospel of the kingdom will be preached in all the world*
*as a witness to all the nations, and then the end will come."*
*(Matthew 24:14)*

It was a daunting task to say the least. Jesus had left His marching orders: "Go therefore and make disciples of all the nations, baptizing them in the name of the Father and of the Son and of the Holy Spirit, teaching them to observe all things that I have commanded you" (Matt. 28:19–20). From a human standpoint, the apostles were not ready for such an undertaking. There were still things they did not understand. Their faith was relatively weak. They had failed in their public witness and in their private faith. Simon Peter, who had been the leader, for all practical purposes, had denied the Lord. How could he now be expected to stand up and proclaim the gospel? How could they do it? Answer: with a power they had never known.

Power is an exciting thing. Most people like power, from fast cars to fast computers. God offers power, but it is power with a purpose—power that is there for a reason.

Uncontrolled power doesn't help anyone. It's like a fire hose that has been dropped. It starts flailing around and could actually kill someone. But if firefighters can get hold of it and direct it, that power can be used to bring a horrible blaze under control.

God's power is not given to us so that we will behave like fools. It is power to be a witness. It is practical power. But because we see excess in this area on the part of some people, we recoil from it and miss out on something we desperately need to effectively bring the gospel to our culture today.

# Thursday

# SIGNED AND SEALED

*And when you believed in Christ, he identified you as his own by giving you the Holy Spirit, whom he promised long ago. (Ephesians 1:13 NLT)*

The question arises, "Was the Holy Spirit already in the lives of the disciples before Pentecost?" Answer: yes. In John 20, we read of an event that took place prior Pentecost: "Then, the same day at evening, being the first day of the week, ... Jesus came and stood in the midst. ... Jesus said to them again, 'Peace to you! As the Father has sent Me, I also send you.' And when He had said this, He breathed on them, and said to them, 'Receive the Holy Spirit' " (vv. 19, 21–22).

The Holy Spirit came and lived within them, and this is true of every Christian. When you put your faith in Christ, the Holy Spirit comes and lives within you. The Holy Spirit of God seals you. It is the mark on your life that you belong to Christ.

Let's say, for example, that a thief was at an airport, looking for a briefcase to steal. As he reaches out to take one, he notices a little ID tag that says, "Property of Mike Tyson." He probably would find someone else's briefcase to steal.

In the same way, when the devil sees you and perhaps says, "I am going to grab that person, he will see an ID tag on you that reads, "Property of Jesus Christ. Sealed by the Holy Spirit." You have been sealed by the Spirit, who gives that inner witness that we are His children. The Bible says, "The Spirit Himself bears witness with our spirit that we are children of God" (Rom. 8:16).

Do you have this power of the Holy Spirit in your life?

# THE SECRET PLACE

*He who dwells in the secret place of the Most High*
*shall abide under the shadow of the Almighty.*
*(Psalm 91:1)*

When you were a kid, did you ever have a hiding place—a place you would run to when you were afraid or wanted to be alone? God wants to be your hiding place. The good news is that you can retreat to this hiding place wherever you are. When you are tied up in bumper-to-bumper traffic, you can retreat there. When you are having a conflict at work and don't know what to say or how to deal with it, you can immediately retreat into that secret place of the Most High as you live in fellowship and communion with God.

It is not only dwelling there, but it is living under the shadow of the Almighty. Have you ever tried to walk in someone's shadow? It can be done, but you have to stay really close. That is exactly the picture here in Psalm 91:1. God is saying, "I want you to be so close that you are actually in My very shadow." If you do that, it will give you the courage to face life.

Remember the story of the great prophet Elijah, who boldly stormed into the court of wicked King Ahab and Queen Jezebel and declared that it would not rain, except at his word? Where did he get the courage to pull off something like that? Though Elijah was in the court of powerful monarchs, he recognized that at the same time, he was in the presence of an even more powerful Monarch. He was dwelling in the secret place of the Most High.

If you kneel before God, you can stand before any man. Are you walking in this fellowship with Him?

# Weekend

# A Way of Escape

*Surely He shall deliver you from the snare*
*of the fowler and from the perilous pestilence.*
*(Psalm 91:3)*

I'm glad that I don't know about every unkind word that has been spoken about me or about everything the devil has tried to snare me with. In that sense, ignorance *is* bliss. But I'm even more glad to know that God's promise to me is: "Surely He shall deliver you from the snare of the fowler and from the perilous pestilence" (Ps. 91:3). What does this mean, exactly? What it *doesn't* mean is that I will avoid all opposition, hardship, or even temptation. But God has clearly promised that I won't be caught up against my will.

The word "snare" used in this verse speaks of a trap, a very primitive object used to catch prey back in those days, which basically consisted of a little noose. If the animal stepped in the trap, the noose would tighten and the animal would be caught.

I think we all know that anyone who has ever fallen into the trap of temptation has clearly cooperated, because God has said in His Word, "No temptation has overtaken you except such as is common to man; but God is faithful, who will not allow you to be tempted beyond what you are able, but with the temptation will also make the way of escape, that you may be able to bear it" (1 Cor. 10:13). He will never give us more than we can handle. There is always a way out. We are responsible for our own actions.

God is saying, "I will keep you from the hidden traps that are out there waiting for you." But what we must do is abide in the secret place—the place of fellowship and communion with Him.

# *Monday*

# FREE FROM FEAR

*You shall not be afraid of the terror by night, nor of the arrow that flies by day, nor of the pestilence that walks in darkness, nor of the destruction that lays waste at noonday. (Psalm 91:5–6)*

History tells of a courageous Christian who was standing before one of the Roman emperors who was persecuting the church. The emperor was demanding that Christians abandon their faith, deny the Lord, and declare Caesar as Lord. But this Christian refused. So the emperor threatened, "Give up Christ or I will banish you."

The Christian said, "You can't banish me from Christ, for He has said, 'I will never leave you nor forsake you.' "

The emperor said, "I will confiscate all your property."

The believer replied, "My treasures are laid up in heaven. You can't touch them."

The emperor said, "I will kill you."

The Christian said, "I have been dead to the world in Christ for forty years. My life is hid with Christ in God. You can't touch it."

The emperor then turned to the rest of his court and said, "What can you do with such a fanatic?"

That so-called fanatic knew something about God's protection. And that is something we all should know about in these frightening times in which we are living. There are so many things we can be afraid of, from getting on a plane to becoming a victim of violent crime to being diagnosed with a life-threatening disease.

It is great to know that God promises, "A thousand may fall at your side, and ten thousand at your right hand; but it shall not come near you" (Ps. 91:7). It isn't over until it's over. Until that time, we can go out with boldness, knowing that God is in control of our lives.

# Tuesday

# KEPT IN HIS WAYS

*For He shall give His angels charge over you, to keep you in all your ways.*
*(Psalm 91:11)*

The angels of God are nearer than you may think. They are all around us all the time, taking care of us and ministering to us, even when we are not aware of their presence. They are essentially God's secret agents, doing the work He has called them to do. Many times they have intervened in our lives and we didn't even know they were doing it.

We could cite many stories in the Bible of angels delivering the people of God, such as Daniel in the lion's den and Peter in prison. But as wonderful as the promise of angelic involvement in our lives is, we must first be aware of what the conditions are for that protection. We find the answer in Psalm 91:11: "For He shall give His angels charge over you, *to keep you in all your ways*" (emphasis mine). The phrase "to keep you in all your ways" is not referring to whatever path you may choose. It is referring to *His* ways, the ways of the Lord.

Some might say, "I believe in angelic protection. I am going to go out and do crazy stuff. God will send His angels to protect me." That is exactly what Jesus was refuting when, during His temptation in the wilderness, He said, "It is written again, 'You shall not tempt the Lord your God'" (Matt. 4:7).

There is a difference between trusting the Lord and testing the Lord by taking unnecessary chances with your life—or even endangering your spiritual safety by doing stupid things and expecting God to bail you out. He will keep you in all of your ways, but your ways should be *His* ways.

# SAFE IN HIS SHADOW

*You shall tread upon the lion and the cobra, the young lion*
*and the serpent you shall trample underfoot.*
*(Psalm 91:13)*

If you have ever seen a lion, then you know this creature is quite a sight to behold. I have had a few opportunities to see lions—once in the wild in Africa and another time in a zoo in Ethiopia, where its roar made my hair stand on end.

The Bible tells us, "Be sober, be vigilant; because your adversary the devil walks about like a roaring lion, seeking whom he may devour" (1 Peter 5:8). Like a lion, sometimes the devil will approach us in obvious ways, frightening ways.

But the Bible also compares the devil to a snake. And sometimes he comes to us subtly like he did with Eve in the Garden: "Now the serpent was more cunning than any beast of the field which the Lord God had made. And he said to the woman, "Has God indeed said, 'You shall not eat of every tree of the garden'?" (Gen. 3:1).

If we could have our way, there wouldn't be any lions or snakes. There wouldn't be obstacles in our lives. But we find this promise in Psalm 91: "You shall tread upon the lion and the cobra, the young lion and the serpent you shall trample underfoot" (v. 13). God is essentially saying, "I will protect you from the enemy, no matter how he comes to you. I will protect you from the obstacles and the opponents that are out there."

Our part is to simply dwell in the secret place of the Most High and abide under the shadow of the Almighty. And if we are, then we have God's Word on it that these promises will be realized in our lives.

# *Thursday*

# ALL FOR HIS GLORY

*Whatever you eat or drink or whatever you do,*
*you must do all for the glory of God.*
*(1 Corinthians 10:31 NLT)*

One of my favorite all-time movies is *Chariots of Fire*, the story of Eric Liddell, a heroic, committed Christian from Scotland who competed in the 1924 Paris Olympiad, winning a gold and bronze medal in the 400-meter and 200-meter races, respectively.

During one scene in the movie, Eric's sister Jenny, also a committed Christian, was upset that her brother was competing. She thought he was wasting his time and reminded Eric that God made him for Himself.

Eric replied, "Aye, Jenny, I know. But He also made me fast, and when I run, I feel His pleasure." As the story unfolds, he glorifies God because of the stand that he makes at the Olympics.

Whatever we do, we should seek to glorify God, whether it is academics, sports, business, or something else. We should do it in such a way as to bring glory to the God who made us. As 1 Corinthians 6:19–20 reminds us, "Or do you not know that your body is the temple of the Holy Spirit who is in you, whom you have from God, and you are not your own? For you were bought at a price; therefore glorify God in your body and in your spirit, which are God's."

You can serve God and glorify Him in whatever He has called you to do. Everyone has abilities that have been given to him or her by God. So you can glorify Him as a construction worker. You can glorify Him in the medical field. You can glorify Him in professional sports. You can glorify Him in graphic design. Whatever it is that you do, you can bring glory to Him.

# PLUGGED IN

*O God, you are my God; I earnestly search for you. My soul thirsts for you; my whole body longs for you in this parched and weary land where there is no water.*
*(Psalm 63:1 NLT)*

When I travel, I take my laptop computer with me, because I try to work on my messages. But often I must work off the battery, so whenever there is an opportunity, I will plug in to the nearest electrical outlet. Why? Because my battery is running down, and I need to recharge.

I think a lot of us function that way as believers. We come to church and get plugged in spiritually. Then we try to run off that energy all week long. We don't realize that the power is wherever we go. We need to be plugged in all the time.

The psalmist David wrote, "O God, you are my God; I earnestly search for you. My soul thirsts for you; my whole body longs for you in this parched and weary land where there is no water. I have seen you in your sanctuary and gazed upon your power and glory" (Ps. 63:1–2 NLT). In other words, "Lord, I want to walk with you all the time. I have seen your glory in the sanctuary, but I want that all week long."

For that to happen in our lives today, we need to plug in. But we have to make time for it. We must grab it where we can get it. Read some Scripture verses when you get up in the morning. Listen to some worship or a Bible study on your way to work or school. Take the moments where you can find them to plug in constantly and stay tapped into all that God has for you.

# Weekend

# A UNIVERSAL PRACTICE

*So, my dear brothers and sisters, be strong and steady, always enthusiastic about the Lord's work, for you know that nothing you do for the Lord is ever useless.* (1 Corinthians 15:58 NLT)

The Bible offers very specific and practical ways regarding how we are to give. And in 1 Corinthians 16, Paul instructed the believers as to how offerings were to be collected: "Now about the money being collected for the Christians in Jerusalem: You should follow the same procedures I gave to the churches in Galatia. On every Lord's Day, each of you should put aside some amount of money in relation to what you have earned and save it for this offering. Don't wait until I get there and then try to collect it all at once" (1 Cor. 16:1–2 NLT).

So what do we learn from these instructions? First, that every believer in every church should give. It is a universal practice: "Follow the same procedure I gave to the churches in Galatia." In other words, he was saying, "They did it in Galatia—you need to do it in Corinth. They did it in Macedonia, and we need to do it here. Every church should do this." It was not just something the Corinthians were asked to do; it is asked of every believer.

Second, we learn that it was to be done every week. "On every Lord's Day," Paul said in verse two, "put aside some amount of money in relation to what you have earned. … " The idea is to take a percentage of your income and set it aside for the work of God. This is what the Scripture tells us we ought to do. And then as you do this, you are able to invest it in His kingdom.

*Monday*

# IS IT THE MESSAGE OR THE MESSENGER?

> *On this rock I will build My church,*
> *and the gates of Hades shall not prevail against it.*
> *(Matthew 16:18)*

A preacher who took a part-time job as a lifeguard was having twenty to thirty people drown on his watch every day. His supervisors thought, "What is with this preacher?" He had gone through the safety training and all the rest. So they went to watch him. Sure enough, when people ran into trouble in the water and began yelling and waving their hands at him, he would notice them from his lifeguard stand and say, "God bless you! I see that hand."

Many times when we share the gospel, people are not rejecting the message as much as they are rejecting the way it is presented. They are not offended by the gospel; they are offended by the way it is portrayed. That is not to say there is no offense in the message of the gospel, because indeed there is. But far too often, people are rejecting the wrapping we are putting on it instead of the actual message that we have to share. So we want to make sure we are effectively sharing the gospel.

But know this: the devil will always oppose the man or woman whom God is using. When Christians, motivated by love for lost people, seek to reach out and invite them to heaven, the devil, motivated by hate, seeks to reach out and pull them into hell. Whenever God's people say, "Let's rise up and build," the devil says, "Let's rise up and destroy." He will always oppose the work of getting the gospel message out. Don't let that terrify you. Let it educate you. After all, Jesus said of His church that the gates of Hades shall not prevail against it.

# Tuesday

# AN ACCURATE
# REPRESENTATION

*And I, brethren, when I came to you, did not come with excellence
of speech or of wisdom declaring to you the testimony of God.*
*(1 Corinthians 2:1)*

I am amazed at how someone can take something as
wonderful and as exciting as the gospel of Jesus Christ
and turn it into a message to condemn people. Some
years ago, I was in Washington, D.C., where I noticed a man
with a megaphone who was standing on the steps of one of
the monuments. He was yelling, "God hates you! God is
going to judge you for your sin!" He quoted every Bible
verse that deals with condemnation for rejecting Christ.
But he did not give one verse that spoke of the love of God
or the forgiveness of God. There he was, waving his Bible,
screaming and yelling. People were walking by saying,
"What an idiot. What a fool." And they were probably
drawing conclusions about the Christian faith because
this man improperly represented our Lord.

Then there are people who can take the gospel message
and water it down in their attempt to make it inoffensive.
They will say something like, "If you ask Jesus Christ to
come into your life, then He will give you joy, peace, fulfillment, and purpose. He will fill that void deep inside of you."
But they leave out something—a place called hell. After all,
part of the good news of the gospel is the fact that we don't
have to go to hell.

By not telling someone there is a judgment, it is failing
to declare the whole counsel of God. If you really love them,
you need to tell them. True, it may make them uncomfortable.
But better for them to be uncomfortable temporarily than
to be sent to hell permanently.

# SIMPLE AND CLEAR

*Now it happened in Iconium that they went together to the synagogue of the Jews, and so spoke that a great multitude both of the Jews and of the Greeks believed.*
*(Acts 14:1)*

If anyone had wanted to present the gospel in a way that would be profound or complex or with human wisdom, it would have been Paul. He was a highly trained, extremely intelligent communicator. This was a man who knew how to get his information across. But he chose to deliver the gospel message in a simple way.

Acts 14 tells us that when Paul and Barnabas came to Iconium, they "so spoke that a great multitude both of the Jews and of the Greeks believed" (v. 1). The word "so" arrests our attention and conveys something to all those who are called to declare the gospel. Is there a way to speak that will cause people to believe? It would appear there is clearly a right way and a wrong way to declare the gospel.

In 1 Corinthians 2, we discover the secret of the "so." Paul said, "And I, brethren, when I came to you, did not come with excellence of speech or of wisdom declaring to you the testimony of God. For I determined not to know anything among you except Jesus Christ and Him crucified" (vv. 1–2). Thus we learn that to effectively share the gospel, we must make it clear. It must be simple. It must be focused on the work of Jesus Christ on the cross and His resurrection from the dead. It must be unapologetically biblical. It must be truthful, yet lovingly shared.

That is what we need to remember as we give this message out. Don't complicate it. Don't add to it. Just proclaim it in its simplicity.

# Thursday

# WHY CREATION MAKES SENSE

*We have come to bring you the Good News that you should turn from these worthless things to the living God, who made heaven and earth, the sea, and everything in them. (Acts 14:15 NLT)*

A lot of people today say that God is not the Creator. They reject the biblical teaching of creationism and embrace the theory of evolution. But I would suggest that most of these people have never taken the time to honestly study the theory of evolution or the biblical teaching of creationism. I would suggest that most haven't read Darwin's book, *The Origin of Species*, nor have they read what the Bible says. Rather, I believe it is a convenient hook on which to hang their doubts and their lifestyles. C. S. Lewis said that even atheists have their moments of doubt.

I find it interesting that the theory of evolution flatly contradicts two known laws of science, the first being the law of energy conservation. Evolution teaches that creation is continually being accomplished by "nature's evolutionary process." But the most basic law of science, the law of energy conservation, states that nothing is now being created or destroyed. Then there is the law of thermodynamics, one of the most well-established principles in all of science, which says that the natural tendency of things is to go from a more ordered state to a less ordered one. Evolution, in contrast, involves universal change upward, whereas the real processes of nature involve a universal change downward.

That is why the biblical concept of creation, the teaching that God made man in His own image and created the heavens and the Earth, fits with the laws of science. Therefore, those who say they believe in evolution do so more as a religious belief than a scientific one.

# HEAVENLY DISPATCHES

*Now when they had gone through Phrygia and the region of Galatia,*
*they were forbidden by the Holy Spirit to preach the word in Asia.*
*(Acts 16:6)*

I find it somewhat comforting that at times in his life,
even the great apostle Paul could be moving the wrong
direction to the point that the Lord had to redirect him.
After his first missionary journey, Paul was concerned for
the churches that were left behind in the area known as Asia
Minor. He wanted to revisit them and check on their progress.
But there was one small problem: God had a different plan.
Paul made very attempt to go to Asia Minor, but he was forbidden by the Holy Spirit.

Have you ever been determined to do a certain thing?
Maybe you were determined to undertake a certain project
or marry a certain person or pursue a certain career when
God redirected you.

Wouldn't it be nice if we could wake up every morning with
a little heavenly dispatch at our door with the itinerary for the
day? Wouldn't it be great if He could just map out our entire
day, telling us what challenges we would face so we could be
prepared and ready and know everything that was about to
happen?

But the Lord has never led me in such a way. I have never
received a heavenly dispatch. Rather, I have found that divine
guidance often comes as a result of taking steps of faith. And
God not only has His will, but He has His timing for each and
every situation. The Bible tells us, "He has made everything
beautiful in its time" (Eccl. 3:11). Therefore, we want to make
sure we are in the will of God and are moving according to
the timing of God.

# *Weekend*

# Divinely Redirected

*And the peace of God, which surpasses all understanding, will guard your hearts and minds through Christ Jesus. (Philippians 4:7)*

God sometimes will use different ways to show us when we are out of His will. One is by giving us His peace when you are in His will and removing it when we are outside of it. The Bible tells us, "Let the peace that comes from Christ rule in your hearts" (Col. 3:15 NLT). Another translation says, "And let the peace (soul harmony which comes) from Christ rule (act as umpire continually) in your hearts deciding and settling with finality all questions that arise in your minds … " (AMP).

Umpires are not always the most popular people at baseball games, because not everyone agrees with the calls they make. The umpire is there to say, "Safe!" and "Out!" The peace of God can act as a spiritual umpire. Perhaps you can think of certain situations, such as a party you went to, a relationship you were involved in, or a place you were going, and suddenly there was a lack of peace, almost like spiritual agitation deep inside. That might have been God saying no.

Another way the Lord sometimes directs us is by closing a door. By that I mean when circumstances in our lives just don't work. Maybe you set out on a big trip, only to get three flat tires. You were trying to do a certain thing when something went wrong, rendering your plan impossible.

Sometimes God can even redirect us through sickness. It has stopped me on a few occasions. However it is the Lord may direct you, remember that it may be in a different way than you wanted to go. But God has His will. And God has His timing.

*Monday*

# ARE YOU SAVED?

> *"All must turn from their sins and turn to God—*
> *and prove they have changed by the good things they do."*
> *(Acts 26:20 NLT)*

You might be able to remember at least one time in your life when someone walked up to you, probably with a Bible in his hand and a determined expression on his face, and asked, "Are you saved?" Before I became a Christian, I would basically laugh it off when I heard people say things like that, thinking it was such a sensationalistic term to use. After all, I wasn't in a burning house. I wasn't drowning at sea. What do they mean am I saved?

In reality, the term "saved" is a very apt description of what happens to a person who puts his or her faith in Jesus Christ, because we really were lost. In fact, our situation was worse than being in a burning house or lost at sea. We were separated from God, facing a certain judgment in a place called hell.

A lot of people today would say they are saved, but many of them probably are not. That is because they have never really met God's requirement to be forgiven of their sins. As a result, they are living with false assurance.

To start with, they have never acknowledged their own sinfulness. They have never really repented of their sins, which is necessary. Acts 3:19 says, "Repent therefore and be converted, that your sins may be blotted out. … " Belief is taking hold of one thing and letting go of another.

There are some who want to believe in Jesus but hold on to the old life, so they have really never repented. But until they have repented of their sins, they have not met God's requirements for salvation.

# Tuesday

## FOLLOW THE DIRECTIONS

*And how can we be sure that we belong to him? By obeying his commandments.*
*(1 John 2:3 NLT)*

When people say, "That whole Christian thing didn't work for me," I would venture to say they didn't do what God told them to do. And I would also suggest that they ask themselves a few questions:

*Did I study and memorize Scripture?* The psalmist said, "I have hidden your word in my heart, that I might not sin against you" (Ps. 119:11 NLT).

*Did I get regularly and actively involved in a church?* Hebrews tells us not to "forsake the assembling of ourselves together, as is the manner of some, but exhorting one another, and so much the more as you see the Day approaching" (Heb. 10:25).

*Did I get baptized?* You don't have to be baptized to be saved, but if you are really saved, then you ought to be baptized.

*Did I turn from all known sin? Did I turn from those things I knew were sin before God?* The psalmist said, "If I had not confessed the sin in my heart, my Lord would not have listened" (Ps. 66:18 NLT).

*Did I develop a prayer life?* The Bible tells us to "pray without ceasing" (1 Thess. 5:17).

*Did I take up the cross and follow Him?* Jesus said, "If any of you wants to be my follower, you must put aside your selfish ambition, shoulder your cross, and follow me" (Matt. 16:24 NLT).

Did I keep His commandments to the best of my ability? As 1 John 2:5 says, "But those who obey God's word really do love him. That is the way to know whether or not we live in him" (NLT). If we truly are Christians, there will be evidence of it in our lives.

# THE REAL DEAL

*For you are a chosen people. You are a kingdom of priests, God's holy nation, his very own possession. This is so you can show others the goodness of God, for he called you out of the darkness into his wonderful light. (1 Peter 2:9 NLT)*

With so many naming the name of Christ today, our impact on the world seems to be null and void. We wonder what difference we are really making. And that is my point: we are allowing secular attitudes to find their way into the church and into our lives. We see people who say they are Christians living in immorality, having sex before and outside of marriage, playing with drugs, getting drunk, stealing, suing one another, and divorcing one another.

It seems like our culture is affecting us more than we are affecting our culture. We need Christians today who will take a stand for what is right. We need more believers today to be both salt and light in our culture.

Sure we could use some more preachers, teachers, evangelists, and missionaries. But we also need Christian journalists. We need Christian broadcasters, Christian artists, Christian doctors, and Christian lawyers. We need believers who will let their light shine in professional sports, in politics, in entertainment, and in the business world. We need truly police officers and military personnel. We need to go out and be true believers who make a difference.

People need to see a real man or woman of God living the Christian life in their neighborhood, in their workplace, and in their school. They need to see the real thing. In short, they need to see you. God can use you. Maybe you are not a preacher, but you can proclaim the gospel through your life and through your words.

# Thursday

## ONE AT A TIME

*"Here on earth you will have many trials and sorrows.*
*But take heart, because I have overcome the world."*
*(John 16:33 NLT)*

The Roman emperor Diocletian relentlessly persecuted the church, causing it to go underground.
Confident that he had succeeded in obliterating
them, he had a commemorative coin struck that said, "The
Christian religion is destroyed and the worship of the Roman
gods is restored." Was he right? No. Where is Diocletian
today? Gone. Where are Christians today? Everywhere.

History tells of many attempts to destroy Christianity.
But those attempts failed and will always fail for one simple
reason: Christianity is Christ. And Jesus Christ will prevail
in the end and establish His kingdom. And because we are
with Him, we will win in the end too.

That is an important thing for us to remember, because
living as a Christian can get real discouraging at times. When
you are the only person standing up for your faith at work,
when you are the only person who believes in the Bible, when
you are the only person who believes in moral absolutes, when
you are the only person who doesn't laugh at the dirty joke,
you feel like a minority, don't you? And you are, because a
true minority today is the authentic Christian.

Are you a Christian who wants to make an impact on the
world? If so, then I want to encourage you to start with *your*
world. By that I mean your sphere of influence: your family …
your friends … your workplace … your neighborhood. The
answer to the question, "How do you eat an elephant?" is
one bite at a time. And when we talk about influencing our
world, it requires the same approach. You just start with
your world—one person at a time.

# THE LIBERATING GOSPEL

*They searched the Scriptures day after day to check up on Paul and Silas, to see if they were really teaching the truth. As a result, many Jews believed, as did some of the prominent Greek women and many men. (Acts 17:11–12 NLT)*

T he gospel had a particular appeal to women in the first century, especially to women of the upper classes who were prominent citizens of Greek cities. There was a reason for that. These were educated women who were instructed in the philosophies of Greece. But they found these Greek philosophies were dead and empty; they offered nothing for the heart and nothing for the spirit within. They instructed the mind, but they did nothing for the soul.

Some of these women had turned to the Judaism of the day and found themselves burdened with difficult and cumbersome regulations they could not keep. They were still searching.

Add to this the fact that in this culture, women were treated like mere possessions. They were not honored and esteemed as they ought to be, but were thought of as nothing more than a piece of property. In this culture, it was possible for a man to divorce his wife for almost any reason. There were actually allowances in divorce court for a husband to unload his wife if she burned his food or if someone more attractive came along.

Then the gospel came upon the scene, with the good news that "there is no longer Jew or Gentile, slave or free, male or female. For you are all Christians—you are one in Christ Jesus (Gal. 3:28 NLT). We are all brought to level ground at the foot of the cross. Some people assert that Christianity is oppressive to women. Yet Christianity didn't oppress women; it liberated them.

# Weekend

# THE ANSWER TO LIFE

*For the greater my wisdom, the greater my grief.*
*To increase knowledge only increases sorrow.*
*(Ecclesiastes 1:18 NLT)*

Maybe you have been searching for a philosophy that you could live by, something you could govern your life by—a philosophy, of course, that you could live out, but still have fun and do what you want to do. Maybe you have thought about creating your own religion. Or maybe you have told yourself, *If I were a highly educated person, that might take care of all the questions I have in life.* While education certainly has its place, you can't study your way to happiness and fulfillment in life.

Solomon, the wisest man who ever lived, wrote, "I said to myself, 'Look, I am wiser than any of the kings who ruled in Jerusalem before me. I have greater wisdom and knowledge than any of them.' So I worked hard to distinguish wisdom from foolishness. But now I realize that even this was like chasing the wind" (Eccl. 1:16–17 NLT). Solomon concluded, "For the greater my wisdom, the greater my grief. To increase knowledge only increases sorrow" (v. 18 NLT).

Of course, Scripture is not condemning the pursuit of knowledge. That is a noble pursuit. But what it is saying is that if you try to fill the void in your life through the pursuit of knowledge, it will be an empty pursuit. Knowledge will not fill that void. Nor is the answer found in the pursuit of pleasure. Nor is it found in possessions. Nor is it found in success. Nor is it found in sex. Nor is it found in education. Nor is it found in religion, even. It is found in Jesus. The answer to your life is only found in a relationship with Jesus Christ.

*Monday*

# CHARACTERIZED BY JOY

*For the kingdom of God is not eating and drinking,*
*but righteousness and peace and joy in the Holy Spirit.*
*(Romans 14:17)*

Today if you were to sum up your life, what truths would you want to emphasize to your family and friends? What regrets would you have?

In Acts 20, we find the final words of Paul to the elders of the church he had started in Ephesus. Here in this chapter, he was delivering his final charge to them. As he looked back on his life, he said, "But none of these things move me; nor do I count my life dear to myself, so that I may finish my race with joy, and the ministry which I received from the Lord Jesus, to testify to the gospel of the grace of God" (v. 24).

There is one word from this verse I want to bring to your attention: joy. Paul was saying, "I am looking back on my life and on what I have done here. One word seems to sum it up well: joy." This word could be translated to say, "exceedingly happy." This was a man who knew what adversity was. This was a man who knew what suffering was. This is a man who knew what hardship was. But he was saying that in the midst of all, there is joy.

The fact of the matter is the happy life is the holy life, the life that is lived for God. Joy is an operative word in the life of the Christian. Jesus said, "I have come that they may have life, and that they may have it more abundantly" (John 10:10). And Jesus not only promises us life beyond the grave, but a dimension of life on this earth that is worth living.

# Tuesday

# THE GREATEST LIFE THERE IS

*But the natural man does not receive the things of the Spirit of God, for they are foolishness to him; nor can he know them, because they are spiritually discerned. (1 Corinthians 2:14)*

When many people think of the narrow way, the life that is dedicated to God, they envision something that is full of misery and rules and regulations. They cannot fathom the appeal of going to church, worshiping, praying, or attending a Bible study, because the Bible tells us, "But the natural man does not receive the things of the Spirit of God, for they are foolishness to him; nor can he know them, because they are spiritually discerned" (1 Cor. 2:14).

But when you know God and you realize the Bible is not a mere book, but God's living Word to each of us, it takes on a whole new meaning. When you realize prayer is not just going through some ritual, but it is communicating with the all-powerful, all-knowing, all-loving God, who is interested in us, that means a lot. And when we sing His praises, we are not just singing a few songs together, but we are lifting up the name of the Lord, that is something the world does not have. There is nothing like it. When you truly come to know God, you realize the Christian life is the greatest life there is.

There are two ways we can live in life: the right way and the wrong way. There are two paths we can take: the narrow way that leads to life or the broad way that leads to destruction. There are two foundations that we can build on: the rock or the sinking sand. The result is that we can either live a happy and holy life or a miserable one.

# SEEING THE WORLD FOR WHAT IT IS

*Yes, everything else is worthless when compared with the priceless gain of knowing Christ Jesus my Lord. I have discarded everything else, counting it all as garbage, so that I may have Christ. (Philippians 3:8 NLT)*

I magine coming out of a restaurant where you just had a wonderful meal, when you happen to look down at the sidewalk and notice a discarded burrito from a nearby fast-food restaurant. Are you going to say, "Oh, a burrito!" and pick it up? Of course not. Why? Because you are satisfied with the meal you just ate. You have had the real thing. You don't want a cheap imitation.

When you are walking with the Lord and have been experiencing the real thing and then the devil offers you some cheap imitation, you see it for what it is. The problem is that often we are not spending enough time seeing who Jesus is. Because when we see who Jesus is, we see what the world is. But if we are only looking at this world and not spending enough time with the Lord, then we will have a diminished view of God and an exalted view of this world. It should be the other way around.

Everything you need in life is found in a relationship with God. You can discover that the easy way or the hard way. You can say, "What do you know? All I want to do is have some fun." You will find out the hard way that what I am saying is true. Not because Greg Laurie says it, but because God says it. What do you really give up to follow Jesus? Not much. What have you sacrificed? Whatever it may be, it is nothing compared to what God has given you in its place.

# *Thursday*

# CALLED TO BE WATCHMEN

*"Son of man, I have made you a watchman for the house of Israel;
therefore hear a word from My mouth, and give them warning from Me."
(Ezekiel 3:17)*

Although the Christian life is a joyful journey, it is also a serious one. We have a solemn responsibility to share the gospel message with others.

When he was giving his final words to the elders of Ephesus, Paul made an interesting statement. He said, "Therefore I testify to you this day that I am innocent of the blood of all men" (Acts 20:26). This may not mean much to us today, but Paul was comparing himself to a watchman who would stand in a tower or on the wall of a city, looking for potential danger.

God told the prophet Ezekiel, "Son of man, I have made you a watchman for the house of Israel; therefore hear a word from My mouth, and give them warning from Me: When I say to the wicked, 'You shall surely die,' and you give him no warning, nor speak to warn the wicked from his wicked way, to save his life, that same wicked man shall die in his iniquity; but his blood I will require at your hand" (Ez. 3:17–18).

So what is our responsibility? If we see someone who is in danger, we are responsible before God to warn that person, to tell him or her the truth. We might think, *I don't want to offend her.* Or, *It would be tense if I had to actually confront him.* The Bible says, "Open rebuke is better than love carefully concealed. Faithful are the wounds of a friend" (Prov. 27:5–6).

What a serious call it is to be watchman. You must stay alert and awake, ready to sound the alarm.

# BLESSED TO BE A BLESSING

*Now may He who supplies seed to the sower, and bread for food, supply and multiply the seed you have sown and increase the fruits of your righteousness.*
*(2 Corinthians 9:10)*

A pastor once asked a farmer in his congregation, "If you had $200, would you give $100 to the Lord?" "Yes I would, Pastor," the farmer said.

So the pastor asked, "If you had two cows, would you give one of those cows to the Lord?"

"Yes, I would," he replied.

Then the pastor said, "Now, if you had two pigs, would you give one of them to the Lord?"

"Now that isn't fair," the farmer said. "You know I have two pigs."

As long as it is theoretical, we are fine with the idea of giving. But for many of us, when it gets down to the reality of what we have, it's another issue. Yet as we give to God, He will give to us. The Bible says, "And God is able to make all grace abound toward you, that you, always having all sufficiency in all things, may have an abundance for every good work" (2 Cor. 9:8). God has blessed you to be a blessing to others. This verse is not saying you should give to get. But it is saying that when you have received from God, you should give, and God will bless your generosity and give you more to give again.

God makes a radical promise in the Book of Malachi: "Prove Me now in this ... if I will not open for you the windows of heaven and pour out for you such blessing that there will not be room enough to receive it" (Mal. 3:10). God will bless as we give to Him.

# *Weekend*

# Giving from the Heart

*Best of all, they went beyond our highest hopes, for their first action was to dedicate themselves to the Lord and to us for whatever directions God might give them. (2 Corinthians 8:5 NLT)*

The Bible offers several examples of people who loved to give. In the Old Testament we read that when the tabernacle was being built, the Israelites were so generous and so blessed by the opportunity to invest in it that Moses had to tell them, "All right, guys. Enough! We have more than we need. Don't bring any more." Those are people who understood the blessing of giving.

And the New Testament tells of believers who just loved to give, believers who, in fact, even begged Paul to allow them to give. Paul said of these believers, "They begged us again and again for the gracious privilege of sharing in the gift for the Christians in Jerusalem" (2 Cor. 8:4 NLT). We hear about pastors begging their congregations for money, yet this was a congregation begging to give.

So what was the secret of the generosity of these believers? Paul mentions it in the next verse: "Their first action was to dedicate themselves to the Lord and to us for whatever directions God might give them" (2 Cor. 8:5). You see, if you give of yourself to God, you will also give of your finances. To put it another way, if you don't give of your finances, have you really yet given of yourself?

You may be thinking, "Well, Lord, you are over all areas except this, You know. This is mine. But the rest is Yours." God can have your money and not have your heart. But He cannot have your heart and not have your money.

*Monday*

# HEALTHY FEAR

*The fear of the Lord is the beginning of wisdom; a good understanding have all those who do His commandments. His praise endures forever.*
*(Psalm 111:10)*

W e all know what it is like to be gripped by fear. We all know what that sensation is like, to have a shiver run down our spine, our mouth go dry, and our hair stand on end.

Fear has a close buddy known as worry, and the two often work in tandem. We can get caught up playing the what-if? game: *What if this happens? What if that happens?* In fact, modern medical research has proved that worry can actually break down our resistance to disease. Excessive worry can even shorten the human life. Charles Mayo, founder of the famed Mayo Clinic, said he never knew anyone who died of overwork, but he knew many who died of worry.

Far too often we are afraid of the wrong things in life, but we are not afraid of the right things—or perhaps I should say the right One. We don't fear God. Yet the Bible tells us the fear of the Lord is the beginning of wisdom.

But what does that mean? First, let me tell you what it doesn't mean: to fear God doesn't mean cowering in terror before Him. Rather the fear of God has been properly defined as a wholesome dread of displeasing Him. So if I have sinned, it is not the fear of what God will do to me, but the fear of what I have done to Him. That is what it is to fear the Lord.

The remarkable thing about fearing God is that when you fear Him, you fear nothing else. On the other hand, if you do not fear God, then you fear everything else.

# Tuesday

# BE OF GOOD COURAGE

*But the following night the Lord stood by him and said,*
*"Be of good cheer, Paul; for as you have testified for Me in Jerusalem,*
*so you must also bear witness at Rome." (Acts 23:11)*

Even the most committed believer has those times when fear and worry can kick in. Anxiety can overtake us. Maybe we are concerned about our future. Maybe we are discouraged or afraid. If that is the case, you might be surprised to know that even the great apostle Paul experienced emotions like this.

Paul had gone to Jerusalem, and the next thing he knew, he was locked up in a cold, damp, dark prison cell. All of this happened as a result of his bold proclamation of the gospel. Acts 23:11 tells us, "The following night the Lord stood by him and said, 'Be of good cheer, Paul.' " That phrase "be of good cheer" could better be translated, "be of good courage." Whenever we read in Scripture that an angel of the Lord appeared and said, "Fear not," it was usually because someone was afraid. So I conclude that when the Lord himself stood by Paul and said, "Be of good courage," the apostle needed that special word of encouragement at that particular moment.

Sometimes it seems like God is the only one standing by us. But if everyone else had forsaken Paul, Jesus was company enough. If all the others despised him, the smile of Jesus was approval enough. Though his circumstances were less than ideal, I am sure he knew it was better to be in the jail with the Lord rather than to be anywhere else without Him.

Jesus is there in your prison as well, whatever and wherever that prison may be. And He knows what you are going through.

# *Wednesday*

# ONLY PART OF THE PICTURE

*But in that coming day, no weapon turned against you will succeed.*
*And everyone who tells lies in court will be brought to justice. These benefits are*
*enjoyed by the servants of the Lord; their vindication will come from me.*
*(Isaiah 54:17 NLT)*

S ometimes when we end up in a certain situation, we say, "Why did God allow this to happen to me?" Then later on as a few years have passed by, we are able to look back on certain circumstances and see why God did what He did or why He did not do what we thought He should do.

When Paul was thrown into prison in Jerusalem, he was ignorant of what was happening, but God knew what was ahead for Paul. And He also knows what is ahead for us. The Lord came to Paul in his hour of need, because He knew he would need this special touch. Basically, Paul was oblivious to what was going on around him. He did not know that as he was in prison, there were forty Jews who had taken an oath not to eat or drink until they had killed him. In some ways, though unknown to him at the time, prison was probably one of the best places he could have been.

To be honest, I am glad I don't always know what is going on around me—both in the supernatural as well as the natural realm. We may not know all the plans against us that may be underway. But we do know this: the Lord is with us. Even if people are plotting against you as a child of God, you don't have to be afraid. God was there with Paul in his prison cell. And He is there with you wherever you are.

# Thursday

## From Start to Finish

*And I am sure that God, who began the good work within you,*
*will continue his work until it is finally finished on that day when*
*Christ Jesus comes back again. (Philippians 1:6 NLT)*

Are you afraid of an uncertain future right now?
Are you discouraged, feeling like you have failed?
If you have invited Jesus to be your Savior and Lord,
then He is with you. And He will complete the work He has
begun in your life. The Bible says, "God, who began the
good work within you, will continue his work until it is
finally finished … " (Phil. 1:6 NLT).

There are many reasons I'm glad that I am not God,
one of them being that I'm the kind of the person who starts
projects and forgets them. I will be cleaning my desk and
almost have it finished when I say, "I'll do it a little bit later.
I want to do something else right now."

Aren't you glad that God isn't that way? He would be
working with me, suddenly lose interest, and say "I'm sick
of Greg. I want to move on to a new life. I'm not going to
finish him." Meanwhile, I am left hanging.

God will complete the work He has begun in our lives.
He will complete the work of making us more and more like
Jesus as well. It is not over, even if you have failed, even if you
have made a mistake. You can still learn from that mistake
and get out of the situation you are in. God knows where you
are at this very moment. He knows what you are experiencing.
He is saying to you, "Be of good courage," because He is with
you. He knows there is a brighter tomorrow for you.

# TOMORROW

*Felix was afraid and answered, "Go away for now; when
I have a convenient time I will call for you."*
*(Acts 24:25)*

Three apprentice devils who were coming Earth to finish their apprenticeship were talking to Satan about their plans to tempt and ruin humanity.

The first said, "I will tell them there is no God."

Satan said, "No. That is not going to work. People know there is a God."

The second said, "I am going to tell them there is no hell."

Satan replied, "No. Most people, deep down in their hearts, know there is a hell and a judgment to come."

The third said, "I am going to tell them there is no hurry."

"Go," Satan answered, "and you will ruin them by the thousands."

That is how procrastination works. It doesn't say, "I'm not going to do it." That is too final, too absolute. Procrastination says, "I'll get around to it later."

Have you ever found yourself procrastinating about something? It is usually something that you don't want to do. There are some things we can put off doing that are not of the greatest significance. If you don't take out the trash, it won't have eternal ramifications. Your house will smell, but you can get away with it. If you don't do your yard work, it won't change where you are going to spend your eternity, although you might have trouble finding your house.

But then there are those issues we must never procrastinate on, chiefly, our relationship with God. Tomorrow sounds so innocent, but it is life's most dangerous word. Tomorrow is the barred and bolted door that shuts people out of heaven. Tomorrow is the devil's word, and so many have been ripped off by his strategy. Don't let it happen to you.

# *Weekend*

# "They've Come Here Too"

*"For we have found him to be a troublemaker, a man who is constantly inciting the Jews. ... He is a ringleader of the sect known as the Nazarenes." (Acts 24:5 NLT)*

The name "Christian" we proudly carry today as followers of Jesus was not really a word we coined ourselves. In fact, it was first used in Antioch. Acts 11:26 tells us, "And the disciples were first called Christians in Antioch." It was a name used to describe the followers of Christ, and I might add that it was used initially in a derogatory way. They said, "These followers of Jesus are like Christians." A literal rendering of the word is "little Christs." In other words, "We thought we had gotten rid of Him when we crucified Him. Now there are all these Christians everywhere, these little Christlike people." Today we wear the name as a badge of honor. We proudly say we are followers of Jesus. But the term didn't originate that way.

It was also said in a critical way of the apostles that they turned their way upside down. When the Jews incited a riot against Paul and Silas in Thessalonica and came looking for them at the home of Jason, Acts 17:6 tells us, "But when they did not find them, they dragged Jason and some brethren to the rulers of the city, crying out, 'These who have turned the world upside down have come here too.' " This was not meant to encourage them. It was meant to discourage them. In reality, what a compliment it was to say they were turning their perverse, wicked world upside down.

I pray that in our day, we will have more Christians who will turn their world upside down, who will impact their culture in a positive way.

*Monday*

# SEIZE THE DAY

> *But exhort one another daily, while it is called "Today,"*
> *lest any of you be hardened through the deceitfulness of sin.*
> *(Hebrews 3:13)*

Repetition dulls truth's potency. The more we hear something, the more immune we can become to it, even if it is the most wonderful thing. Take music, for example. You've just heard the greatest song. You just love it. So what do you do? You go and buy it. You load it on your iPod or put it in your CD player. You play it over and over again, because you love it. Then you like it. Then you like it a little less. Then you are getting sick of it. Why? Because you have heard it over and over again. Repetition has dulled your appreciation for it.

Or let's say, for example, that you go out to eat with a friend, and he orders a malt. It looks really good, so he lets you have a taste. So you order one too. That first taste is sweet, but the more of it you take in, the less you appreciate it.

The same is true of the gospel. If we hear it and then put it off responding to it, our hearts will begin to harden. Our continual exposure to the truth and our refusal to respond to it causes our hearts to grow more calloused. When someone does this, his or her heart becomes hardened to the very truth that might have softened it. That person becomes judged by the very message that might have set him or her free. The most difficult people to reach with the gospel are those who know it best but are unmoved by it.

The Bible warns about being hardened through the deceitfulness of sin. Has this happened to you?

# Tuesday

# What It Takes

*He saved us, not because of the good things we did, but because of his mercy.*
*He washed away our sins and gave us a new life through the Holy Spirit*
*(Titus 3:5 NLT)*

If you were to ask the average person on the street what one must do to be a Christian, some of the answers might go along these lines: "You need to believe Jesus Christ is the Son of God." "You need to believe that there is heaven and hell." "Believe in miracles." "Believe Jesus is coming back again." "You need to go to church." "You need to pray." "You need to keep the Ten Commandments." "You need to have a change in your lifestyle."

I would not argue with any of those things in and of themselves. But you could do all of t and not necessarily be a Christian.

You can pray with all of the passion in the world, but if your sin has not been confessed to God, it will not do you any good. You can believe in heaven and hell and that Jesus is coming back again and not necessarily be a Christian. James 2:19 tells us, "You believe that there is one God. You do well. Even the demons believe—and tremble!" You can even make some visible changes in your life and not necessarily be a Christian. Doing good things in and of themselves will not convert you.

So then what does it take to be a Christian? The Bible says, "Believe on the Lord Jesus Christ, and you will be saved" (Acts 16:31). To believe means to put your faith in, your trust in, Jesus Christ as your Savior and Lord. The outward change is often without the inward. But the inward change is never without the outward.

# *Wednesday*

# TURN ON THE LIGHT

*Yes, I am going to send you to the Gentiles, to open their eyes so they may turn from darkness to light, and from the power of Satan to God. (Acts 26:17–18 NLT)*

S ome people are trying to live in two worlds. They want to walk in the light on Sunday and live in darkness the other six days of the week. But they need to decide. The devil loves darkness. It's worth noting that a lot of crimes are committed at night. Hell is described as outer darkness. Darkness is the devil's domain.

But God lives in the light. That is why Scripture tells us to wake up from our sleep and cast off the works of darkness. Ephesians 5:8 says, "For though your hearts were once full of darkness, now you are full of light from the Lord, and your behavior should show it!" (NLT).

That is why the Bible says, "Don't team up with those who are unbelievers. How can goodness be a partner with wickedness? How can light live with darkness?" (2 Cor. 6:14 NLT). This doesn't mean that Christians can't have friends or associates who are not Christians. The Bible is speaking here of being yoked together in a close union where you are walking with someone.

The Bible says you can't live in two worlds. If you are going to be a true Christian, then there will be things you have to say no to. You will have to decide.

Have you been trying to live in darkness? It is hard to hide light, because it leaks out. A little light can go a long way. We need to let our lights shine before others—not try to hide our light or hide our Christianity. Let's hold it up for all to see.

# Thursday

# KEPT SAFE IN CHRIST

*For God has reserved a priceless inheritance for his children.*
*It is kept in heaven for you, pure and undefiled, beyond the reach*
*of change and decay. (1 Peter 1:4 NLT)*

One of the questions I am often asked is, "Can a Christian lose his or her salvation?" Certainly that is a vital question, because what is more important than our eternal salvation, which gives us the very hope of heaven? Yet there are many people who struggle with doubt and uncertainty in this very important area.

On the other hand, there may be those who lack the assurance of salvation because, quite frankly, they haven't met God's requirements to be saved. The reason they lack assurance is because it isn't there.

Young believers, especially, can be easily misled. The devil whispers in their ear, "You were never saved to start with." Or, "God has rejected you. Christ has left you." He will challenge their salvation. Not only does this happen to young believers, but it also happens to those who have walked with the Lord for many years—even those who are facing death. The devil may try to rob them of their great assurance.

But we need to remember the devil is a liar and that this is a tactic he has been using with great effect ever since the Garden of Eden, where he said to Eve, "God has said, 'You shall not eat it, nor shall you touch it, lest you die'?" (Gen. 3:3). His essential challenge was, "Did God really say that?"

The devil will whisper in the ear of the believer on many occasions: "Do you really think you are saved? Do you really think God would accept you or forgive you?" But don't listen. He is a liar and the father of lies.

# Fruit Inspection

*For every tree is known by its own fruit. For men do not gather figs from thorns, nor do they gather grapes from a bramble bush. (Luke 6:44)*

In my understanding of Scripture, for someone to truly be a Christian means that he or she needs to repent. To repent means to change your direction. And if that is not taking place, then I would question whether there was a legitimate salvation experience.

There are certain results that should follow as an outcome of meeting Christ. Understand, it is not works that save us; it is the work of Christ that saves us. But at the same time, if we are truly saved, then there will be results in our lives. Works don't save a person, but they are good evidence that he or she is saved. It is faith alone that justifies, but faith that justifies will never be alone.

When someone says, "I am a Christian," but we don't see any evidence of that, then it would not be incorrect for us to assume that this person might not be saved. You may be thinking, *Careful, Greg. The Bible says, 'Judge not, that you be not judged.'* "Let's understand that the phrase "judge not" means that we can't pass final judgment. But we can make an observation.

We are told in the Bible to make certain evaluations and judgments. Jesus said, "Therefore by their fruits you will know them." (Matt. 7:20). I think of myself as a fruit inspector. I look for fruit. If I don't see fruit in a person's life, then it would indicate to me that he or she is not a Christian. I can't make the ultimate judgment, but I can make an observation. And people can do the same with us.

# Weekend

# ONCE AND FOREVER

*Therefore he is able, once and forever, to save everyone who comes to God through him. He lives forever to plead with God on their behalf. (Hebrews 7:25 NLT)*

Maybe the question is not whether someone who was saved could lose his or her salvation. Maybe the real question is was this person ever saved to begin with. The issue may not be that he or she lost it. In many cases, it just may be that he or she never had it to begin with.

Some people say, "I tried the whole Christian thing. It didn't work for me. I tried Christ. He didn't work for me," as though they are talking about toothpaste. But Christ is not a product that works for some, but not for others. He will change any man or woman who comes to Him in honest faith.

That would be like getting very sick and going to the doctor only to just sit in the waiting room. You never actually see the doctor and end up more sick than you were before. Then you tell your friends, "I tried the whole doctor thing. It didn't work for me."

You have to go a little further than the office. Sitting out there in the waiting room isn't going to help you. You have to see the doctor. More importantly, you have to listen to what he or she says. Then you have to follow His directions. But to just sit and wait in the room there isn't going to do it for you.

Here is what it comes down to. When people say, "I tried the Christian thing. It didn't work for me," I say nonsense. If you were really converted, if you really met Christ, then He will work in you and through you.

# *Monday*

# A Prodigal or a Pig?

*It would be better if they had never known the right way to live than to know it and then reject the holy commandments that were given to them. They make these proverbs come true: "A dog returns to its vomit," and "A washed pig returns to the mud." (2 Peter 2:21–22 NLT)*

A re you a prodigal? Or are you a pig? If you are a prodigal, then you will always come back to God. You might go astray for awhile. But you will always return. But if you are a pig, then you will never come back.

In 2 Peter 2:22, we read, "A washed pig returns to the mud" (NLT). A lot of people today have taken pigs such as potbellied pigs and have turned them into pets. But the nature of a pig is still a pig. Personally, I think they would really prefer to be living in their natural element. You can take a pig, bring him into your house, and even have a little tuxedo outfit designed for him, complete with a little top hat and tails. That pig may be looking fine, but the first chance he gets, he will go out to where pigs like to hang out. Why? Because he is still a pig. Pigs are pigs. It is their nature.

In the same way, a prodigal will always return home, because a prodigal is a child of God. But a pig will always go back to the mud.

Just as the prodigal went astray, believers can go astray. They can have temporary lapses in their Christian life. But just as the prodigal never ceased to be his father's son, a Christian will never cease to be a child of God. And a true Christian will always come back home again.

# Tuesday

# THE ANSWER TO EMPTINESS

*A Gentile woman who lived there came to him, pleading, "Have mercy on me, O Lord, Son of David! For my daughter has a demon in her, and it is severely tormenting her." (Matthew 15:22 NLT)*

Everyone has a god. Everyone has a passion. Everyone has a pursuit that drives them on in life. Even atheists have a god: some ideal, some purpose, some belief they subscribe to. Some people worship the god of success. Others worship the god of pleasure. Others worship the god of materialism.

But there comes a point in each of our lives when we see the futility and emptiness of these gods. I have found that when most people come to Christ, it is usually preceded by a recognition of the emptiness of life.

I remember that is exactly what I was experiencing before I became a Christian. I had seen the emptiness of the lifestyle I had been pursuing. I went into what might be described as a search mode, telling myself there had to be something more.

That is what happened with a Gentile woman who came to Jesus seeking help for her demon-possessed daughter. She saw the futility and the emptiness of the false gods she was raised with. She realized she could receive no help from objects of stone. Therefore, she left behind that false belief and came to the only One who could help her.

Some people dismiss Christianity. They say, "You Christians turn to God because you are weak. Your religion is a crutch." Christianity is not a crutch; it is a whole hospital. I am glad of that. I acknowledge that I need help. But I need more than a crutch. I need open-heart surgery. And I am so glad God is there to offer it to me.

# OUR SPIRITUAL INFLUENCE

*"Woman," Jesus said to her, "your faith is great. Your request is granted." And her daughter was instantly healed. (Matthew 15:28 NLT)*

Any parents know there is nothing they wouldn't do for their own kids. If their kids are hurting or sick, they would gladly take that pain upon themselves to spare their children of what they are going through.

In Matthew's Gospel we find the account of a Gentile woman who came to Jesus, anxiously seeking help for her child. Demon powers had taken control of her little girl, and there was nothing she could do to drive them away. She probably had already gone to her pagan temple. And maybe her daughter got worse and worse.

Then she heard about this Jesus, this Teacher who could dismiss a demon at His very word, who could raise the dead and give sight to the blind. So she found Him and cried out to Him in desperation, "Have mercy on me, O Lord, Son of David!" (Matt. 15:21 NLT).

I don't know how her child became demon-possessed. I think we can safely say that it was related to her own beliefs. If this woman worshipped in pagan temples and essentially opened herself up to demonic power, then it should not come as any surprise that the same thing had a direct effect on her child.

In a very real way, the sins of the parents are visited upon the children. It reminds us that what we do as parents has a direct effect on our children. The positive side is that if you live a godly life, then that will affect your children. Sometimes you wonder whether you're getting through. The best thing you can do for your kids is not just tell them how to live, but show them.

# *Thursday*

# WORTHY OF WORSHIP

*"Worthy is the Lamb who was slain to receive power and riches and wisdom, and strength and honor and glory and blessing!" (Revelation 5:12)*

God has uniquely wired into humanity a desire for something more, a recognition that life is more than mere existence. And that causes us to worship. So the smart thing to do is to worship the true God. The word worship comes from an English word "worthship," which means to ascribe value or worth to someone or something. In other words, we worship someone who is worthy. Gods of our own making are not worthy of our worship. Gods of our own making won't save us when we are in trouble. They won't be there to forgive us of our sin. Only the true and living God can do that. God is worthy of our praise.

There are a number of words in the Bible translated "worship." The one used most often means "to bow down and do homage." Another means "to kiss toward," the idea of showing reverence. Put those two words together, and you have a good idea of what real worship is. We worship God because He is worthy. And in doing so, we bow down and pay homage to Him. That speaks of reverence and respect for God. But we also "kiss toward" Him, which speaks of tenderness and intimacy.

Some people are too informal with God, as though He were their celestial big buddy. They are flippant and casual. Others recognize God as holy and all-powerful and tremble before Him, but they don't realize God wants to be known in an intimate and a personal way.

We are to revere Him. We are to honor Him. But we also are to embrace Him in closeness. That encompasses what true worship is.

# TRUE AND FALSE WORSHIP

*And every creature which is in heaven and on the earth and under the earth and such as are in the sea, and all that are in them, I heard saying: "Blessing and honor and glory and power be to Him who sits on the throne, and to the Lamb, forever and ever!" (Revelation 5:13)*

Worship is something we ought to be learning more about, because it will be one of the primary activities in heaven. But Jesus made it clear that there is true and false worship.

The Pharisees, who thought they were experts at worship, were by and large not even close. Jesus said of them, quoting Isaiah, " 'These people draw near to Me with their mouth, and honor Me with their lips, but their heart is far from Me. And in vain they worship Me, teaching as doctrines the commandments of men' " (Matt. 15:8–9).

Just because someone takes on a posture of worship doesn't necessarily mean he or she is worshipping. You can be in church singing very loudly, and people may look at you and say, "Look at that guy. He is really worshipping God." Maybe you are. But maybe you are thinking about other things, like, *After church, I'm going to drive through In-N-Out Burger and get a Double-Double. I'll get some fries. Should I get onions? No ... I'd better not. I hate it when I drop them in my car and it smells for a month.* Just because you are doing something outwardly doesn't mean you are doing it inwardly. That is why Jesus said, "God is Spirit, and those who worship Him must worship in spirit and truth" (John 4:24).

The worst thing to do is to pretend to be worshipping when we are not. We should engage our hearts.

# *Weekend*

# PREPARED TO GIVE

*I have shown you in every way, by laboring like this, that you must support
the weak. And remember the words of the Lord Jesus, that He said,
"It is more blessed to give than to receive."*
*(Acts 20:35)*

Have you ever noticed that when you go out to eat with
certain people, they can never find their wallet when
the check arrives? When the check is placed on the
table, we all know what that means. And when you know the
check is coming, you prepare yourself, because it is a polite
gesture to at least make an effort to pick up the check.

In the same way, we should prepare ourselves to invest in the
work of God. The apostle Paul told the believers to "put aside
some amount of money in relation to what you have earned and
save it for this offering. Don't wait until I get there and then
try to collect it all at once" (1 Cor. 16:2 NLT). This means being
ready when the offering comes. Your check has been written
already. You have the money set aside. Still, some people seem
to be mystified each week by this thing called the offering. Yet
the offering is an opportunity to be an obedient Christian. It's
an opportunity to invest in the work of the kingdom of God.
And everything we give for the work of the kingdom is used to
impact the lives of people for the gospel of Jesus Christ.

This is one of the disciplines of the Christian life. But I
want to emphasize that it is not about the money; it is about
the heart. If we say, "Well, Lord, You can have your way in
other areas of my life, but not this one," there is something
wrong. True, giving is a responsibility, but even more so,
it is a blessing. And as Jesus said, "It is more blessed to give
than to receive."

*Monday*

# WHAT FRIENDS ARE FOR

> *Run from anything that stimulates youthful lust. Follow anything that makes you want to do right. Pursue faith and love and peace, and enjoy the companionship of those who call on the Lord with pure hearts.*
> *(2 Timothy 2:22 NLT)*

One morning after one of our services at Harvest Christian Fellowship, a young woman walked up and asked if I would pray for her and a relationship she was in. "What kind of a relationship is it?" I asked.

"It's a relationship with a guy."

"Let me ask you a question. Is this guy that you are in a relationship with a Christian?"

"Well," she said, "I ... think he is. I am not really sure if he is or not."

I said, "You know what? I am not going to pray that God will heal your relationship. I am going to pray that God will give you the courage to terminate the relationship. That is what needs to happen. Here you are in church, and you are struggling and having a hard time with a guy who doesn't walk with the Lord." As we talked further, it was apparent that this is exactly what was happening. The relationship was dragging her down spiritually.

Many times we will pray for the Lord to fix something, and He will say, "You are in a place you don't belong. You are hanging out with people you don't belong with. This is bringing about many of your problems."

In 2 Timothy 2:22 we read, "Pursue faith and love and peace, and enjoy the companionship of those who call on the Lord with pure hearts" (NLT). Are you enjoying the companionship of those who call on the Lord with pure hearts? Or are you hanging around with people who are dragging you down spiritually?

# *Tuesday*

# STANDING STRONG

*Watch, stand fast in the faith, be brave, be strong. (1 Corinthians 16:13)*

There will come times in all of our lives when we will be tested in our faith. There will be times when what we believe will be challenged. There will be temptations to do the wrong thing.

We might ask ourselves, *Will I be able to stand strong spiritually when this happens?* That is entirely up to you. It isn't up to God. It is up to you. God wants you to stand. But He is not going to force you to stand. He will give you all the resources you need. He will give you the power to resist. He will even give you a way out. But you have to cooperate. There are some things only God can do. And there are some things only you can do.

Only God can forgive sin. But only you can fall into sin. Only God can give you the power to change your life. But you need to be willing to have your life changed. You need to cooperate with Him. He is not going to force you to resist what is evil. You have to be willing to resist it on your own, then take hold of the resources that He gives you. You decide today whether or not you will fall tomorrow. The stand you make today will determine what kind of stand you make tomorrow.

When you are building a house, the most important time is not when you lay carpet or paint; it's when you lay the foundation. If you don't do that well, then all of your decorative additions will be for nothing. You have to get the foundation right.

Therefore, you determine today what kind of situation you will be in tomorrow.

# *Wednesday*

# WITH THE END IN MIND

*But you, O man of God, flee these things and pursue righteousness,*
*godliness, faith, love, patience, gentleness.*
*(1 Timothy 6:11)*

M any of us will put ourselves into situations we don't
need to be in. We hang around with people that we
don't need to be hanging around with. We watch
movies that we don't need to be watching. We listen to music
that we don't need to be listening to. And it will affect us.

Granted, we cannot control every circumstance we will face
in life. I would acknowledge that all of us end up in situations
in which we think, *I wish I hadn't seen that. ... I wish I hadn't been exposed*
*to that.* But if we live in the real world, then we will see and hear
things that we don't want to see. Unfortunately, it is part of life.

Some may say, "Oh, it doesn't affect me. I can handle it." But
it does. As the saying goes, "Garbage in, garbage out." We will
reap what we sow. It may not be dramatic. It may not be overt,
initially. But it will have its effect.

It is a lot like sowing seeds. You don't sow a few seeds today
and have a forest tomorrow. You sow a few seeds today, and
then down the road, you have some sprouts. A little bit later,
you have plants. And in time, you will have your forest.

The seeds we are sowing today will be reaped eventually.
And if we are sowing seeds of corruption, then we will reap
the tragic results later. If we are sowing spiritual seeds by
doing the right thing, then we will reap the blessed results
of that as well. The seeds we are sowing today will be reaped
in the years to come.

# *Thursday*

# DARE TO BE A DANIEL

*But Daniel purposed in his heart that he would not defile himself with
the portion of the king's delicacies, nor with the wine which he drank.
(Daniel 1:8)*

We serve a living God. And if we serve a living God, then that means we will take Him everywhere we go. It will affect everything we do. It will affect our relationships. It will affect our ethics. It will affect our work. It will affect our play. It will affect the way we think. It will affect the way we live. It will affect the way we vote. It will affect everything we do. Because if Jesus is not Lord of all, then He is not Lord at all.

The Bible tells us about a man who had this kind of faith in God in the midst of tremendous peer pressure. His name was Daniel, and the Bible also gives us an indication as to how he did it: "But *Daniel purposed in his heart* that he would not defile himself. ... " (Dan. 1:8, emphasis mine). The word to underline in your Bible is "purposed." He purposed in his heart.

That is what we need a lot more of today. How we need men and women of conviction. We need men and women of purpose, people who will say, "This is right. I don't care if it is popular. I have to do what is right."

Be a man, be a woman, of purpose. Be a man, be a woman, of conviction. As Philip P. Bliss wrote in his classic hymn, "Dare to be a Daniel, dare to stand alone! Dare to have a purpose firm! Dare to make it known." Daniel purposed in his heart that he would not defile himself. What have you purposed in your heart today?

# LIVING WITH PURPOSE

*When he came and had seen the grace of God, he was glad, and encouraged them all that with purpose of heart they should continue with the Lord. (Acts 11:23)*

I f you were asked to complete the sentence, "My purpose of life is … ", what would you say? As Christians, I know we would quickly say, "God." But let's be honest and not just say what we think is the right thing to say. What *really* is your purpose in life?

To put it another way, where do you channel most of your energy? What do you think about the most? What is the most significant thing to you in life?

Some people, if they answered honestly, would say, "My purpose in life is to have fun." Someone else might say, "My purpose in life is to experience pleasure." Another might say, "My purpose in life is to be successful." Another might say, "My purpose in life is to make money."

The Book of Acts tells us that when Barnabas came to Antioch, he exhorted the believers there "that with purpose of heart they should continue with the Lord" (Acts 11:23). And Paul said, "For my determined purpose is that I may know Him that I may progressively become more deeply and intimately acquainted with Him, perceiving and recognizing and understanding the wonders of His Person more strongly and more clearly … " (Phil. 3:10 AMP). Paul knew where he was going. And if you don't know where you are going, then you won't know if you get there. Paul was essentially saying, "My purpose in life is to know Him. Yes, there are other things that I do, but my primary purpose is to intimately, deeply, and personally know God."

Is that your purpose in life right now?

# *Weekend*

# Didn't Miss A Thing

*It is better to have little with fear for the Lord than to have great treasure with turmoil. (Proverbs 15:16 NLT)*

A little with God is better than much without Him. As believers, we will make sacrifices in our lives. There are times, if we were honest, that we will see some people doing certain things, and we think, *That looks like fun.* You might even be a little tempted. You look at people who live for selfishness. Or they live for partying. Or they live for sex. But then let the years pass. Look at the course their lives took and the course your life took, and then compare notes.

I had friends from high school who didn't accept Christ when I did. They went their way, and I went mine. I run into them every now and then, and I think, *Thank God that I went the way that I went!* Did I miss a few parties? Yes—a lot of them. Did I miss some good times? I missed a few. But I also missed a lot of hangovers and other problems that are associated with that kind of lifestyle. Did I miss out on a few things? Sure I did. But what God gave me in their place is so much better.

It has been said, "One must wait until sunset to see how splendid the day has been." I know that when you are young, many things look so tempting: *Go out and party? Or go to church? Go out and have fun? Or go sing songs about God?*

The point is that you will make some sacrifices. You will deny yourself at times. But then, when you look back on your life someday, you will come to realize that you didn't really miss anything.

*Monday*

# RIGHTEOUS REBELLION

*"When you pass through the waters, I will be with you;*
*and through the rivers, they shall not overflow you. When you walk*
*through the fire, you shall not be burned, nor shall the flame scorch you."*
*(Isaiah 43:2)*

At one time or another, every Christian will be asked to make a stand. It may not be quite as dramatic as what Shadrach, Meshach, and Abed-Nego faced, however. But every believer will be confronted with that challenge.

Shadrach, Meshach, and Abed-Nego were three Israelite teenagers who were put into a very difficult situation as they, along with their nation, were dragged off as captives into Babylon. God had warned the Israelites, His people, not to worship false gods. So when King Nebuchadnezzar decided to build a gigantic golden image of himself and have everyone in the kingdom bow down and worship it, these three young men refused. Maybe they even stood up a little taller. It was teenage rebellion channeled in the right direction.

As believers, let's rebel against the right things. Let's rebel against the mob mentality that tries to squeeze us into its mold. Let's rebel against the empty lifestyles our culture follows after. If you want to be a true rebel, then follow Jesus Christ. That takes courage in this day and age.

When King Nebuchadnezzar got word that these three young men didn't bow, he issued an ultimatum: bow or burn. They chose the latter. But God miraculously delivered them, and as a result, King Nebuchadnezzar gave the glory to God.

When you are challenged to make a stand as a Christian, remember that Jesus said, "I will never leave you nor forsake you" (Heb. 13:5). That is His promise to you. Just as He walked with Shadrach, Meshach, and Abed-Nego, He will walk with you.

# Tuesday

# A LION AND A LAMB

*Then Jesus stood up again and said to her, "Where are your accusers?*
*Didn't even one of them condemn you?" "No, Lord," she said. And Jesus said,*
*"Neither do I. Go and sin no more." (John 8:10–12 NLT)*

I find it interesting that Jesus never really rebuked your rank-and-file sinner, the garden-variety unbeliever. He saved His most scathing words for the religious hypocrites of His day: the Pharisees and Sadducees. The only time we see Him showing righteous indignation was because these religious leaders had falsely represented God to the people. But when Jesus came into contact with sinners—with people who had broken His commandments—He would reach out to them in love.

When the religious leaders brought a woman caught in the act of adultery before Him, they pointed out how the Law said they should stone her. Jesus, being God, could have said, "What do I say? I say let's go." Yet he showed compassion. He said, "All right, stone her. But let those who have never sinned throw the first stones!" (John 8:7 NLT).

We see Jesus going into the little town of Jericho and reaching out to a man named Zacchaeus, who was hated by everyone because he was a tax collector.

Time and time again, we see Jesus showing compassion toward people. So if you really want to know what God is like, then all you have to do is look at Jesus. On the one hand, the Bible teaches that God is perfect, that He is holy, that He is righteous, and that He has indeed established standards that we should all seek to live by. But it also tells us that God recognizes our shortcomings and weaknesses. Therefore, He has made a way for us to know Him through Jesus Christ.

# An Ending and a Beginning

*What then shall we say to these things? If God is for us, who can be against us?*
*He who did not spare His own Son, but delivered Him up for us all,*
*how shall He not with Him also freely give us all things?*
*(Romans 8:31–32)*

Once we commit our lives to Jesus Christ, things change. Most things will change for the better. The emptiness will be gone. The guilt will be removed. A sense of certainty will replace that lack of purpose in life. Best of all, there is a hope of heaven beyond the grave.

While it is true that one set of problems will cease to exist, it is also true that an entirely new set of problems will begin.

We see this in the life of David. Once God's anointing came upon him, the problems began. Once David was doing what God wanted him to do, the devil was there opposing him. Saul was trying to kill him.

It has been said that conversion has made our hearts a battlefield. Once you decide to follow Jesus Christ, you had better expect satanic opposition. The good news is that God will be with us and will never give us more than we can handle. The Bible gives us this promise: "For I am persuaded that neither death nor life, nor angels nor principalities nor powers, nor things present nor things to come, nor height nor depth, nor any other created thing, shall be able to separate us from the love of God which is in Christ Jesus our Lord" (Rom. 8:38–39).

You had better know that temptation will come knocking on your door, and it will be appealing and attractive. You will have to commit yourself to resist it. Because it *will* be there.

# *Thursday*

# DROPPED

*Now David said, "Is there still anyone who is left of the house of Saul, that I may show him kindness for Jonathan's sake?"*
*(2 Samuel 9:1)*

Mephibosheth was only five years old when his father Jonathan and his grandfather Saul were killed on the battlefield. Imagine, if you will, life as he had known it up to this point. The privilege and potential of his present could not have prepared him for the hard life he would face in the future. There was life in the palace as a young prince … people waiting on him hand and foot … being raised by his godly father Jonathan. Life was good for this young boy.

But there were dark clouds gathering in his world. In one moment, through no fault of his own, his entire life would change forever. Jonathan knew things were going to change. Thus, he persuaded David to make an agreement to look out for his descendants. He made David promise to show kindness to his family forever. David made that promise. And he kept it.

When news hit the palace that Saul and Jonathan had been killed on the battlefield, the nurse who was caring for Mephibosheth, in her frenzied state, dropped this little boy on the ground. As a result, he was crippled for life.

Perhaps you have gone through hardships in your childhood. Maybe something traumatic has happened to you. You have been dropped in life, so to speak. You wonder if anything good can come out of your life.

Mephibosheth was dropped in life, but God intervened. In fact, God specializes in taking people who have been dropped in life and picking them back up again. That is just what David did for Mephibosheth. That is just what God will do for you.

# LIVING IN LO-DEBAR

*"As for Mephibosheth," said the king, "he shall eat at my table like one of the king's sons."... So Mephibosheth dwelt in Jerusalem, for he ate continually at the king's table. And he was lame in both his feet.*
*(2 Samuel 9:11, 13)*

The Bible tells us that when David sought out Jonathan's son to show him kindness, Mephibosheth was living in Lo-debar. When the prophet Amos spoke of this place, he said, "And just as stupid is this bragging about your conquest of Lo-debar ... " (Amos 6:13 NLT). The name really means "the place of no pasture." You didn't want to live in Lo-debar. It was a dry, parched, crummy place to live.

But where were we when Jesus Christ found us? We were living in Lo-debar, a parched, dried-up place. And just like David sought out Mephibosheth, Jesus Christ sought us. It is worth noting that it was not Mephibosheth who looked for David; it was David who looked for Mephibosheth. That might not seem significant, but it really is. David wanted to have a relationship with him. We read in 2 Samuel 9:5, "Then King David sent and brought him out of the house of Machir the son of Ammiel, from Lo Debar." David was persistent. He would not give up on Mephibosheth.

This is a reminder to us that we need to reach out to our friends, neighbors, and even enemies who don't know Christ. They don't realize it, but they are living in Lo-debar. They are living in a parched place—separated from God. So we need to ask God to place an urgency in our hearts. We all know people who need someone to reach out to them. That is exactly what David did. And that is what we need to do.

# *Weekend*

# CHECK YOUR FACTS

*But God, who is rich in mercy, because of His great love with which
He loved us, even when we were dead in trespasses, made us alive
together with Christ (by grace you have been saved).
(Ephesians 2:4–5)*

There are a lot of people today who think God is out to
get them, that He is out to make their lives miserable.
They believe He is there to impose rules and regulations on them and generally make their lives hard. But that is
a false concept of God. We should not base our opinion of God
on something that someone may have told us. Rather,
we should find out what God says about himself.

How many unbelievers have you met who have actually
taken time to look at what the Bible says? How many of them
have even read one Gospel, not to mention all four of them?
How many have bothered to even search out what Christianity
really teaches and what it truly means to be a Christian?

So many will base their entire opinion of God on someone
who falsely represents Him. To be honest, if all I knew of
Christianity was limited to what I saw on television, then I
would be turned off too. If all I knew about Christians is
what I read in the news, then I would say they were a bunch
of weirdos.

But thank God that I came into contact with genuine
believers who loved Jesus and reflected His love. Thank
God that I had someone share the gospel with me and
heard it for myself.

Here is my point: Don't base your opinion of God on
a fringe group of weird people who misrepresent Him.
Base your opinion of God on what He says about himself
in His Word.

*Monday*

# THE GOD OF KNOWLEDGE

*Talk no more so very proudly; let no arrogance come from your mouth, for the Lord is the God of knowledge; and by Him actions are weighed.* (1 Samuel 2:3)

If intellectualism alone were the major key to purpose and fulfillment, then our universities and college campuses would be bastions of peace and purpose. Yet as you walk around your typical secular university today, you will see the emptiness of academic pursuit without God. On these campuses you will often find the most bizarre and aberrant ideas circulating today.

Certainly the pursuit of knowledge and wisdom is a good one. Very few things this life offers are greater than the pursuit of knowledge and wisdom, the pursuit of a good education. But if in that pursuit we leave God out, then it will indeed be an empty one.

The year before he died, J. Robert Oppenheimer, the brilliant physicist who was known as "the father of the atomic bomb," said this about his life: "I am a complete failure." In looking back on his achievements, he said they were meaningless. That sounds a lot like Solomon, who said, "But as I looked at everything I had worked so hard to accomplish, it was all so meaningless. It was like chasing the wind ... " (Eccl. 2:11 NLT).

We celebrate our dramatic advances in science and technology, which have been breathtaking to say the least. But as Tom Brokaw once said, "It is not enough to wire the world if you short-circuit the soul. Technology without heart is not enough."

With global telecommunications, we truly have become a global village. Yet there is a sense of isolation and detachment, and all this technology almost seems to numb the soul a little bit more. It is the pursuit of knowledge without God.

# Tuesday

# Nothing New

*History merely repeats itself. It has all been done before.*
*Nothing under the sun is truly new. (Ecclesiastes 1:9 NLT)*

Joy Davidman, the wife of C. S. Lewis, made this insightful statement about the pursuit of pleasure: "Living for your own pleasure is the least pleasurable thing a person can do. If his neighbors don't kill him in disgust, he will die slowly of boredom and powerlessness." And that is true. It has been said that the only cure for hedonism is to try and practice it.

The pursuit of pleasure is nothing new. As Solomon reminds us a number of times in the Book of Ecclesiastes, when you boil it down, there is nothing new under the sun. Though our technology has changed and we have had certain advancements since Solomon wrote those words, the basic cravings of humanity have not changed, nor have the basic things we look to. The philosophy of eat, drink, and be merry has been with us for a long time.

When Solomon decided he would pursue everything this world offer had to offer, He was not considering God in all of it. He was living horizontally—he had adapted a worldview that omitted God. Eventually he came to realize there was nothing to profit from under the sun. It was only when Solomon looked above the sun and looked to God that he found the answers he was seeking. When we see God for who He is, we will see the world for what it is.

If you have a close relationship with God and are walking closely with Him, you will recognize philosophies, concepts, and ideologies being propagated that are contradictory to what the Bible teaches. When you are walking closely with God, you will see this world for what it is.

# CHASING HAPPINESS

*You will show me the path of life; in Your presence is fullness of joy;*
*at Your right hand are pleasures forevermore.*
*(Psalm 16:11)*

Only humanity has a longing for meaning in life. I can assure you that my dog does not sit around pondering the reason for his existence. He won't be looking back on his life and saying, "I tried it all as a dog. I chased cats. I drank toilet water. I tried bones. But deep inside of me, there was a void. … " Dogs don't think that way. They just think, *Food … sleep. …* They are not made in the image of God.

But you are. And I am. We are living souls. We are designed to know God and live above this mundane existence that we call life. We have been on a quest. And the answer to all of our questions is found in a relationship with God. God can give us pleasure that far surpasses the pleasures this world offers. The good news is that there is no hangover in the morning. There is no guilt that accompanies it. As Psalm 16:11 says, "In Your presence is fullness of joy; at Your right hand are pleasures forevermore." There is pleasure in knowing God, not in chasing after happiness.

I have discovered that I will never find happiness by chasing it. But what you will find is that as you chase God, if you will, as you pursue God and walk with Him, then one day you will realize you became a happy person. Happiness comes not by seeking it, but just getting your life in its proper balance. Happiness is the byproduct. Joy is the byproduct. It is not from chasing after those things, but from pursuing God and knowing God.

# *Thursday*

# THE MISSING PIECE

*The night is almost gone; the day of salvation will soon be here.*
*So don't live in darkness. Get rid of your evil deeds. ...*
*(Romans 13:12 NLT)*

Have you ever tried to put a puzzle together and when you were almost done, you realized that someone had lost the final piece? It can be incredibly frustrating. Maybe you have tried to put your life together: *If I put this here and that there, it will work. ... Where is that other piece?* God holds the missing piece. You will not find it in your pursuits. The missing piece is a relationship with God through Jesus Christ. Have you found that missing piece? Or, do you still have a hole in your heart that you've tried to fill with everyone and everything, but nothing satisfies?

I was raised around many of the empty pursuits this world offers. And I pursued enough of them to know they were empty—enough to know they weren't the answer to what I was looking for. So when I first heard about Jesus Christ, the idea of having a relationship with God held great appeal for me. But the Christians I knew were so nice and loving. I thought, *I don't know if I can become one of these people.* But God started working in my life. He changed my heart. And if He can do it for me, then He can do it for you. In fact, when I told people I was a Christian, they didn't believe it. Then a few years later when they learned I was a pastor, they laughed even harder. It was the last thing anyone ever envisioned for me. But God had a different plan for my life.

Who knows what kind of plan He has for you?

# As If It Were Your Last

*You have decided the length of our lives. You know how many months we will live, and we are not given a minute longer.*
(Job 14:5 NLT)

The writer of Hebrews tells us, "It is appointed for men to die once, but after this the judgment" (Heb. 9:27). That is why we want to always heed the biblical admonition to prepare to meet our God. We don't when the day is coming.

Here is the good news: It will happen when it happens. That day has already been predetermined by God. This takes the stress out of life, because you can easily live in fear and paranoia with all that is happening in our world. You can commit your ways to the Lord and say, "If this is my day, Lord, then I am ready to meet You. If it is not, then I will serve You one more day." As Paul said, "For to me, to live is Christ, and to die is gain" (Phil. 1:21). This doesn't mean we should be foolish and test the Lord unnecessarily. There is a difference between trusting the Lord and testing the Lord. But it does mean that we should accept each day as a gift from God Almighty and live it to its fullest, totally committed to God. We should live each day as if it were our last.

Let's say, for example, that this day was your last. Think back on it. What did you do with your life today? Would you be ashamed of how you lived it? Or would you say, "I think I lived it well. I did what I should have done. I have no real embarrassment to speak of. It was a well-lived day." Good. That is how you should live each and every day.

# Weekend

# GOOD DAYS AND BAD DAYS

*"To everything there is a season, … A time to weep, and a time to laugh; a time to mourn, and a time to dance." (Ecclesiastes 3:1, 4)*

Sorrows come into all of our lives. And while none of us enjoy them, they are a reality. You will experience heartache. If you ever choose to love anyone, if you ever choose to extend your friendship to another person, then you will be disappointed. You will be let down. You will be heartbroken. There will be great disappointments for you in life.

You also will lose loved ones. And as you get older, you will lose more loved ones. There might even come a day when you will recognize that you actually have more friends who have gone to heaven than you have on Earth, and that it probably won't be long until you join them.

But there also will be times of laughter, times of great joy and celebration. One of the lessons I've learned from life is to enjoy the good times. Don't take them for granted. Savor the moment, because you can be sure some bad times will come down the road. But thank God they will first go through Him, because He continues to be in control of all circumstances that surround our lives.

God can use suffering. He can use it to deepen you and to teach you compassion. He can use it make you into a different person. And sometimes God even uses suffering to bring you to your spiritual senses.

If your heart is filled with sorrow right now, if it is filled with heartache, then I want you to know that Jesus Christ can bring you comfort. Cast your cares upon Him, and He will give you strength in your time of need.

# *Monday*

# SCATTERING AND GATHERING

*There is a time for everything, …*
*a time to scatter stones and a time to gather stones.*
*(Ecclesiastes 3:1, 5 NLT)*

I have noticed that with the passing of time, friendships come and go. Your friends that you had in elementary school or high school are probably not the friends you have today, although there may be some exceptions, of course. It might even be true that friends you were so close to ten years ago aren't even a part of your life today. People move. Things change. And God brings new friends into your life.

Therefore, it is important not to let your friends make your decisions for you. Think of some things that you have done because your friends pressured you into it. Then realize they may not even be your friends ten years from now.

Some people will not give their lives to Christ because they are afraid of what their friends would think—as if that even matters, as if their friends will be with them on Judgment Day, standing around nudging each other and laughing. That is not the case. Each of us will be all alone before God. Our friends will come and our friends will go. The Bible says "there is a friend who sticks closer than a brother (Prov. 18:24), referring to Jesus Christ.

The Bible also tells us there is a "time to cast away stones, and a time to gather stones" (Eccl. 3:5). It might be a relation-ship that suddenly has become counterproductive in your life. Instead of building you up spiritually, it is beginning to do the opposite. It just may be that it is time for it to end. It might feel horrible at the time. But it could be the best thing that ever happened to you.

# *Tuesday*

# WHEN WE MUST TURN AWAY

*There is a time for everything, … a time to embrace and a time to turn away.*
*(Ecclesiastes 1:5 NLT)*

The Bible tells us that "open rebuke is better than love carefully concealed. Faithful are the wounds of a friend" (Proverbs 26:5–6). If you really care about someone, there may come a time when you must turn away so that he or she will know what the truth is.

Let's say, for example, that you know someone who claims to be a Christian, yet he is getting drunk or living immorally. You may think, *I need to love him as my Christian brother, and even though what he is doing is sinful, I will keep hanging out with him.* But the Bible tells us there is a time to turn away.

Paul addresses that very subject in 1 Corinthians 5: "I wrote to you in my epistle not to keep company with sexually immoral people. Yet I certainly did not mean with the sexually immoral people of this world, or with the covetous, or extortioners, or idolaters, since then you would need to go out of the world" (vv. 9–10). Paul was saying that we are not to associate with anyone who claims to be a Christian, yet indulges in sexual sin or is greedy or worships idols and so forth.

Yet a lot of Christians today ignore this command. "Just be loving," they say. I would suggest that they don't know what love is. Love cares enough to say, "What you are doing is wrong." Then the pressure is on, because what they will be sensing is the conviction of the Holy Spirit. It is good for them to feel the heat. It is far less than the heat they could ultimately feel if they don't repent.

# A Closed Mouth Gathers No Foot

*To everything there is a season, a time to keep silence, and a time to speak.*
*(Ecclesiastes 3:1, 7)*

I can think of so many times when I should have kept silent, but just had to speak. Have you ever done that? Have you ever said something, and the moment it left your lips, you thought, Why did I just say that? But you said it.

The Bible says, "My dear brothers and sisters, be quick to listen, slow to speak, and slow to get angry." (James 1:19 NLT). So much better it would be if we were to stop and think for a moment: *Is this the right thing to say? Would this be an appropriate statement to make? Lord, would this glorify You?*

Peter was very outspoken, which is why I like him so much. One of my favorite stories about him was when he was on the Mount of Transfiguration with Jesus, James, and John. Jesus told His three disciples to stay awake with Him. Yet Peter and the boys fell asleep. When they woke up, Jesus was shining like the sun and talking with Moses and Elijah. So Peter stood up and said, "It is good for us to be here … " (Mark 9:5). I like the commentary Mark's Gospel adds: "He didn't really know what to say …" (v. 6 NLT).

Have you ever been in a situation like that, when you wanted to say the perfect thing, yet you ended up saying the lamest thing possible?

An old proverb advises, "Better to be silent and be thought a fool than to open your mouth and dispel all doubt." Or as another proverb says, "A closed mouth gathers no foot."

There is a time to speak. And there is a time to be quiet.

# *Thursday*

# Cut It Loose

*All things are lawful for me, but not all things are helpful; all things are lawful for me, but not all things edify. (1 Corinthians 10:23)*

Often the question is asked, "Can I do this and still be a Christian?" I might be going to certain kinds of movies or listening to certain kinds of music or going to a certain type of place.

Whatever it may be in life, be it relationships, friendships, habits, indulgences, or whatever things they are, if they entangle you, if they hinder your walk with God, if they make the reading of the Bible more dull, your prayer life more dead, and the reality of eternity more dim, then they should be cut loose.

A question to ask regarding that thing you are wondering about is: "Is it slowing you down in the race of life?" Is that relationship impairing your progress? Is that habit impairing your performance? If so, then cut it loose. This is why Hebrews 12:1 tells us, "Therefore, since we are surrounded by such a huge crowd of witnesses to the life of faith, let us strip off every weight that slows us down, especially the sin that so easily hinders our progress" (NLT).

If you ever wonder whether something is allowable for you to do as a Christian, then ask yourself these four questions:

1. Does it build me up spiritually?
2. Does it bring me under its power?
3. Do I have an uneasy conscience about it?
4. Could it cause someone to stumble?

Paul said, "All things are lawful for me, but not all things are helpful; all things are lawful for me, but not all things edify" (1 Cor. 10:23).

Is some activity or pursuit gaining a hold on you? Maybe you need to cut it loose.

# GOOD FRICTION

*"But whoever denies Me before men, him I will also deny before My Father who is in heaven. Do not think that I came to bring peace on earth. I did not come to bring peace but a sword." (Matthew 10:33–34)*

If you are going to follow the Lord, then it will create friction. Jesus said, "Do not think that I came to bring peace on earth. I did not come to bring peace but a sword" (Matt. 10:34). For example, let's say that you go home to your family, who are unbelievers, and tell them, "I got saved."

"You got what?"

"Saved. Jesus came into my heart."

"He came into what? Who?"

"Jesus. I am a Christian now."

"Oh, great! I have a holy roller in my house now. I have a Jesus freak living with me."

By following Christ, you will create friction, but it is a good friction, because unbelievers around you will become aware of their lack of a relationship with God. And ultimately, that temporary friction can bring about the ultimate unity when they also commit their lives to Christ because of your witness.

The Bible tells us that when Jesus said to one man, "Follow Me," he said, "Lord, let me first go and bury my father." It wasn't that his father had just died. Rather, he was describing his responsibility to help his father in the family business until he died and the inheritance was distributed.

Jesus replied, "Let the dead bury their own dead, but you go and preach the kingdom of God" (Luke 9:60). Jesus was saying there has to be a commitment. Sometimes it means saying good-bye to friends. It means saying good-bye to things that would hold you back. It means that you can't live in two worlds.

# Weekend

# A REASONED COMMITMENT

*But Jesus replied, "Foxes have dens to live in, and birds have nests,
but I, the Son of Man, have no home of my own, not even a place to
lay my head." (Luke 9:58 NLT)*

Jesus was quickly approaching the zenith of His popularity when someone approached him and said, "Lord, I will follow You wherever You go" (Luke 9:57). Matthew's Gospel tells us this man was a scribe. The scribes were authorities in Jewish law and were closely associated with the Pharisees. These were the theologians of the day, great intellects who had committed themselves to the careful study of Scripture. They generally were teachers themselves—not followers of other teachers.

So it is significant that this scribe, this respected individual, would say to Jesus, "I will follow You wherever You go." It was the equivalent of a big-time convert.

One could have expected Jesus to say, "Let's welcome this great celebrity! You come along with us. You will be good for the cause." But Jesus said, "Foxes have holes and birds of the air have nests, but the Son of Man has nowhere to lay His head" (Luke 9:58). He was actually discouraging him. Why? Because Jesus was God and could see into the human heart.
He could see that this man was indeed acting on the impulse of the moment. He was acting out of emotional excitement, not on a reasoned commitment.

There will come a point when you must say, "I am following Jesus not because my best friend is, not because my boyfriend or girlfriend is, not because my parents are, but because I choose to follow the Lord." Sometimes people that you know are going to fall away. Are you going to follow them? Or is your commitment to Him and Him alone?

*Monday*

# REJOICE ALWAYS

*Even though the fig trees have no blossoms, and there are no grapes on the vine; even though the olive crop fails, and the fields lie empty and barren; even though the flocks die in the fields, and the cattle barns are empty, yet I will rejoice in the Lord! I will be joyful in the God of my salvation. (Habakkuk 3:17–18 NLT)*

Solomon said, "For the happy heart, life is a continual feast" (Prov. 15:15), and the psalmist wrote that in the presence of God there is fullness of joy, and at His right hand pleasures forevermore (see Ps. 16:11). Jesus said, "My purpose is to give life in all its fullness." (John 10:10 NLT). God wants us to experience joy as believers—not a fickle happiness that depends on circumstances, but a joy that is there in spite of what is taking place around you.

Anyone can be relatively happy when things are going well. But when you face adversity or sickness or hardship and then rejoice, you show yourself to be a real Christian. This is a unique trait of believers—that we can rejoice when things go wrong.

How do we do it? We find the key in Philippians 4:4: "Rejoice in the Lord always. Again I will say, rejoice!" Paul didn't say to rejoice in circumstances. Rather, he said to rejoice *in the Lord.* In other words, God is still on the throne. You are still going to heaven. You are still forgiven. God still has a plan for your life; He has not abandoned you. We need to rejoice in the Lord always. That is the key. I recognize that in spite of what I am going through, His plans for me are still good. And He will never leave or forsake me.

# *Tuesday*

# JUST WAITING FOR YOU TO ASK

*"Call to Me, and I will answer you, and show you great and mighty things, which you do not know." (Jeremiah 33:3)*

Why should I pray? The short answer is because Jesus told us to. The Bible says in Luke 18:1, "Men always ought to pray and not lose heart." There is no better reason. That is not to even mention the blessings that come from watching our prayers get answered, such as the salvation of a loved one or a divine healing or God's provision in our lives. We should pray because Jesus told us to.

Another reason we should pray is because prayer is God's appointed way for our obtaining things. James 4:2 says, "You do not have because you do not ask." There are potential answered prayers waiting for you.

Maybe you have wondered, *Why is it that I never seem to know what the will of God is for my life?* You do not have because you do not ask. *Why is it that I never have the opportunity to lead people to Christ?* You do not have because you do not ask. *Why am I always just scraping by and never seem to have enough?* You do not have because you do not ask. *Why do I have this affliction or problem that won't go away?* You do not have because you do not ask.

I am not suggesting that if you pray, you will never be sick again, will never have an unpaid bill, or will never wonder what God's will is for your life. But I am saying there are many times when God will indeed heal you, when God will indeed provide for you, and when God will indeed reveal His will to you. He is just waiting for you to ask.

# BREAK THE GLASS

*You keep track of all my sorrows. You have collected all my tears*
*in your bottle. You have recorded each one in your book.*
*(Psalm 56:8 NLT)*

When you are hurting about something, although people may not understand, God understands. You can bring a burden before the Lord that may seem insignificant to someone else.

David understood this when he wrote, "You keep track of all my sorrows. You have collected all my tears in your bottle. You have recorded each one in your book (Ps. 56:8 NLT). That is a wonderful insight into the personal compassion that God has for each and every one of us.

We are prone to only pray about the big things. We tend to think of prayer as last resort, like the fire alarms that say, "In case of emergency, break this glass." If it is a little fire, so to speak, we think, *I can handle this,* and we will put the fire out. But if half the building is burning, then we go ahead and break the glass.

Yet God is telling us to break the glass, no matter what it is. Don't wait for a small thing to become a big thing. Bring the small thing before the Lord and pray about it. Your heavenly Father is interested in every detail of your life. Do not reduce the infinite to the finite by placing a limit on God, because He says, "Is anything too hard for the Lord?" (Gen. 18:14).

Philippians 4:6 tells us, "Don't worry about anything; instead, pray about everything" (NLT). Note the word "everything." It doesn't say, "Pray about *some things*." Nor does it say, "Pray about *really big things*." In the original language, that could be translated to say "everything." And what it really means is everything.

# Thursday

# IT STARTS WITH A THOUGHT

*Fix your thoughts on what is true and honorable and right. Think about things that are pure and lovely and admirable. Think about things that are excellent and worthy of praise. (Philippians 4:8 NLT)*

If you want peace in your heart, then the Bible says you need to get your thoughts in order. You need to keep your mind stayed on God. As Isaiah 26:3 tells us, "You will keep him in perfect peace, whose mind is stayed on You, because he trusts in You."

What we think about ultimately affects what we do. Therefore, we want to nip in the bud any thoughts that would be impure or spiritually destructive. The Bible says, "For as he thinks in his heart, so is he" (Prov. 23:7). Maintaining personal peace involves both the heart and the mind.

When the devil approached Eve in the Garden, notice that did not come and say, "Hi, I'm Lucifer. I fell from heaven. Listen, Eve, I hate your guts. I hate Adam. I hate the descendants that are going to come. In fact, I have been thinking about getting you thrown out of the Garden of Eden and wreak havoc on your life." He is not going to do that. He subtly tempted her. We learn from 2 Corinthians 11:3 that he attacked her mind, because Paul wrote, "But I fear, lest somehow, as the serpent deceived Eve by his craftiness, so your minds may be corrupted from the simplicity that is in Christ."

What do you allow to fill your mind? My point is that we need to have a right mind. If we don't, then it is only a matter of time until we fall into sin. If we allow garbage into our minds, then ultimately, it will work its way into our lives.

# MEMORY FULL

*Casting down arguments and every high thing that exalts itself against the knowledge of God, bringing every thought into captivity to the obedience of Christ.*
*(2 Corinthians 10:5)*

We all live in the same world. We see and hear things we wished we had never seen, things we didn't even go out of our way to see. But if you live in this world, then you will be exposed to things that you don't want to be exposed to at times.

Then there is your free time, the time when you pick up that little thing called a remote control. Then there is the radio. There are CDs and books and magazines. You have control over these things.

On my computer I have six gigabytes of storage. I have every Bible program I can get my hands on loaded onto the hard drive. That way, I can access them when I am traveling, so I can still study and prepare for my messages.

But I only have so much space on my hard drive. Even if I have six gigs, I will eventually fill it up. When I try to load a new program, a little message will come up on my screen that tells me no more memory is available. If I want to load a new program, then I have to throw something out. Otherwise, I need to get a new hard drive.

Wouldn't it be great if, when the devil comes with his temptations, a little sign would appear that says, "Memory full. Heart and mind are filled with the things of God."

After all, the best defense is a good offense. So instead of being open and vulnerable to the attacks of the devil through our imaginations, let's fill our minds with the things of God.

# Weekend

# AT PEACE IN HIM

*"Peace I leave with you, My peace I give to you; not as the world gives do I give to you. Let not your heart be troubled, neither let it be afraid."*
*(John 14:27)*

You cannot separate outward action from inward attitude. Sin always results in unrest. Isaiah 57:20 says, " 'But the wicked are like the troubled sea, when it cannot rest, whose waters cast up mire and dirt. There is no peace,' says my God, 'for the wicked.' " When you live a wicked life, it is constantly in turmoil.

In contrast, when you live right before God, you will have His peace. Isaiah 32:17 says, "The work of righteousness will be peace, and the effect of righteousness, quietness and assurance forever."

Maybe you are filled with anxiety and worry right now. Maybe you have done some things you know you shouldn't have, and you are afraid. And in many ways, you ought to be, because you are worrying about the results of sin. That is what sin brings into your life.

It is so great when you are able to lay your head on the pillow at night and not have to worry about those things—not because you have lived flawlessly or perfectly, because we have all made our mistakes, but because you are at peace in Christ.

Do you know that peace right now? You might be full of guilt for the wrong things that you have done. You might be afraid. You might be lonely. You might be filled with worry and anxiety.

I want you to know that Jesus Christ has the answer to your problems. He will get to the heart of them. He won't gloss these things over. He will get to what you really need changed, which is your heart.

*Monday*

# UNPOPULAR WORD, UNPOPULAR MESSAGE

*John came baptizing in the wilderness and preaching a baptism*
*of repentance for the remission of sins. (Mark 1:4)*

Repent—there is an interesting word. When we hear it, we usually think of someone who seems to be very angry, who perhaps is wearing a sandwich board painted with flames, and is yelling, "Repent!" It is a word we don't hear very much of today.

You might be surprised to know that the first word to fall from the lips of Jesus Christ after He began His public ministry was the word "repent." And in the New Testament, we find the story of a man who talked quite a bit about the subject. In fact, this man was the cousin of Jesus Christ. We know him as John the Baptist or John the Baptizer. In the eyes of many, John was a radical and a revolutionary, even a troublemaker who was not content to leave well enough alone. He had a life and ministry that directly confronted people with the truth. He was not afraid to say what was right, whether people liked it or not.

This was a man who had a job to do. He realized that he had a relatively short period of time to get a lot done. It was John's task to prepare the nation for the Messiah and then to present the Messiah to them. And he wasn't very popular for it.

John came at a strategic time in human history. He stood as a herald to proclaim the coming King. We, too, stand at a strategic time in human history. Like John, we don't know how much time we have. So we have to make every moment count. We don't want to waste time. We want to make our lives count for something.

# Tuesday

# THE QUESTION OF LIBERTY

*"And do not be drunk with wine, in which is dissipation;*
*but be filled with the Spirit" (Ephesians 5:18)*

Sometimes I am asked the question, "What do you think about Christians drinking? Do you think that it's a good idea?" I think it is a dangerous thing for a Christian to drink, because I have never seen a person drunk who did not drink first.

I was raised in an alcoholic home. I saw the devastation that it could bring not only to my family, but also to other families. As a pastor, I have also seen the destruction that alcohol brings. I cannot think of one single good thing about it, but I can certainly think of a lot of bad things.

Many times the Bible warns us of what alcohol can do in our lives. Proverbs 23:32–33 says of alcohol, "At the last it bites like a serpent, and stings like a viper. Your eyes will see strange things, and your heart will utter perverse things." Paul wrote in 1 Corinthians 6:2, "You may say, 'I am allowed to do anything.' But I reply, 'Not everything is good for you.' And even though 'I am allowed to do anything,' I must not become a slave to anything" (NLT).

Another thing to consider is whether it will cause someone else to stumble spiritually. Romans 14:15 says, "Yet if your brother is grieved because of your food, you are no longer walking in love. Do not destroy with your food the one for whom Christ died." What we do and what we are has a direct effect on others.

Here is the way I look at it. I don't want to be under the influence of spirits. I want to be under the influence of the Spirit of God.

# Genuine Salvation

*"Beware of false prophets, who come to you in sheep's clothing, but inwardly they are ravenous wolves." (Matthew 5:14)*

I believe in Jesus Christ, but my god is not judgmental, and my god would never send a person to hell," some people say.

One cannot have it both ways. We cannot say "My god … " and then make it up as we go. If He is the true God, then we need to see what He says of himself in Scripture. Yet there are many people, even in the church, who have a watered-down belief in God. This watered-down gospel may be the most dangerous plague the church is facing today, because it gives a sense of false assurance to the person who believes it.

The Bible warns of false prophets who give false assurance. In Jeremiah 6:14, God says of them, "They offer superficial treatments for my people's mortal wound. They give assurances of peace when all is war" (NLT). It would be like going to see a doctor when you are having a heart attack, but the doctor says, "Oh, you are fine. You are *so* dramatic! You will be okay." That doctor would not be doing his job.

Yet today there are ministers who say, "God loves you and everything is fine. You can do whatever you want to do and live however you want to live. It's all okay. Let's just love one another and have a great time." That is a false gospel.

Sure, God loves you. Sure, God receives any person who comes to Him. But He also asks you to turn from your sin. And if you are not willing to do that, then you are not experiencing biblical faith, and thus, you will not receive what the Bible describes as genuine salvation.

# Thursday

# AN ESSENTIAL STEP

*"For godly sorrow produces repentance leading to salvation, not to be regretted; but the sorrow of the world produces death." (2 Corinthians 7:10)*

A hospital chaplain kept a record of some two thousand patients he had visited, all of whom were apparently in a dying state, and all of whom had shown signs of repentance. This chaplain said that among those who had been restored to health, he could only think of two who showed a marked changed in their spiritual lives after their recovery.

As it has been said, there are no atheists in foxholes. When the chips are down, people want God's help. But when He answers their prayers, many of them seem to say, "Thanks, God. See You next crisis."

That is how a lot of people are. They have never really repented of their sins. They have never really brought forth fruit in keeping with repentance. But this is absolutely necessary if we want to be forgiven of our sins. A recognition of personal sin is always the first step toward receiving forgiveness. But a person can recognize the need to repent and still not do it. A person can recognize his or her personal sin and not necessarily take action.

For example, the Bible tells us in the Book of Exodus that Pharaoh was hardened against God, even when he saw miracle after miracle done by the hand of Moses. Finally he summoned Moses and Aaron and admitted that he had sinned. But then he deliberately sinned against God and His people.

It is not enough to say we are sinners. We need to say we are sinners and that we are sorry enough for our sin that we want to stop doing it. Until we have taken this step, we are not there yet.

# THE FRUIT OF REPENTANCE

*But now having been set free from sin, and having become slaves of God,*
*you have your fruit to holiness, and the end, everlasting life.*
*(Romans 6:22)*

The question has been asked, "If you were arrested for being a Christian, would there be enough evidence to convict you?" It is not a matter of how often you go to church, how many Christian CDs you own, or how many Bible you have. While all those things are fine, the question at hand is have you brought forth fruit in keeping with repentance?

A lot of people today think they are Christians but are not, because they have not really changed. There are people today who say, "I am a Christian," but they are out getting drunk. They say, "I am a Christian," but they are having sex with their boyfriend or girlfriend, or they are being unfaithful to their husband and wife. They say, "I am a Christian," but they lie to people every day in their business.

I am not saying a Christian cannot sin. I am not saying a Christian won't slip up. But I am saying there is a big difference between a person who sins, is sorry for it, and wants to change, and a person who lives in continual, willful, habitual sin. The Bible says that if you live that way, then you don't know God.

Is there evidence in your life that you really know Jesus Christ? Are you just hiding behind some profession you made a decade ago, a year ago, or a month ago? Are you hiding behind the fact that you were raised in a Christian family and have gone to church your entire life? Do you really know Christ? If so, have you brought forth fruit in keeping with repentance?

## Weekend

# Spiritual Multimillionaires

*Blessed be the God and Father of our Lord Jesus Christ, who has blessed us with every spiritual blessing in the heavenly places in Christ. (Ephesians 1:3)*

Hettie Green was known as America's greatest miser, but she was worth a lot of money. When she died in 1916, she left an estate valued at $100 million. That is a lot today, but it was even more back then.

What is amazing about Hettie Green is that she lived as through she were poverty stricken. She would eat cold oatmeal every day to save the expense of heating the water. She debated the value of skim milk compared to whole milk and how much money she could save. When her son had a severe leg injury, she took so long trying to find a free clinic to treat him that his leg had to be amputated because of advanced infection. She even hastened her own death by not taking care of herself. She lived like a pauper when, in reality, she was a multimillionaire.

Like Hettie Green, some Christians might not realize how much is actually in their spiritual bank account. Such believers are experiencing spiritual malnutrition, because they have not taken advantage of the great storehouse of spiritual nourishment and resources that are at their disposal. Because of what God has done for us, we can live full, productive, and effective Christian lives. We don't have to find insufficient funds when we go to our spiritual ATM machine. God's heavenly bank has no such limitations or restrictions. No Christian has to be spiritually deprived or undernourished or impoverished. The Lord's heavenly resources are more than adequate to cover the cost of all of our past debts, our present liabilities, and our future needs and still not reduce our heavenly assets.

*Monday*

# BY THE WILL OF GOD

*Paul, an apostle of Jesus Christ by the will of God.*
*(Ephesians 1:1)*

We may look today at people in the church who are called to be pastors or evangelists or worship leaders or elders and conclude they are the spiritual elite. Meanwhile, someone is laboring away as an accountant or a waitress or a nurse or a teacher and might be thinking, *I am not as significant as them. They are really making a difference for the kingdom of God.*

Understand, every one of us is called to be something by the will of God. Paul was called to be an apostle by the will of God. But Steve can be called to be an architect by the will of God. Mary can be called to be a nurse by the will of God. Joan can be called to be an attorney by the will of God. Jack can be called to be a policeman by the will of God.

Each of us has a part to play. The highest calling of God is what God has called you to be. There is no higher thing. We need to be faithful to what the Lord has called us to.

You may think it is a higher calling to preach. Granted, it is a high calling and it is a privilege. But the highest calling is what God has called you to do. So don't feel like a second-class citizen if you are not in full-time ministry.

When certain people at church are highly visible, you think they are important. Maybe they are. And maybe they aren't. But then there is the person you don't know anything about who is very important to God. You might be one of those people. Be who you are by the will of God.

# Tuesday

# TWO-DIMENSIONAL LIVING

*For he raised us from the dead along with Christ, and we are seated with him in the heavenly realms—all because we are one with Christ Jesus. (Ephesians 2:6 NLT)*

A Christian is someone who lives in two dimensions. There is the spiritual dimension, which means that as we walk in the Spirit, we know God in the Spirit. Yet we live on Earth. So as believers, we need to transfer what we have in the spiritual realm into the earthly realm.

For example, when I travel to another country, I still maintain my U.S. citizenship. When I went to Israel a few years ago, although I had my passport that indicated I am an American, I had to live in their culture. There were things I needed to adapt to. For example, I needed money. So I took funds from my bank in the U.S. and converted them into shekels to use in the Israel. Of course, I didn't know what the exchange rate was, so on my first day there, I may have tipped someone fifty dollars to carry my bags to my room. (He was really nice to me the rest of the day.)

As Christians, we have riches, or treasures, waiting for us in heaven. And when the Bible speaks of the heavenlies, we need to recognize that it is not talking about something that is merely waiting for us in heaven. Rather, it talking about the supernatural realm. So before we can effectively walk as believers, much less engage in spiritual battle, we need to learn about the resources that God has given to us. We also need to understand they are treasures that God wants us to start utilizing here, spiritual resources that are available to the believer who is walking with God.

# BEFORE THE WORLD BEGAN

*Long ago, even before he made the world, God loved us and chose us in Christ to be holy and without fault in his eyes. (Ephesians 1:4 NLT)*

**B**efore the world was made, even before sin entered into this world that was made, God predestined you. He chose you to be His child. We use phrases like, "The day I found the Lord," and that is true in one sense. But in another sense, God chose us before we chose Him.

Jesus said, You did not choose Me, but I chose you and appointed you that you should go and bear fruit, and that your fruit should remain … " (John 15:16). God chose us before we were ever around to choose Him. We may wonder, *What merit or goodness did He find in me that He would choose me to be His child?* There was no merit. In spite of our best intentions or the high opinion we may hold of ourselves, God's choosing had nothing to do with our merit or goodness.

If you knew what would happen before it took place, would you choose something that worked in your favor or against it? God knew exactly how you would turn out. And He chose you from the foundation of the world. You might say, "I think the Lord made a mistake here, because I am a loser." God chose you to win. God chose you to be something that He will make you into. You may look at yourself and see your flaws and shortcomings, but just remember that you are still a work in progress. God is not finished with you yet. He is going to complete what He has begun in your life. So rejoice that He chose you from the foundation of the world.

# *Thursday*

# The Joy before Him

*The Lord Jesus on the same night in which He was betrayed took bread; and when He had given thanks, He broke it and said, "Take, eat, this is My body which is broken for you; do this in remembrance of Me." (1 Corinthians 11:23–24)*

It is amazing to me that on the night the Lord was betrayed, just moments from this event, that He was giving thanks. He was giving thanks as He was about to face a horrendous time of suffering and anguish. He was giving thanks with the foreknowledge that His own disciples would temporarily abandon Him. He was giving thanks with the full knowledge that the man who was about to betray Him would do so in just a few moments.

Yet He gave thanks. How could He give thanks at a time like that? Because He had a goal, and the way to reach it was through His death on the cross. Hebrews 12:2 tells us, "For the joy that was set before Him [He] endured the cross, despising the shame, and has sat down at the right hand of the throne of God." What kept Him going—all the way to the cross? You did. "For the joy that was set before Him. … " He did it for you.

Jesus told the story of a shepherd who had one hundred sheep and one went astray. So he left the ninety-nine and went searching until he found that one, wayward lamb, wrapped it around his neck, and came back rejoicing. There was joy in finding a lost sheep.

The joy that was set before Jesus was knowing that we could have our sins forgiven, have our lives right with God, and be able to approach His throne twenty-four hours a day. And He gave thanks.

# Adopted

*Having predestined us to adoption as sons by Jesus Christ to Himself,*
*according to the good pleasure of His will, to the praise of the glory of His grace,*
*by which He made us accepted in the Beloved. (Ephesians 1:5–6)*

W e can get so hung up on the hows and the whats of predestination that we miss the why. Why did God choose us from the foundation of the world? He predestined us to be adopted into His family as His very children.

Imagine for a moment that you once were a slave who had been put up for sale. Different slave traders walked by and looked at you, but they all said they didn't want you. Then one day Jesus walked by. He looked at you and smiled. He said, "I will take that one." He paid the price, and you were so thankful. You had heard about Jesus. You had heard that He was a great guy to work for. As you were following Him, you said, "Lord, I am going to be the best slave you ever bought. Thank you so much."

He said, "Let me unlock those shackles."

"I am going to be your most faithful and loyal slave," you say. "Where to, Master?"

"We are going to go over to the courthouse."

You walk in, and they give Him some papers. He is filling them out. He is writing your name.

"Why are you writing my name?"

"These are adoption papers," He says. "I bought you out of the slave market to adopt you as My child." That is what God has done for you. You were a slave to sin, separated from God. But He adopted you as His own child. He ordained you. He predestined you to be adopted into His family.

# *Weekend*

# ACCEPTED

*He made us accepted in the Beloved. (Ephesians 1:6)*

All that God has done has been because of His grace, which means "unmerited favor." You are not merely forgiven, not merely justified, not merely cleansed of your sins, but you have been received in love by God himself. This is because of His deep love for His own Son Jesus. Because His Son lives in you, you have found His favor. You have the approval of God because of what Jesus has done.

Some people have been raised in homes in which their father may have never demonstrated any kind of love toward them. Maybe he was cold and distant. Or maybe they, like me, were raised in a home where there wasn't a father at all. We can transfer those emotions to God the Father. We can walk around in life feeling as though we don't have the approval of God: *If I just did this, God would notice. If I worked a little harder, then God would love me.*

God approves of you. The Bible says, "He made us accepted in the Beloved" (Eph. 1:6). You are accepted in the Beloved—not because you read your Bible a little bit longer, share Christ with more people, or give a little more in the offering. You are accepted in the Beloved when you don't do all of that. You are accepted in the Beloved when you fail, when you trip up. You are accepted in the Beloved not because of what *you* have done, but because of what *He* has done.

But in understanding this great truth, you should want to do these things for His glory—not to earn His approval, because you already have it. Isn't that a great thing to know? You are accepted in the Beloved.

# BY FAITH ALONE

*"How then can man be righteous before God?" (Job 25:4)*

I am surprised at how many of those who have put their faith in Christ don't have a basic understanding of the Bible's foundational teachings on what salvation really is. We need to fully understand and grasp the meaning of salvation. I like this description from the great evangelist D. L. Moody:

1. There is repentance that is a change of mind, where we receive a new mind about God.

2. There is conversion, which is a change of life. We receive a new life from God.

3. There is regeneration, which is a change of nature, and we receive a new heart from God.

4. There is justification, which is a change of state. It is a new standing before God.

5. There is adoption, which is a change in family. That is a new relationship toward God.

6. There is sanctification, which is a change of service. It is a new condition with God.

All these things are a part of what we call being saved. The question is how is a person justified? In Paul's day, some were saying it was done through religious works. Specifically they were saying that if a person really wanted to know God, they had to go through the Jewish rituals and then keep the law—not only if you were a Jew, but even if you were a Gentile, a non-Jew. The apostle Paul addressed that issue head-on. In his letter to the Romans, he said, "Therefore we conclude that a man is justified by faith apart from the deeds of the law" (Rom. 3:28). As C. H. Spurgeon said, "It is admitted by all evangelical Christians that the standing or falling in the church is that of justification by faith."

# Tuesday

# Lapses of Faith

*For what does the Scripture say? "Abraham believed God, and it was accounted to him for righteousness." (Romans 4:3)*

The Bible doesn't teach that if you are a Christian, you will never stumble. It doesn't teach that if you are a true believer, you will not periodically fall short. But it does teach that if you are a true believer, when you have had a lapse or a stumble, you will always get up and move forward. That is the way to determine whether a person is really a believer or not.

When God came to Abraham in Ur and told him to break away from his family, Abraham basically refused and did not go for years. Even after he left, he partially obeyed God by dragging his nephew Lot along. This only resulted in more friction down the road. Eventually he and Lot parted company. On through his life we would see other lapses of faith. Abraham told his beautiful wife Sarah to say that she was his sister, because he was afraid someone would kill him if they realized he was indeed her husband. He did that on two occasions. There were a number of acts of disobedience on Abraham's part. Having said that, it is also important to point out that although he deviated occasionally from the straight and narrow, he always came back.

If a person says he or she is a believer and falls away and never comes back, then that person is not a believer. As 1 John 2:19 says, "When they left us, it proved that they do not belong with us." (NLT). But if a person is a true believer, then he or she will be miserable in sin and will eventually beat a quick path back to the cross of Calvary.

# Gone for Good

*He will again have compassion on us, and will subdue our iniquities.*
*You will cast all our sins into the depths of the sea.*
*(Micah 7:19)*

Have you ever done anything that you were ashamed of? Have you ever done things you wished you had not done? If you have repented of that sin and have turned your back on it, then the Bible clearly declares that you are forgiven.

In speaking of our sins, God says, "I, even I, am He who blots out your transgressions for My own sake; and I will not remember your sins" (Isa. 43:25). And Micah 7:19 tells us that God will cast all our sins into the depths of the sea.

Have you ever lost anything in a lake or in the ocean? It is pretty much a lost cause. Once it goes down, it goes way down.

Years ago I was scuba diving in Hawaii. As we started making our way out, it was about fifteen feet deep, then about twenty feet deep, then about seventy feet. We kept going, and the shelf of sand kept lowering and lowering. Then all of a sudden, it dropped straight down. I looked down and could not see the bottom. It was scary. I looked at that and hovered there for a minute. Although I wasn't any deeper than I had been three minutes before, it was just that I couldn't see the sand anymore. I turned around and started swimming back. I can guarantee that if you dropped something down to those depths, you would never it again.

God has taken your sin and has thrown it into the deepest part of the sea. To put it another way, it is gone. Therefore, you need to accept God's forgiveness and put it behind you.

# Thursday

# CHECK YOUR ACCOUNT

*I no longer count on my own goodness or my ability to obey God's law, but I trust Christ to save me. For God's way of making us right with himself depends on faith. (Philippians 3:9 NLT)*

Justification includes forgiveness, but it is only part of it. Justification is more than just forgiveness and the removal of guilt and the condemnation that accompanied it. Justification also includes what God has done for you and what He has given to you. It is a legal act of God, declaring the sinner guiltless before Him. Justification not only speaks of what God has taken away; it also speaks of what God has put in its place.

Imagine, for a moment, that you were in debt for $10 million. There was no hope of ever paying this enormous debt back. Then you find out that you have a wealthy relative somewhere with the last name of Gates. You weren't aware of this before. So you call up Mr. Gates and ask for $10 million. He says no problem and writes a check for $10 million. Your debt is paid in full. You are so relieved and so thankful.

Then he calls you a little later and says, "I was thinking about this propensity you have for getting yourself into debt. So I put a little money into your account. You might want to go check it out." So you get on your bicycle and ride down to the bank. You pop in your ATM card to check your balance, only to discover that it is $15 billion.

That is what God has done for you. He forgave you of all of the wrongs you have ever done. He removed your sins. And not only that, but He has put righteousness into your account.

# TAKE IT TO THE BANK

*We put no confidence in human effort. Instead, we boast about what
Christ Jesus has done for us. (Philippians 1:3 NLT)*

A homeless man was on a street corner asking for
money when a well-dressed attorney came walking
by. The attorney looked at him and said, "Haven't I
seen you somewhere before?"

The man recognized the attorney and said, "Remember
third-period English in high school?"

"You sat right next to me," the attorney said. "What
happened?"

"I just fell on hard times."

The attorney said, "Don't say another word." He pulled out
his checkbook and wrote out a check for $500. Then he said,
"I want to help you out. Take this money, get cleaned up, and
get a new set of clothes. Don't thank me. It is the least I can do."
And off he went.

With the check in hand, the man made his way down to the
bank where the attorney's account was. But when he saw how
nicely dressed the people were and how clean and tidy the bank
was, he felt unworthy and didn't go in.

The next day, the attorney was walking down the same street
when he saw the same man asking for money. He said, "What
are doing here?"

The man said, "I felt ashamed. I didn't feel worthy to go into
the bank and cash your check."

The attorney told him, "That check has my signature on it.
You take that down and cash it. It is not based on who you are.
It is based on me. My signature is on it, and it is good. Cash it."

That is what God has done for us in justification. God's
grace has been extended to us. We are wrong when we think
we have to do something to somehow earn it.

# *Weekend*

# YOU DON'T HAVE
# TO WORK FOR IT

*When people work, their wages are not a gift. Workers earn what they receive.*
*But people are declared righteous because of their faith, not because of their work.*
*(Romans 4:4–5 NLT)*

As a young Christian, I remember thinking that the reason God was blessing me was because of my disciplined Bible study. I would get up well before school every morning and study the Scripture for about an hour. Then I would pray for an hour or more (I know because I kept checking my watch). I could say to my friends, "While I was studying the Bible for an hour and praying for over an hour today, the Lord showed me. …" It gave me bragging rights. I thought that when I got to school, God would use me because I had done so much for Him. Look at how faithful I was! Look at how diligent I was! I was so proud.

Then one morning my alarm didn't go off. I woke up very late. I didn't have time to pray or read my Bible. It turned out to be one of the most blessed days of my life. God even allowed me the privilege of leading someone to Christ that day. I thought, *What does this mean? Don't read the Bible or pray?* I think what God was trying to say to me was, "Greg, don't do those things to seek My approval. Rather, do those things because you have My approval."

It is not because of what we have done that we have God's approval. It is because of what God has done for us. We put our faith in Him, and then God puts His righteousness into our account. He loves us when we do well. But He also loves us when we stumble.

*Monday*

# TEMPORARY TROUBLES

*So we don't look at the troubles we can see right now; rather,*
*we look forward to what we have not yet seen. For the troubles we see will*
*soon be over, but the joys to come will last forever. (2 Corinthians 4:18 NLT)*

There are times in our lives as Christians in which everything is going along wonderfully. There are no real problems to speak of. The sky is blue. The sun is shining. The birds are singing. Then suddenly, without warning, the bottom drops out. It may be a tragedy. It may be something completely expected.

Or maybe for you it is not that the bottom has dropped out, but it is just that you feel as though nothing seems to be happening in your life. It seemed as though God was preparing you for something. Doors were opening. God was going to do great things in your life. Then it was as though everything went into freeze frame. You are waiting. You are praying, "God, I thought you were coming back soon. I thought time was short. I am available. You don't seem to be calling on me."

Surely Moses could have felt that way. I am sure when he saw that Egyptian mistreating the Hebrew that it seemed like a good idea at the time to kill him. Obviously he found out that it was the worst thing he could have done. He spent forty years in the backside of the desert just tending sheep. Then unexpectedly, God recommissioned him at the burning bush.

If you are going through a time of testing and trials, recognize that God has a purpose in it. Who knows that God is not preparing you and training you today for what He is going to do in your life tomorrow?

# Tuesday

# THE PROMISE OF PEACE

*For God in all his fullness was pleased to live in Christ, and by him God reconciled everything to himself. He made peace with everything in heaven and on earth by means of his blood on the cross. (Colossians 1:19–20)*

M any of the blessings the Bible promises are still in our future. The hope of heaven is still ahead. Glorified bodies are definitely ahead. But the peace of God is something that is ours here and now. When we put our faith in Christ, we can begin to experience the peace of God.

Philippians 4:7 promises, "The peace of God, which surpasses all understanding, will guard your hearts and minds through Christ Jesus." I know this peace in my life. I am sure you know it as well. I can think back to the day when I put my faith in Christ at age seventeen. One of the first things I remember is a sense of peace filling my heart. It was as though someone had lifted a heavy burden from me. It wasn't until later that I read that the Bible promises peace.

Peace has been given to us as a gift from God, because we have been justified by faith. It is not describing a feeling; it is describing a fact. It does not come from what we are, but from what He has done. The cause of this peace is being justified by faith. The effect is the peace we experience. This is very important. We cannot have this wonderful effect without the beginning cause. In other words, we cannot have the peace of God until we first have peace with God.

If we are fighting with God, if we are resisting His plan and purpose for our lives, then we will not experience His peace.

# NO PLACE FOR NEUTRALITY

*For the sinful nature is always hostile to God. It never did obey God's laws, and it never will. That's why those who are still under the control of their sinful nature can never please God. (Romans 8:7–8 NLT)*

Make no mistake about it: prior to our conversion, we were at war with God. Many unbelievers probably do not think of themselves as enemies of God. Maybe they don't have any conscious feelings of hatred toward Jesus Christ or His followers. They feel they are not opposed to God or at war with God. They would probably describe themselves as neutral.

In reality, no such position exists. There is no place for neutrality. Romans 8:5 says, "Those who are dominated by the sinful nature think about sinful things, but those who are controlled by the Holy Spirit think about things that please the Spirit" (NLT). The sinful mind is hostile toward God. If a person has not met God's requirement for salvation, which is unconditional surrender, then he or she is at war with God. I will give you a sneak preview of what is ahead: unbelievers will lose this war. They might as well surrender while they can.

Speaking to the self-righteous Pharisees, Jesus said, "If God were your Father, you would love me, because I have come to you from God. I am not here on my own, but he sent me. ... For you are the children of your father the Devil, and you love to do the evil things he does." (John 8:42, 44 NLT).

This is why Jesus said, "He who is not with Me is against Me, and he who does not gather with Me scatters abroad" (Matt. 12:30).

Once we have surrendered, we have the peace of God and peace with God.

# *Thursday*

# It's Already Yours

*Now hope does not disappoint, because the love of God has been poured out in our hearts by the Holy Spirit who was given to us. (Romans 5:5)*

Have you ever owned something that you didn't use? Have you ever gone shopping for something, only to come home and find it in your closet already? I have done that. I get this idea that I need a blue shirt. I have exactly what it should look like in my mind. Then I go shopping, come home, hang it up, and see that I already have that blue shirt. No wonder I had such a vivid idea of what it should look like.

This is how we can be as Christians. We are searching for things that are already hanging in our spiritual closet, so to speak. Many times we ask God for what He has already given us.

For example, we pray, "God, give me peace." But the Bible says, "We have peace with God through our Lord Jesus Christ" (Romans 5:1). God is saying, "Enjoy it to the fullest."

We might say, "God, I need more love," when actually, we need to use the love God has given us. We are praying for more of an emotional feeling of the love God already has given us. God will not necessarily answer a prayer like that. When we love someone, when we forgive someone, it is an act of obedience, believing "the love of God has been poured out in our hearts by the Holy Spirit who was given to us" (Rom. 5:5).

God has given us everything we need for spiritual growth. Many of us simply need to read His Word to find out the balance in our spiritual bank account. And then we need to start appropriating it.

# UNLIMITED ACCESS

*Because of our faith, Christ has brought us into this place of
highest privilege where we now stand, and we confidently and
joyfully look forward to sharing God's glory. (Romans 5:2 NLT)*

P eace with God takes care of our past, because He will
no longer hold our sins against us. Access to God takes
care of our present, because we can come to Him at any
time for the help we need. The hope of the glory of God takes
care of the future, because we are confident that one day we
will share His glory.

When I was a kid, I went to Disneyland every birthday.
I still remember to this day making a vow as a child in the
backseat of the car that one day, when I became an adult
and made my own money and had my own car, that I would
go to Disneyland every single day.

A few years ago, someone gave me an annual pass to
Disneyland. I could go any time I wanted, free of charge.
Do you know how many times I used it? Not that many. It
is a funny thing, because I would even brag about it: "I
can go to Disneyland anytime I want, free of charge."

"Do you want to go right now?"

"I can't go now. Maybe next week." I kept putting it off.

We can be that way when it comes to our access to the
presence of God. As believers, we can go into God's presence
24/7—any time we want. When is the last time you went?
*Oh, I am so busy. I have so many things that I am doing.* We can go any
time we want.

God has opened this incredible door for us. But we
have to walk through it.

# *Friday*

# TRIALS THAT TEACH

*We can rejoice, too, when we run into problems and trials, for we kno w that they are good for us—they help us learn to endure. (Romans 5:3 NLT)*

The fact that God has chosen us, that He has forgiven us, that He has given us free access into His presence means that our lives are not some accident and that we are not victims of chance or luck. It means we are guided by His providence.

Therefore, there is a meaning and a purpose when I go through tribulation. Before, we might have counted hardships or difficulty as the effect of nature and something merely to be endured. But now we can know that God is in control of all circumstances that surround our lives as believers.

As Paul said, "We can rejoice, too, when we run into problems and trials, for we know that they are good for us—they help us learn to endure" (Romans 5:3 NLT). Paul was not simply enduring these experiences; he was glorying in them. This doesn't mean Paul was a masochist. Rather, he was saying, "I glory in it, because tribulation produces something I need." He made a choice. When he was going through hardship, he decided that he was not going to become bitter; he was going to become better.

Hardship will come into our lives. Tribulation will come into our lives. The Bible is clear on that. So when hard times come, you have choice. You can get mad at God and turn your back on Him. Or you can embrace that difficulty and attempt to learn what God is trying to teach you so you will become better instead of bitter. It is a choice. Hardships will come, but how you react to them is entirely up to you.

# HEROIC ENDURANCE

*And not only that, but we also glory in tribulations, knowing that tribulation produces perseverance; and perseverance, character; and character, hope.*
*(Romans 5:3–4)*

If you want to build yourself up physically, then you will need to go through the process of tearing your muscle down and building it up. The first day of working out is not so hard. But the next day, everything hurts. The next day, you feel so weak. A couple of days later, you are still weak and sore, but a little stronger. So you raise the weights a little bit. Then you do a little more. You are getting stronger. It is through the breaking down that the building up comes.

James says much the same: "Count it all joy when you fall into various trials, knowing that the testing of your faith produces patience. But let patience have its perfect work, that you may be perfect and complete, lacking nothing" (James 1:2–4). The word James used here for patience is the Greek word *hupo-mone*, which means "perseverance, endurance, steadfastness, or staying power," or as one translator puts it, "heroic endurance." We need to toughen up as Christians. We need to build up our spiritual muscles.

God lets us go through difficulties. He raises the weights on us. And pretty soon, we are benching a whole lot more than we ever thought possible. We are learning more than we ever thought we would learn. We are doing more than we ever thought we would do. Iron is entering our souls, and we are developing that heroic endurance, perseverance, and strength that only comes through difficulty.

It is not so easy to do at the time. But one day, you will be able to look back and say that God meant it for good.

# Tuesday

# AN ANCHOR OF HOPE

*This hope we have as an anchor of the soul, both sure and steadfast,
and which enters the Presence behind the veil. (Hebrews 6:19)*

I grow very impatient waiting for fruit to ripen, especially
bananas. I can't stand a mushy banana. I like them when
they are not quite green but barely yellow. Sometimes in
my impatience, I will eat a green banana. Then I will have a
stomachache for an hour because I couldn't wait for it to ripen.

God is doing a work in us, waiting for the fruit to ripen. As
Romans 5:5 tells us, "Now hope does not disappoint, because
the love of God has been poured out in our hearts by the Holy
Spirit who was given to us." As we come through tribulations,
not only do we ripen spiritually, but we also develop hope.

What hope does this world have? Is it in some politician that
is supposed to come and solve all our problems? Is it in the
White House? Is it in government programs? I hope not. Even
the best-intentioned leaders cannot resolve the basic conflicts
inside us. God offers us a hope that is far greater. A hope that
is an anchor of our soul, according to Hebrews 6:19.

I love that old hymn, "The Solid Rock," which says, "My
hope is built on nothing less than Jesus' blood and righteousness; I dare not trust the sweetest frame, but wholly lean
on Jesus' name. On Christ the solid rock I stand. All other
ground is sinking sand, all other ground is sinking sand."

Those are good words. Our hope is not in this changing
world. We have free access to God, and that is where we need
to anchor ourselves. That is where we draw our strength in
times of trouble.

# Wednesday

# WHY WE NEED A SAVIOR

*Do not enter into judgment with Your servant,*
*for in Your sight no one living is righteous.*
*(Psalm 143:2)*

It is hard for us to understand a love like God's, because our love tends to be so fickle. Generally, we love lovable people. We love people who do something for us: *Let's spend time together because … you make me laugh … I have a good time with you … I find you encouraging … You do something that I like. Therefore, I will be your friend. But if you are a complete drag and I don't like to be around you and I am miserable when I am in your presence, then I don't want to spend time with you.* Our love is fickle. We love people who are lovable or who can do something for us.

The Bible says, "God demonstrates His own love toward us, in that while we were still sinners, Christ died for us" (Rom. 5:8). He did this for us when we were sinners. That is hard for us to accept, because we like to think we are basically good.

Let me just say that there are good people. I have met unbelievers who are good people in one sense. They are kind. They are considerate. And to be quite honest with you, I have met unbelievers who have more traits of human goodness than some believers I have known.

The Bible is not saying that people are not capable of good things. It isn't even saying that people can't be good in one sense. It is simply saying that no one is *good enough*. Not one person is good enough, righteous enough, to meet the requirements of God. No one is. That is where Jesus comes in. That is why we need a Savior.

# *Thursday*

# OUR INTERCESSOR

*Who is he who condemns? It is Christ who died, and furthermore is also
risen, who is even at the right hand of God, who also makes intercession for us.
(Romans 8:34)*

If you were going through a hard time, would it bring you
some measure of comfort if Billy Graham called you?
"This is Billy Graham. I wanted to talk to you. I heard you
were going through a hard time. I would like to pray for you."

"Please do."

So Billy Graham prays for you. Wouldn't you feel good
about that?

Then let's say the phone rings again. "This is Pastor Chuck
Smith. I heard you were experiencing some difficulties. I
could pray for you if you would like me to." So Chuck Smith
prays for you.

The phone rings again. "This is Chuck Swindoll. I heard
you were having a tough time. Can I pray for you?" So Chuck
Swindoll prays for you.

How would you feel? You would feel good. Why? Because
Billy Graham, Chuck Smith, and Chuck Swindoll just prayed
for you.

I have something even better than all those guys—and they
are all great, without a doubt. You would definitely want them
praying for you. The Bible teaches that Jesus Christ is praying
for you. Jesus Christ is interceding for you. What more do you
need?

Hebrews 7:25 tells us, "Therefore He is also able to save to
the uttermost those who come to God through Him, since He
always lives to make intercession for them." And in Hebrews
9:24, we read, "For Christ has not entered the holy places
made with hands, which are copies of the true, but into heaven
itself, now to appear in the presence of God for us." Jesus is
standing for you. He is interceding for you.

# Angry with Adam?

*So you see, just as death came into the world through a man, Adam,*
*now the resurrection from the dead has begun through another man, Christ.*
*(1 Corinthians 15:21 NLT)*

Sin has infiltrated the human race. None of us escape its effect. Every day that we feel pain, every day that we see a new wrinkle on our face, it is a reminder that we are sinners. Sin has affected everything about us, not just our nature that gives us a propensity to do the wrong thing. Sin has affected us physically. If Adam had not eaten of the forbidden fruit, we never would have grown old. For that matter, I probably never would have lost my hair. We might protest, "It is not fair. Why am I held responsible for what Adam did so many years ago?"

Adam was acting as the head of the human race, even as the president is the head of the U.S. government. When the president acts, it is really the American people acting through him. We, in theory, voted him into power. He represents us.

In that same sense, Adam was our representative in the Garden. What he did affected all of us. But don't be too quick to jump down Adam's throat. The fact of the matter is that had we been in his position, we would have done the same thing. Don't think you wouldn't have. Not a day goes by that you are not faced with hundreds, even thousands, of choices to do the right or wrong thing. How often have you chosen the wrong thing? The answer is many times. Just like I have. But Jesus offers us the solution. At the cross of Calvary, He took the curse upon himself that came for those who break the law.

## Weekend

# It Comes Down to the Cross

*For the message of the cross is foolishness to those who are perishing,*
*but to us who are being saved it is the power of God.*
*(1 Corinthians 1:18)*

I once asked Billy Graham, "If you had it to do it all over again, are there things you would have emphasized as a younger preacher that maybe you are emphasizing now?" His response surprised me.

Without any hesitation, he said, "The cross of Christ and the blood. That's where the power is." And I remembered that. I took note of it as a preacher: the cross of Christ and the blood. That is what he would emphasize more. That's where the power is.

It comes down to the cross. Any accurate presentation of the gospel comes down to the cross. You can talk about loneliness. You can talk about hope and life beyond the grave. But it comes down to the cross.

Paul said, "Now let me remind you, dear brothers and sisters, of the Good News I preached to you before. ... that Christ died for our sins, just as the Scriptures said. He was buried, and he was raised from the dead on the third day, as the Scriptures said" (1 Cor. 15:1, 3–4 NLT).

We need to remember this as Christians. Perhaps you don't consider yourself a theologian or the greatest intellect of all time. But you can tell the story of what Jesus did on the cross and how He died and shed His blood for us. There is power in that message. I have watched it transform people time and time again, because God anoints it. He blesses it. And He uses it to penetrate the defenses that people can put up. Jesus died on the cross for us. That's where the power is.

*Monday*

# THE SON OF GOD

*And the angel answered and said to her, "The Holy Spirit will come upon you, and the power of the Highest will overshadow you; therefore, also, that Holy One who is to be born will be called the Son of God."*
(Luke 1:35)

Some would say they don't have to believe in the virgin birth of Jesus; they simply need to believe in His death and resurrection. But if Jesus was not conceived supernaturally in the womb of Mary, then the Bible is not true. If Jesus was not conceived supernaturally in the womb of Mary, then He was not God's Son, but just a mere man. It wouldn't have been enough for Mary to say she was having a baby with Joseph and would call him the Messiah. There would be a problem, because that baby would have a sinful nature.

But what was unique about Jesus is that He was God. He had a body; that is true. But He did not have sinful nature, because His father was not Joseph. His father was God.

A child will have the same blood type as his or her father. The blood type of Jesus was the same as His Father's. Who was the father of Jesus? It was none other than God Almighty. So when Jesus' blood was shed on the cross, it was not the mere blood of a man. That blood was such as had never been shed before, nor ever will be again. It was God shedding His blood for us.

That is why Jesus Christ is the only way to have a relationship with God. That is why His death was unique. That is why He and He alone qualifies to bridge the gap between a perfect, flawless, and holy God and sinful, flawed humanity.

# Tuesday

# THE GIFT THAT
# KEEPS ON GIVING

*Thanks be to God for His indescribable gift! (2 Corinthians 9:15)*

I heard that someone actually tried to figure out how much it would cost to give all the gifts mentioned in the song, "The Twelve Days of Christmas." It came to about $15,000. Some items were affordable, like a partridge in a pear tree. That would set you back about $34.99. Six turtledoves would run you somewhere around $50. Six geese-a-laying would cost around $150. But the price soars when you add eleven pipers piping. That is $1,000 there. Twelve drummers drumming, with current union scale for musicians, would be another $1,000. Then the price really soars when you get twelve lords a leaping. We are talking about $3,000 for that, although I don't know where you would find them. It can get very expensive.

Christmas is a time when we give gifts one to another. Some criticize this and say it is just is not right, because we miss the whole purpose of the season. In reality, I think it is a good custom of giving gifts to other people. I know that I like receiving them. But I enjoy giving them even more. It is a joy to give something to someone. There is also a good biblical premise for it. The wise men brought gifts to the child Jesus. We also know that Jesus himself was God's gift to us as we celebrate at this time of year. As we give and receive these gifts, it is a reminder and a reflection of what God has done for us.

The real message of Christmas is not the gifts we give to each other, but the gift that God has given to each of us. It is the only gift that truly keeps on giving.

# HUMBLE WRAPPINGS

*"And this will be the sign to you:*
*You will find a Babe wrapped in swaddling cloths, lying in a manger."*
*(Luke 2:12)*

What would you think if you looked under a tree and saw beautifully wrapped presents with ornate ribbons, but then you spotted a box over in the corner wrapped in newspaper and string? At first you would probably think that a guy wrapped that gift.

Allow me to digress for just a moment and say to women that wrapping gifts for men is basically a waste of time. For a man, wrapping is nothing more than an obstacle that slows him down in getting to what is inside. Women appreciate a well-wrapped gift. They will look at something you've just given them and say things like, "What a nice bow! I am going to save this for later." Then they will neatly undo the paper. Men, on the other hand, will just tear through it.

But let's think about God's gift to us. Jesus was not born in a palace of gold. He was not wrapped in silk, but in rags. He was not laid in a bed of gold befitting a king, but in a feeding trough. He was not attended by doctors and nurses, but by common barnyard animals. We like to romanticize the birth of Christ in that stable in Bethlehem some two thousand years ago. But the fact of the matter is that it was cold, damp, and unsanitary.

This does not diminish the story of His birth in any way for me. If anything, it enhances it when I realize the great sacrifice that God made for us, His gift to humanity, the ultimate gift of eternal life through His Son Jesus Christ, came in the simplest and most humble of wrappings.

# Thursday

# A GIFT WE DON'T DESERVE

*For scarcely for a righteous man will one die; yet perhaps for a good man someone would even dare to die. But God demonstrates His own love toward us, in that while we were still sinners, Christ died for us. (Romans 5:7–8)*

At Christmas, we generally give gifts to family, friends, and coworkers. Some people even give gifts to their pets. But we don't give gifts to our enemies. We don't give a gift to someone who has been slandering our name. We don't give a gift to someone who is trying to run us out of business. We don't give a gift to a thief who just broke into our house. We only give gifts to those we care about and people who treat us well—or at least people who give us a gift first.

But think about this: God gave His gift to us when we were His enemies. He didn't give His gift to us because we deserved it. He did just the opposite. The Bible tells us that when we were in rebellion against Him, while we were yet sinners, Christ died for us (see Rom. 5:8).

What did we ever give to God? Absolutely nothing. What do we deserve from God? Certainly not a gift. If anything, we deserve a certain judgment. We have done nothing to merit a gift. We have broken God's laws time and time again. We have sinned against Him repeatedly. All of us have fallen short of the standards of God (see Rom. 3:23). Unless you are one hundred percent, flawlessly perfect, then you don't measure up. We have all crossed the line. We have all broken His commandments. None of us merit this great gift that God has given us. But He chose to give it anyway.

# WELL IN ADVANCE

*This truth gives them the confidence of eternal life, which God promised them before the world began—and he cannot lie. (Titus 1:2 NLT)*

When you are going to give someone a gift, you start thinking about it ahead of time. You usually don't wait until an hour before you're planning to give that gift and then run out to find something. A good giver thinks about the gift well in advance. Hopefully you try to find what that person wants or needs. You save and you prepare for it. Then you give that person your gift.

So when did God decide to give us the gift of eternal life? Was it something that He thought of on the fly? *Things haven't worked out, have they? I thought Adam and Eve would do so well in the Garden of Eden. What a pity this is. What am I going to do now?*

God knew that Adam would blow it in the Garden. God knew that he would eat of the forbidden fruit. Long before there was a town called Bethlehem, long before there was a garden called Eden and for that matter, a planet called Earth, a decision was made in eternity that God would send forth His Son, "born of a woman, born under the law, to redeem those who were under the law" (Gal. 4:4–5). It was an appointed time that God had set when the Son of God would come to Earth to die for our sins. The Bible says of Jesus that He was "slain from the foundation of the world" (Rev. 13:8).

Make no mistake about it. This gift that God has given to you was the most sacrificial thing that He could have possibly offered. And it was planned before the world began.

# *Weekend*

# WHAT CHRISTMAS
# IS ALL ABOUT

*For the wages of sin is death, but the gift of God is eternal life
in Christ Jesus our Lord. (Romans 6:23)*

Imagine for a moment that I went out and bought you the most expensive gift imaginable. Let's say that I liquidated all of my assets and had nothing left to my name so I could buy you this gift. Then I came to you and said, "I want to give this to you. Merry Christmas."

You could immediately see that this gift was incredibly expensive. You looked at it and said, "I can't believe that you did this for me!"

"I can't either," I might say, "but I did."

"Here, Greg. I am really touched that you would think enough of me to give me a gift like this. I am glad of that. Here take it, Greg. I know you paid a lot for that gift. I can never repay you for this gift. I want you to know that I have done nothing to deserve this gift."

"That is true. But take it anyway."

"I really couldn't. You keep it. You need to take it, Greg. Take it back and get your refund."

"I can't get my money back," I say. "I can't return this gift. I have sold everything. I want you to have it. It gives me joy to give you this. Will you take it now?"

"I really can't. I am so sorry."

That would offend me deeply, because I had gone to such lengths to get you this gift, only to have you turn it away.

That is what it is like when we reject Jesus Christ. To not accept God's gift is to completely reject it. God offers us the gift of eternal life. That is what Christmas is all about.

# MORE BLESSED TO GIVE

*"And remember the words of the Lord Jesus, that He said,
'It is more blessed to give than to receive.'" (Acts 20:35)*

Jesus said, "It is more blessed to give than to receive."
Have you found that to be true?

Most kids don't get that. They don't really like to give.
In fact, one of the first words they learn is "mine." Just watch
two children with one toy. One child picks up the toy, and the
other child, who showed no interest in it previously, now wants
the toy also. Children seem so sweet and innocent, and they
are to a certain degree. But I can assure you they have a sinful
nature. Therefore, we have to teach our children to share.
And as the years pass and they become adults, hopefully they
will start realizing that it is a joy to give.

I love to give presents. I love to give them more than get
them. My problem is that I can't wait to give them. I will start
shopping and get something for Christmas for my wife and
kids and others, and I want to give them right away. I don't
like to wait. My wife always has a way of knowing what I get for
her. But I still want to give her the gift. It brings me pleasure,
because it is more blessed to give than to receive.

We could simply apply that principle to our lives in general.
What would happen if, instead of asking, "What about my
needs?", we started asking, "What about the needs of others?"
What would happen if we reached out to someone who was in
desperate need? What would happen if we took our eyes off
ourselves and began thinking about someone else? It could
change our lives.

# Tuesday

# THE PRESCRIPTION FOR HAPPY LIVING

*" 'You shall love the Lord your God with all your heart, with all your soul, and with all your mind.' This is the first and great commandment. And the second is like it: 'You shall love your neighbor as yourself.' " (Matthew 22:37–39)*

Conventional wisdom says that if you want to be happy, then you have to look out for number one. You have to go do whatever it takes to succeed and whatever it takes to fulfill your own desires and needs. It doesn't matter who you step on. It doesn't matter who gets hurt in the process. You have to think about yourself. That is what the world says.

The question is does it work? No. Because all of us know from the experience of having probably tried it that it is a complete failure to some degree. We know that our happiness ebbs and flows, and it isn't lasting.

Here is God's formula for a life that is meaningful and full. Here is how God tells us to live:

> Therefore if there is any consolation in Christ, if any comfort of love, if any fellowship of the Spirit, if any affection and mercy, fulfill my joy by being like-minded, having the same love, being of one accord, of one mind. Let nothing be done through selfish ambition or conceit, but in lowliness of mind let each esteem others better than himself. (Phil. 2:1–3)

Everyone says, "Look out for yourself. Think of yourself." But the Bible says, "Let each of you look out not only for his own interests, but also for the interests of others" (Phil. 2:4).

The Bible teaches that we already look out for number one. That comes with human nature. It is not something we need to learn how to do.

# No License to Sin

*What shall we say then? Shall we continue in sin that grace may abound?*
*(Romans 6:1)*

Sometimes we confuse God's leniency with His approval. By that I mean, we think because we have committed a certain sin and have not paid an immediate price for it, that somehow God doesn't care. If we allow sin to twist our thinking, we can take it a step further and assume that maybe God even approves of what we are doing. *Nothing bad has happened. There have been no real ramifications to speak of. Maybe God is saying that you are the exception to what the Bible says. You have a special relationship. You can do whatever you want. You can have your cake and eat it too.* This is what the devil whispers in our ear.

But the apostle Paul clearly refutes this: "What shall we say then? Shall we continue in sin that grace may abound? Certainly not! How shall we who died to sin live any longer in it? Or do you not know that as many of us as were baptized into Christ Jesus were baptized into His death?" (Rom. 6:1–3).

The fact of the matter is that you may sin and not immediately pay for it. But no one really gets away with sin. You can sin for a time and not have to pay for it. Yet it will eventually catch up with you. The Scripture is clear in saying your sin will find you out (see Num. 32:23). Do you realize the long-term price you can pay? Do you realize that your credibility as a Christian may be irreparably damaged in the eyes of many people? Though God will forgive you, many people will not. You still are going to have to pay a price.

# *Thursday*

# KNOW, KNOW, KNOW

*His divine power has given to us all things that pertain to life and godliness, through the knowledge of Him who called us by glory and virtue. (2 Peter 1:3)*

Many of us think the way to overcome sin is by saying no, no, no. But the method for overcoming it is to know, know, know. We can say no to sin, but we cannot do it in our own strength or ability. However, when we know what God has done for us, when we know about the resources at our disposal, when we know what can be appropriated in our lives, then it can change the way that sin affects us.

Often we are defeated in our day-to-day living as believers because we don't understand what God has done for us. It would be like going into battle and trying to hold back the enemy without any ammunition, when all the time we had in our possession more ammunition than we ever could have used in a thousand battles. Our defeat on the spiritual battlefield lies largely in our ignorance of the facts.

There is in Jesus Christ the power to live a new life and no longer be under sin's control. Yet a lot of us don't realize that. We think we are destined to be the devil's punching bag. So we need to know what God has done for us.

We cannot avoid sin's power by merely imitating Jesus. It is not just "What would Jesus do?" It is Jesus living in you. It is Jesus living through you. It is not just imitation; it is impartation. It is appropriating the divine provision that God has for you. Let Christ who is in you give you the power to do what He has called you to do.

# SPIRITUAL LONGEVITY

*"Now therefore, give me this mountain of which the Lord spoke in that day. ... "*
*(Joshua 14:12)*

W hat is the secret to spiritual longevity? Caleb, one of the unsung heroes of the Bible, stands as a shining example of someone who never lost his edge spiritually. He was faithful to the very end. When he was eighty-five years old, Caleb said, "I am as strong this day as on the day that Moses sent me; just as my strength was then, so now is my strength for war, both for going out and for coming in. Now therefore, give me this mountain ... " (Josh. 14:11–12). But there is another statement of Caleb's that we should take note of: "I wholly followed the Lord my God" (v. 8).

What does that tells us? To be winners in this spiritual race, we, like Caleb, must follow the Lord our God completely—not half-heartedly, but fully. It means giving 100 percent of ourselves to God.

When Caleb said, "Give me this mountain," it is worth noting that Hebron was one of the most treacherous, mountainous areas of the Promised Land. In fact, there were some formidable adversaries there. No one wanted to take them on—except for eighty-five-year-old Caleb. Caleb trusted in God's promises. He had waited forty-five years. So he said, "Give me this mountain. In fact, I have already picked out the area. I want Hebron." People must have thought Caleb was out of his mind.

But I love Caleb's boldness. He took the mountain. He overcame his adversaries. And he was victorious. While others looked back, Caleb looked forward. That is an essential key to spiritual longevity. You are always moving forward. You are always seeking to grow spiritually—and never looking back.

# *Weekend*

# FINISHING WELL

*Having loved His own who were in the world, He loved them to the end.*
*(John 13:1)*

When Billy Graham was asked the question, "What has been the greatest surprise of your life?", he answered, "The brevity of it." That is so true. Time passes quickly, and we don't want to squander this precious thing that God has given to us called life. Over the years, I have been surprised by some people who I thought were going to do great things for God, but actually fell away from Him. I have also been surprised by people who I thought would never make it as a Christian, but are now serving the Lord with great effectiveness.

It's important to remember that we are not mere victims without any say-so as to whether or not we are going to do well spiritually. We need to realize that people fall away because they choose to. By that I mean, their spiritual failure usually isn't a result of a deliberate decision to backslide. Rather, it's the result of wrong choices they make in life that lead to a spiritual breakdown. If you want to make it in the Christian life, then you are going to make it. Jude I says, "To those who are called, sanctified by God the Father, and preserved in Jesus Christ." The original language used the perfect tense. The nearest equivalent of it is, "They are continually kept by Jesus Christ." Whatever difficulties you are facing today as a believer, you are preserved in Christ. He is going to keep you.

I am thankful for those people I know who have started well, are doing well, and look as though they will cross life's finish line with flying colors. I want to be one of those people. Don't you?

# Afterword

Have you put your faith in Jesus Christ? By that I mean, have you admitted to God that you are a sinner? Have you admitted to God that you cannot reach His standards in your own strength or by your own merit? Do you realize that God loves you so much that He sent His Son Jesus to die on the cross and shed His blood for every sin you have ever committed? That same Jesus who died on the cross and rose again three days later is ready to come into the heart of anyone who will ask Him and will turn from his or her sin. He can come into your heart right now.

Not only will you have a life worth that is worth living, not only will you find the meaning of life, but you also will have the hope of life beyond the grave. What a deal—life during life … and life after death.

If you would like to invite Christ into your life, simply pray a prayer like this one, and mean it in your heart:

> Dear Lord Jesus, I know I am a sinner. I believe You died for my sins. Right now, I turn from my sins and open the door of my heart and life. I confess You as my personal Lord and Savior. Thank You for saving me. Amen.

To help you grow in your newfound faith, be sure to make the following a part of your life each day: read the Bible regularly, pray, spend time with other Christians by going to church, and tell others about your faith in Christ.

For additional resources to help you learn more about what it means to know God and to be a follower of Jesus Christ through every season of your life, please visit http://www.harvest.org/knowgod/.

# NOTES

1. C. S. Lewis, *Mere Christianity* (San Francisco: HarperSan Franscisco, 2001), 125.

2. Samuel Rutherford, letter to John Ewart, Bailie of Kirkcudbright, "Samuel Rutherford (1600–1661); The Letters of Samuel Rutherford," *A Puritan's Mind.com,* http://www.apuritansmind.com/SamuelRutherford/SamuelRutherfordLetters.htm (accessed July 7, 2006).

3. C. H. Spurgeon, *Sermons of Rev. C.H. Spurgeon of London,* second series (New York: Robert Carter & Brothers, 1883), 169–170.

4. C. S. Lewis, *Mere Christianity,* 155.

5. "Quotables: Wealth and Poverty," *Ministry in Daily Life,* InterVarsity, http://www.ivmdl.org/quotables.cfm?quoteid=137&cat=Wealth%20and%20Poverty (accessed August 8, 2006).

# ABOUT THE AUTHOR

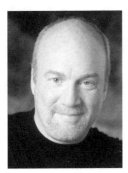

Greg Laurie is the pastor of Harvest Christian Fellowship (one of America's largest churches) in Riverside, California. He is the author of over thirty books, including the Gold Medallion Award winner, *The Upside-Down Church,* as well as *Every Day with Jesus; Are We Living in the Last Days?; Marriage Connections; Losers and Winners, Saints and Sinners;* and *Dealing with Giants.* You can find his study notes in the *New Believer's Bible* and the *Seeker's Bible.* Host of the *Harvest: Greg Laurie* television program and the nationally syndicated radio program, *A New Beginning,* Greg Laurie is also the founder and featured speaker for Harvest Crusades—contemporary, large-scale evangelistic outreaches, which local churches organize nationally and internationally. He and his wife Cathe live in Southern California and have two children and one grandchild.

# OTHER AllenDavid BOOKS PUBLISHED BY KERYGMA PUBLISHING

*The Great Compromise*

*For Every Season: Daily Devotions*

*Strengthening Your Marriage*

*Marriage Connections*

*Are We Living in the Last Days?*

*"I'm Going on a Diet Tomorrow"*

*Strengthening Your Faith*

*Deepening Your Faith*

*Living Out Your Faith*

*Dealing with Giants*

*Secrets to Spiritual Success*

*How to Know God*

*10 Things You Should Know About God and Life*

**Visit:** www.kerygmapublishing.com
www.allendavidbooks.com
www.harvest.org